THE
SCIENCE OF
KNOWING

SUNY series in Contemporary Continental Philosophy

Dennis J. Schmidt, editor

THE SCIENCE OF KNOWING

J. G. Fichte's 1804 Lectures on the Wissenschaftslehre

J. G. Fichte

translated by
Walter E. Wright

State University of New York Press

Published by
State University of New York Press, Albany

For information, address State University of New York Press,
194 Washington Avenue, Suite 305, Albany, NY 12210-2384

Production by Diane Ganeles
Marketing by Susan Petrie

Library of Congress Cataloging-in-Publication Data

Fichte, Johann Gottlieb, 1762–1814.
   [Lectures. English. Selections]
   The science of knowing : J. G. Fichte's 1804 lectures on the Wissenschaftslehre / J. G. Fichte
; translated by Walter E. Wright.
      p. cm. — (SUNY series in contemporary continental philosophy)
   Includes bibliographical references and index.
   ISBN 0-7914-6449-0 (hardcover : alk. paper) — ISBN 0-7914-6450-4 (pbk. : alk. paper)
   1. Philosophy. I. Title. II. Series.

B2805 2005
193—dc22
                                                                              2004017162

10   9   8   7   6   5   4   3   2   1

Dedicated to
Charles Scott and John Lachs

Contents

Acknowledgments

This translation of Johann Gottlieb Fichte's 1804 *Wissenschaftslehre*, lectures delivered at his home in Berlin, has been the intermittent work of many years. I initially undertook the project in order to learn something about Fichte's mature philosophy; however, as I have returned to it repeatedly over the years, it has taken on a life of its own. When I began, I. H. Fichte's edition of his father's unpublished works was the only source for this text, and my first complete draft for this translation was made from it. Subsequently, I have compared my translation carefully with the two newer, more carefully edited, editions.[1]

In attempting to enter the strange world of nineteenth-century transcendental philosophy, I have been guided by many helpers—too many to name them all. However, a few cannot go unmentioned. Robert Ehman's Timothy Dwight College Sophomore Seminar at Yale (1962–63) established the framework within which I understand the history of philosophy and remains a memorable educational experience. Charles Scott and John Lachs at Vanderbilt first introduced me to Fichte. The writings of Joachim Widmann and Wolfgang Janke—together with the editorial genius of Reinhard Lauth, and (again) Joachim Widmann—helped me begin to go deeper into this remarkable text. Along the way Dan Breazeale, Tom Rockmore, Joseph Naylor, and Gunther Zöller have contributed immeasurably to my understanding of Fichte, as have all the many participants in the North American Fichte Society. Ken Foldes provided helpful encouragement. Finally, without the friendship, support, and encouragement of Joe Lawrence and Jeffrey Bernstein—delivered at critical moments—this project might still be unfinished. Likewise, without the generous support of the Higgins School of the Humanities at Clark University, this work would not have come to fruition.

I also thank my colleagues at Clark University, Judith Wagner DeCew, Patrick Derr, Scott Hendricks, Gary Overvold, and Michael Pakaluk. Although none of you have given Fichte much thought, you all have been continuously and generously supportive of my work. Professor Nancy Mardas provided invaluable assistance by reviewing a late draft of this translation against the German, suggesting many improvements. An anonymous reviewer at Cornell University Press pointed out several remaining mistakes and infelicities. Of course all the remaining errors are my sole responsibility. I am deeply grateful to my late father, Walter Menzies Wright, who was unfailingly curious and supportive about whatever I worked on. Additional thanks for a wide range of things are also due to Hansjurgen Verweyen, Fredrick Beiser, Pamela Wright, John Riker, Susan Curewitz Arthen, Robert Nelson Beck, Eric Leventhal Arthen, Bernard Kaplan, Kaki Green, Jack Lund, Lois Mayer, and many others, too numerous to mention.

Many excellent people at SUNY Press have helped this project happen. Thanks to Dennis Schmidt, Jane Bunker, Diane Ganeles, Susan Petrie, and all the staff for their encouragement, help, and professionalism.

Finally, I owe a special debt to my wife and colleague Sarah Buie for her ongoing love and support.

Introduction

Wissenschaftslehre

If there is one word that describes Johann Gottlieb Fichte's contribution to philosophy, that word is *Wissenschaftslehre*. Fichte coined this word to name his distinctive pathway for philosophical thinking. This way exerted an important influence on his times. It was studied, discussed, and "refuted" by F. W. J. von Schelling, Georg Wilhelm Friedrich Hegel, and other important contemporaries. Fichte's works have been published in two major collected editions in German, have been translated into many languages, and have elicited a large and growing critical literature. There are several professional societies devoted to the study of his ideas. Despite all of this activity, it remains remarkably difficult to say just what *Wissenschaftslehre* really is.

When Fichte was called abruptly to the chair at Jena, he claimed to have found a revolutionary new idea of philosophy as a science, but he was not ready to present it publicly. Responding to the necessities of his new position, Fichte worked rapidly to assemble his *Grundlage der gesamten Wissenschaftslehre* (1794). He intended these writings as a private text for students in his initial lectures at Jena. However, given the widespread interest in his new philosophical system, the *Grundlage* was published, and it quickly became the primary source for people's understanding of Fichte's thinking. At Jena, Fichte surrounded the *Grundlage* with lectures and supplementary writings,[1] and he amplified it with works that applied his fundamental perspective to the more particular domains of philosophical inquiry, ethics and social philosophy. The confusion and misunderstanding that continued to greet these efforts led Fichte to reformulate his fundamental ideas in the *Wissenschaftslehre novo methodo*.[2] Unfortunately, he had not yet fully worked this material out for publication, when his rethinking was interrupted by the "Atheism Controversy" and its resulting turmoil. This affair, its charges and counter-charges filled with moral posturing on both sides, culminated with Fichte's dismissal from Jena in the spring of 1799. Fichte then moved to Berlin, seeking some way to support his family and to vindicate the importance of what he believed to be his revolutionary new ideas in philosophy. So, at the turn of the nineteenth century, Fichte, the unemployed philosopher, had still not made good on his commitment to present his new insight, his core philosophy, his *Wissenschaftslehre* in a definitive form.

1

The 1804 Lectures

Near the beginning of January 1804, Fichte published a notice in the *Berlin Reports on Governmental and Scholarly Affairs* (*Berlinischen Nachrichten von Staats-und gelehrten Sachen*, no. 2, January 5).[3] This notice announced that he would be holding a new series of public lectures on the *Wissenschaftslehre*. Those who wished to attend could see a "more detailed plan for the arrangements" at Saunders Bookstore, where, for a fee, they could also enroll.

This announcement was itself a very noteworthy event. Since his dismissal from his professorship, Fichte had been struggling. Without a university appointment, he had pieced together a living by republishing earlier works and teaching privately, while he labored to bring his system into a finished form. Disappointed at the uncomprehending and frequently hostile reception that had greeted the first published presentation of his system, Fichte attempted to develop a new approach to expressing and communicating his philosophical path. His deep belief that "it is the vocation of the scholar to be the teacher of the human race"[4] made this work especially urgent for him. His philosophy was to be part of elevating European culture and humanity to new levels. His announcement in the *Berlin Reports* suggested that at last Fichte believed his work was sufficiently complete, and that he was ready to bring a new account of his *Wissenschaftslehre* before the public.

Although Fichte had promised more than once to publish a new version of his *Wissenschaftslehre*, he proved unable to produce something that he found entirely satisfactory. In 1802 he had lectured privately to a limited group on a "New Presentation of the *Wissenschaftslehre*," with the idea of preparing this manuscript for eventual publication. He also lectured privately in 1803. However, with the unrelenting—and to his mind uncomprehending—attacks on his work by his former associate Schelling, as well as by Hegel, and the Berlin popular philosophers, Fichte finally concluded that his best strategy for communicating his system would be a living engagement between himself and a group of students. Therefore, abandoning the idea of publication at least temporarily, he set out to lecture.

These public lectures were to be something new. Fichte planned to lead a group of educated and active citizens into the central and deepest parts of philosophical reflection. Although a number of young scholars attended, these lectures were not primarily for a specialist audience within the small world of academic philosophy. Rather, they were another installment in Fichte's project of educating the human race.

Hence, for those interested in Fichte's work, the announcement in the *Berlinischen Nachrichten* was very welcome news. True, Fichte had already been lecturing on philosophy in Berlin, but these new lectures were something quite different both in their openness and in their promise to provide a new, comprehensive account of the science of knowing. In his *pro memoria* for the Royal cabinet of ministers in Berlin, Fichte wrote:

> Lately, there is a system, completed in its external form, which boasts that it—purely self-contained, unalterable, and immediately manifest—provides all other sciences with their first principles and their guide. In this way, it alleviates forever all conflict and misunderstanding in the scientific disciplines. It shows every spirit *(Geist)*, which has established itself properly within its domain, the proper field for its endless advance to greater clarity, to *empirical reality*, and leads it infallibly on this field.

During the year that followed, Fichte held three different series of lectures on his system. He conducted all three courses in his house at number 9 Commanders Street, in Berlin. The first series, consisting of thirty lectures, ran from January 17 through March. Because a number of interested people had been unable to attend the initial lectures—and perhaps more because Fichte believed that he had underestimated the difficulty of this first series— he conceived the second as a repetition. After a two-week pause for Easter, he began the second series on April 16, and gave twenty-eight lectures, ending on June 8. The third series consisted of twenty-three lectures, held in November and December. The lectures of the second series, with which we are concerned here, took place four days a week between 5:30 pm and 7 pm.

Apparently, all of these lectures, for which Fichte charged a fee, had good attendance. Fichte lectured to a mixed audience of men and women, older and younger people. Scholars have established with some confidence the identity of sixteen men who very probably attended the second series of lectures. They have also identified about another twenty-five who, with varying degrees of probability, may have been present. For our purposes, it is enough to report I. H. Fichte's description of the group as "the king's first advisors and the most important men of the court." It is very probable that in addition a group of aspiring young professionals and educators from the first series continued into the second. So far as we know, the fifteen women who attended were primarily the daughters and spouses of other attendees.[5]

Fichte's Post-Jena *Wissenschaftslehre*

The second set of lectures from 1804 is widely regarded as particularly important in Fichte's philosophical development. Scholars have generally viewed this text as the crucial beginning point for all the later, post-Jena versions of Fichte's system. It has been the focus for a number of very important studies by philosophers associated with Reinhardt Lauth and the Munich Group.[6] Günther Zöller calls it "a major document for this phase of [Fichte's] thinking."[7] Beyond that, I believe that these lectures may well be the pinnacle of Fichte's efforts to present his fundamental philosophical system. In depth and clarity of expression, they are accurate and succinct in a way that none of the earlier versions can match. In their emphasis on philosophical insight as emergent, arising in the individual in consequence of that person's performance of specific reflective acts, they introduce a bold refinement in Fichte's accounts of what philosophy is. Although these lectures are certainly difficult, once one grasps the principle of their composition they are no more difficult than Hegel's *Phenomenology*, or Martin Heidegger's *Being and Time*. Indeed, they stand with those texts as one of the masterworks in the European philosophical tradition.

The reasons why many scholars hold these lectures in such esteem are not far to seek. First, they go to the conceptual heart of Fichte's "first philosophy." Here, in striking and original language, Fichte explores the transcendental foundations of experience and knowing in ways that go beyond the familiar arguments of Immanuel Kant's *Critique of Pure Reason*. Moreover, he also goes beyond Karl Leonhart Reinhold's attempt to discover an indubitable "first principle" for philosophy in the concept of "representation" and his own attempt in the *Grundlage der Gesamten Wissenschaftslehre* to ground knowing transcendentally in a primal act of self-positing. Here, in a rigorous process of calling up and working through the many contradictions that arise in awareness, Fichte claims to open the path to an insight into the final, highest oneness. This oneness grounds and explicates the self and its finite experience, while transcendentally annulling any claim to the self's ultimacy in the face of the incomprehensible, absolute, whether we call it being, light, God, or whatever.

Thus, these 1804 lectures chart a pathway for German idealism that is both promising and unfamiliar. Because they took place in Fichte's home and were not published during his lifetime, their contents were not widely known to Fichte's contemporaries. The philosophical community continued to judge Fichte almost exclusively through the early Jena writings, which he himself viewed as seriously defective. Until recently, therefore, Fichte has generally been viewed within the familiar *Von Kant bis Hegel*[8] framework as a transitional figure, who contributed to the development of German idealism, a movement that passed through Schelling's philosophy and culminated in the Hegelian system. These lectures help to refute this theory, if such refutation is still needed. They reassert the centrality of human finitude, ground themselves in philosophical realism about what is ultimate, and avoid the hermetic self-enclosure of the absolute spirit, which Hegel takes to be the *telos* for all development. The Fichte who emerges in the 1804 lectures stands in a continuous line of development with the radical thinker who introduced the *Wissenschaft-*

slehre at Jena in 1794. However, this presentation of his philosophical system has deeper, more carefully articulated, and more perspicuous roots. In its continuities and discontinuities with the tradition, Fichte's profound system of transcendental philosophy stands on its own alongside both Kant and Hegel.

Further, given their uncompromising commitment to the centrality of truth, these lectures provide a novel voice that can contribute to the postmodern conversation. They are relevant both in their energetic arguments for human finitude and in Fichte's unwavering commitment to the ideal of truth, a commitment that some thinkers working under the influence of postmodernism have—perhaps too easily—abandoned. Fichte's independent approach has not already been subverted by the criticisms directed against Kant's and Hegel's more familiar forms of classical German philosophy. Further, it stands beyond both realism and idealism as theoretical accounts of "what there is." Therefore, contemporary thinkers would benefit from making the effort to encounter it afresh. His entirely immanent, and radically immediate exploration of the foundations of knowing raises new possibilities for transcendental phenomenology.

Although these lectures contain more than their fair share of conceptual and linguistic difficulties, they also have moments of economy and clarity, which can grant the reader a wonderful overview of Fichte's (and his age's) philosophical landscape. For instance, his comments about his contemporaries (especially Kant, Reinhold, and F. H. Jacobi) are masterful, and his brief engagements with Benedict de Spinoza are richly suggestive.[9] Further, his fundamental theory is challenging and significant. In short, these lectures contain some of Fichte's richest work. While the precise relationship between Fichte's Jena works and his so-called later philosophy remains to be resolved, there are indisputable continuities connecting the various phases of his career. The 1804 *Wissenschaftslehre* can therefore provide a felicitous and comprehensive introduction to Fichte's philosophical work as a whole.

There are two extant versions of the German text for the second series of lectures from 1804. First, I. H. Fichte claimed to have a "completely worked out" manuscript for the entire lecture series, which he published in his edition of his father's unpublished works.[10] However, as Lauth, Joachim Widmann, and Peter Schneider clearly demonstrate, this edition introduced many mistakes into its text of the 1804 lectures. Based on internal evidence, they argue that I. H. Fichte must have given the manuscript directly to a typesetter. They infer that, when the typesetter returned the proofs, he did not include the manuscript, so that I. H. Fichte had to correct them without being able to refer to the original. Consequently, he missed some typographical errors introduced by the printer, and—correcting the proofs from his memory instead of the written version—introduced additional mistakes of his own. As a result, his published text is editorially defective, even though complete.

For more than half a century, this was the only known text of these lectures. Fortunately, early in the twentieth century the librarian K. Wendel discovered a gray, half leather volume in the Halle University library. The title of this book read:

Copia.
Wiederholung
der Wissenschaftslehre
28 Vorlesungen 1804

It contained the entirety of what can only be Fichte's second set of lectures from 1804. Irregularities in pagination and binding, together with notations in the upper right hand corner of some pages, suggest that, at some point, the volume had been rebound from a set of ten notebooks, each of twenty or twenty-four pages. The text reveals idiosyncratic spellings familiar from Fichte's other manuscripts, leading the editors to assume that it is (as it says) a copy (by someone unknown) of an earlier manuscript that was probably from Fichte's own hand. A close comparison of these two texts shows many things. Their extensive similarity supports I. H. Fichte's claim to have had "a completely worked out" version. There are also important differences. Each contains clearly erroneous words and sentences. Each contains brief passages missing in the other. Each has sections containing concentrated sets of mistakes. The editors attribute this latter circumstance to copyist fatigue in the *Copia* and unequal attention by the typesetter in I. H. Fichte's edition. Because both versions contain many (and different) obvious mistakes, Lauth, Widmann, and Schneider[11] judge the two versions to be of equal worth, with each providing reasons to correct particular passages in the other. In one volume of the ongoing modern critical edition of Fichte's works by the Bavarian Academy of Science,[12] I. H. Fichte's text and the *Copia* are printed on facing pages, allowing us to compare them in detail. By means of such comparison, it is possible to approximate more closely to what the author's handwritten version may have been.

Still, attempting to translate these celebrated 1804 lectures might still seem impossible, or at least reckless. Remember, after all, that Fichte himself decided not to publish a new version of his first philosophy in light of the problems raised by its initial reception. More importantly, in these lectures themselves, Fichte repeatedly emphasizes the *performative* aspect of the new philosophy that he is attempting to promulgate. For Fichte, philosophy is not expressible through any set of propositions; rather, it is a spiritual attainment. He puts great weight on the living presentation of his ideas, which he invites his listeners to reproduce inwardly through their own acts of conceptualization and attention. He constantly reinforces the necessity for this type of active listening, and for reproducing his presentation inwardly. The regular conversation sessions, held at intervals during his lectures, allowed Fichte to confirm that his listeners were following him properly. In short, Fichte saw himself as engaged in a living work with the particular audience assembled before him, attempting to awaken them to create their own insight into the fundamental structures and enactments that compose knowing, consciousness, and truth. He wanted to elicit the *Wissenschaftslehre* directly within his listeners, in response to their own enactment of it. This individual event was, for him, the central task of philosophy. If Fichte did not think that he could awaken this spark of his science without direct engagement with his students, why should anyone 200 years later think it possible to translate the written record of such a process?

Despite the difficulty, not to say impossibility, of this task, there are nonetheless many reasons for attempting it. First, there is the importance of these lectures for a correct appreciation of Fichte's mature philosophical project. In the words of his son and editor, I. H. Fichte, these lectures are a masterpiece "in the energy of thinking, as in the power and virtuosity of supple presentation and auspicious views."[13] Widmann goes even further, asserting that this work "counts among the greatest classical texts in the history of philosophy."[14] In these lectures Fichte pushes his transcendental philosophical program to its deepest point. Second, this text allow us to make a more comprehensive assessment of Fichte's significance in relation to important later schools of thought, including Sigmund Freud, Karl Marx, Heidegger, phenomenology and various postmodernist groups. It is here above all that Fichte claims to bring together, in a single philosophical enactment, the absolute in its full transcendence and the finite conditionedness of consciousness as it actually occurs. Finally, Fichte's radical attempt to bring about complete consistency between the content of his theory and its enactment in each individual who thinks it, between what is said and the saying of it, is a powerful philosophical project in its own right. It has enduring lessons for contemporary philosophical practice.

Fichte Today

Fichte thought that he had discovered something of great significance. As one of the continuing line of philosophers who, following Kant, believed they had found the key to a comprehensive system of philosophy, Fichte wanted to elevate humanity to a higher level of culture though his philosophical activity. He thought that there was a deep truth of things and that he had found a way to awaken knowledge of it. Now, however, at the dawn of the twenty-first century, such ideas can only seem thoroughly alien. Two world wars, achievements in social science, widespread historicism and pragmatism, modern psychology, the incredible growth of technology, and an expanding, global capitalist economy have left us very far away from the vigorous speculative optimism of classical German idealism. We have grown up nourished on ubiquitous claims regarding the constructed character of individual consciousness. Philosophers and theorists almost universally accept that consciousness in its occurrence depends on underlying linguistic, biological, neurological, instinctual, economic, cultural and/or historical factors. Both modern analytic philosophy and Continental postmodernism have turned from dreams of system to a demolition of any such hopes in a process of perpetual skepticism and critique. We have gone to school in the lessons of finitude, learning from such disparate figures as William James and John Dewey, as Heidegger and Hans Georg Gadamer, Theodor Adorno and Richard Rorty, not to mention Ludwig Wittgenstein, Jacques Derrida, Michel Foucault, and Donald Davidson.

Yet, in some strange way, Fichte may be closer to this contemporary spirit than any of the other philosophers usually grouped under the heading German idealism. Despite his insistence on a single ultimate truth, his transcendentalism (which seems to favor subjectivity and idealism), and the painful abstractness of his vocabulary, the deeper trajectory of his thinking is surprisingly contemporary. Zöller has already pointed out the persistent realism in Fichte's insistence on the lack of self-identity in consciousness and in its necessary reference to an other.[15] One must always keep in mind Fichte's unwavering grasp of the finitude of human subjectivity. As he understands it, human consciousness taken generally—including our consciousness as philosophers—always operates within limits. As consciousness, it can never be unconditioned or absolute. Nor can we, as individual persons, be what exists ultimately. Likewise, as already indicated, one must always keep in mind Fichte's emphasis on the *performative* element in philosophy. That is to say, philosophical insight is something we become in doing rather than any discursively expressible object of awareness. For Fichte, philosophy is an art or praxis rather than any proposition, set of doctrines, or argument. Therefore, he always regards the expression of philosophy in words as strategic: aiming to ignite philosophy's essentially inward process and to arouse the event of philosophical insight. Finally, we must keep in mind Fichte's methodological emphasis on identifying and undermining oppositions within every position posed as ultimate. Fichte's philosophy is fundamentally critical. It is an endless, minute paring away of possibilities until only a final, unremovable insight remains. Fichte's underscores this critical method by the importance he assigns to skepticism. As he asserts at the end of Lecture XIII in this presentation of his system:

> Just the possessor of this science who surveys all disjunctions in consciousness (disjunctions which, if one assumes the validity of consciousness in

itself, become contradictions) could present a skepticism which totally negated everything assumed so far; a skepticism in the face of which those who have been playing with all kinds of skeptical doubts as a pastime might blanch and cry out: "Now the joke goes too far!"

Thus, Fichte thinks that his *Wissenschaftslehre* could produce the most thoroughgoing skepticism imaginable by pointing out the disjunctions, and hence contradictions, within all philosophical systems so far developed (and indeed in every finite mode of awareness).

In these ways, Fichte's philosophical practice displays important analogies to contemporary critical theory. However, there are important *dis*-analogies as well, perhaps the most important of which arise from Fichte's insistences on system and on an immanent method. He thought that consciousness, working within its own resources, would be able to carry philosophy through to its highest point. He also thought that this highest point would bring a systematic structure of reason's enactments into view. We, however, true to our postmodernity, suspect any claims to systematic finality, as well as any purely immanent theorizing.

Yet, Fichte's immanent method also includes deeply critical moments. His method claims to demonstrate in just what way consciousness is always an unreliable guide for knowing. He insists that philosophy can make progress toward a scientific form only by identifying and overcoming the discontinuities in this consciousness. Fichte insists that consciousness always occurs within the "form of outer existence," or as a "projection through a gap." This concept of projection enters Fichte's discussion in Lecture XIV. In that context, it names the structure of consciousness we might now call intentionality. Consciousness, for Fichte, always involves a break between the occurrence of awareness itself (Husserl's *noesis*) and the object intended in consciousness (Husserl's *noema*). So Fichte says, "Your consciousness of thinking should contain a thought, actual, true, and really present, without your being able to give an account of it; therefore this consciousness projects a true reality outward, discontinuously . . ." (XIV). On this view, there is necessarily something fundamentally and completely inexplicable within consciousness, something underivable. Yet, the philosopher must offer a genetic explanation of this very inexplicability itself. Fichte undertakes to do this in the second part of his science. One might think of this "projection through a gap" or "form of outward existence" as the principle of objectivity. Experience always includes some content that is present directly and inexplicably, and consciousness always occurs under this "form of outward existence." Therefore, Fichte asserts, consciousness always intends a being that differs from its own being as an enactment (and hence defers oneness and truth). In its nature, enacted consciousness *cannot* be adequate to its object. Fichte's account of projection defines consciousness in a way that undermines Hegel's image of final reconciliation as an event of self-knowing. At the same time, it supports modernity's general rejection of conscious awareness as a test of truth. In fact, one might say that, despite his opposition to some of its deepest tendencies, Fichte, arguably more than any other German idealist, has explored the soil from which contemporary Continental philosophy has grown up.

Translating Fichte

In translating Fichte, one faces a number of terminological difficulties. Not the least is determining what his system should be called. Fichte's own term, *Wissenschaftslehre*, has caused consistent discomfort for English-speaking Fichte scholars. In his early translation of the *Grundlage der Gesamten Wissenschaftslehre* 1794, A. E. Kroeger rendered this word "science of knowledge." Lachs and Peter Heath follow that same path in their 1971 re-translation of the *Grundlage*. Consequently, this remained the prevailing practice among English-speaking philosophers for many years. French translators, with greater fidelity to this compound word's German root meanings, call it *Doctrine de la science*.

   Both of these solutions soon enough came under critical scrutiny. Perhaps the best concise statement of the problems with this initial English solution comes from Daniel Breazeale who writes in a "Note on Translation" at the beginning of his *Fichte: Early Philosophical Writings*:

> *Wissenschaft* means "science"; the German term, however, especially in its late-eighteenth-century usage, is by no means limited to "natural science" but includes any disciplined study and systematic body of knowledge. For these reasons, "science" is not an entirely satisfactory translation. . . . But it is certainly superior to "knowledge." There are several German words that might plausible be rendered simply as "knowledge," but *Wissenschaft* is not one of them. . . . *Lehre* means "teaching," or "theory" or "doctrine," as in "theory of evolution" or "Spinoza's doctrine of freedom." It most certainly does not mean "science." For these reasons, it is unacceptable to translate Fichte's *Wissenschaftslehre* as "science of knowledge," despite the unfortunate fact that this is the name by which it has long been known in English. Either it should be translated as something like "Doctrine of Science" or "Theory of Scientific Knowledge," or else it should not be translated at all.[16]

   If one understands the task of translation as requiring, above all, fidelity to lexicographically literal renditions of root words, these remarks are exactly right. Moreover, they provide solid grounds for Professor Breazeale's decision in his own work to leave this word untranslated as a "term of art." Others (including Tom Rockmore, Frederick Neuhouser, and Zöller, to name three) have also made his choice. In fact, it is now the most common practice among English-speaking Fichte scholars. However, this does not entirely settle the matter. While leaving *Wissenschaftslehre* untranslated imposes no burden on the specialist reader, it does have drawbacks for others, and it may possibly serve to make Fichte's philosophy less accessible than it might otherwise be.

In my view, translation is less a matter of literal transference of content, or fidelity to root meanings, than of something larger. In his essay "The Task of the Translator,"[17] Walter Benjamin asserts that translation is not the transmission of information or the imparting of meaning. Rather, its ultimate purpose is to express "the central reciprocal relationship between languages." In it, the original rises into a "higher and purer linguistic air." In that context, he says that:

> The task of the translator consists in finding the intended effect *[Intention]* upon the language into which he is translating which produces in it the echo of the original. (p. 76)

Leaving *"Wissenschaftslehre"* untranslated avoids that task. It risks situating Fichte's philosophical thinking within a technical (or antiquarian) perspective from which it may prove difficult to free it. His words then become something of historical or specialist interest, but they have less connection to public discourse about contemporary concerns. Above all, however, Fichte conceived philosophy as a civic duty connected with the cultivation and elevation of human life. Therefore, if we wish to do justice to Fichte's philosophical activity (which is always more a matter of its inner spirit than its outer form), I believe that we must face the problem squarely and find a way of producing an "echo of the original" within the English of our time.

As a way of approaching the problem, we might ask how Fichte characterizes his project. At the beginning of the 1804 Lectures, Fichte describes the *Wissenschaftslehre* as "one of the possible philosophies." Philosophy, in turn, he describes as the disciplined search for absolute unity in knowing, beyond all distinctions and differences. "Philosophy," he says, "traces all multiplicity back to oneness." As Fichte conducts it, the *Wissenschaftslehre* is a genetic investigation into knowing, which aims to search out the original genesis, the original truth, which is antecedent to everything merely factical. He conceives this task as leading to genuine knowledge, which he thinks we perceive with manifestness *(Evidenz)*, that is as unquestionably true.

For Fichte, *Wissenschaftslehre* is not a "doctrine" or a "theory," which is merely contingently true. Nor, indeed, is it a collection of propositions at all. One cannot write it down. Neither is it knowledge as a body of material, or any kind of objectivity. Instead, as I have indicated, philosophical truth necessarily involves a performative element—it is an enactment. Although knowledge may be a body of propositions, knowing, as an enactment, never is. With that in mind, one might say that *Wissenschaftslehre* is the event of genuine philosophical knowing. The teacher can help the student create the conditions for the occurrence of this event, but the event itself, if it is to occur at all, must ultimately create itself in us as we fulfill these conditions. What the successful student of the *Wissenschaftslehre* (if there could be one) would come to know would be the unitary genetic principle of all knowing, and such a student's knowing of this would be a "knowing by acquaintance." In short, the *Wissenschaftslehre*, if it is anything at all, can only be the event in which knowing knows itself. Fichte regards the path toward this event as something that can be pursued systematically—in a word, as a "science." Indeed, as we have already seen, sometimes in these very lectures Fichte refers to his project as a science. For these reasons, I have chosen to translate *Wissenschaftslehre* here as the "science of knowing."

Besides the title, these lectures present the translator with other difficult linguistic problems. One of the most fundamental derives from the fact that Fichte steadily modified and reshaped the terminology of his system from presentation to presentation. He insisted that only directly grasping the spirit of his work internally could lead to true understanding. Therefore, he thought that the philosopher must not reify any particular set of concepts, as if *they* could contain the truth. He enacted this belief by progressively recasting his vocabulary in each new version, introducing novel terminologies with which to approach the *Wissenschaftslehre*'s transcendental terrain, and reducing previously central terms to marginal roles. Thus, for example, although "positing" *(setzen)* is arguably the most important term in the 1794 Jena *Grundlage*, it plays only a minor role in these lectures. Such continual shifts require the translator to look past the literal meanings of Fichte's words to his work's deeper structure. At the same time, within each of his various presentations, Fichte uses certain crucial terms repeatedly, often without ever giving them any exact definition. In such cases, context and use are decisive. Fichte's linguistic strategies for expressing his unique philosophical insights include altering or shifting meanings, using simple words in technical ways, and introducing neologisms.

I will illustrate these strategies by providing brief explanations for a few central concepts that appear in the lectures that follow.

First, consider the fundamental terms *Genesis* and *genetisch,* which I render consistently as "genesis" and "genetic." To Fichte's educated contemporaries, these terms might evoke the Hebrew account of the world's creation in the first book of the Pentateuch. Alternatively, they might perhaps bring to mind the philosophy of Johann Gottfried Herder. Fichte undoubtedly intended the Biblical resonance, as his Protestant Christian roots run deep. The question of Herder's use of "genesis" is something else again. For him, the genetic method was historicist and relativistic. It involved tracing a text, act, or idea back to the specific historical matrix from which it had arisen. Further, Herder believed that there were several such matrices, each incommensurable with the others: "Every nation has the center of its happiness within itself just as every ball has its own center of gravity" (Herder *Werke*, V, 509). To understand a thing, for him, was to trace it to its origins:

> With the origin of a thing, one part of its history escapes us that can explain so much of the thing, and indeed its most important part. Just as a tree grows from its roots, so art, language, and science grow from their origins. In the seed, there lies the creature with all of its members; and in the origin of a phenomenon there lies all the treasure of its interpretation, through which our explanation of it becomes genetic. (Herder, *Werke*, II, 62, my translation)

Fichte shares with Herder both the term "genesis" and the concept of a developmental method. However, they use these elements very differently. In Fichte's text, these terms characterize the process or relation that links given concepts, or conscious contents, back to their source. Thus, for him, their meaning is transcendental rather than historical. The language here recalls Fichte's references in the *Grundlage* to a "pragmatic history of the human spirit." It also evokes the *Grundzüge des gegenwärtigen Zeitalters* (1806) and its a priori theory of the world's ages. For Fichte, apparently historical and factical aspects of human culture have a priori, transcendental grounds. Accordingly, his references to genetic thinking invoke an archaeological dis-covery of the transcendental roots for whatever view, argument, or fact is under investigation. Because they also imply a process that unfolds an implicit character into external expression, I sometimes add the clarifying qualifier "development" or "developmental."

Another aspect of Fichte's deployment of the term "genesis" connects with the priority that he always grants to act over fact. Frequently, his genetic/developmental analyses involve taking up some datum given factically and then attempting to discover an act from which it arises. At the end, nothing should remain that presents itself merely as given. Rather, all givenness must derive from some activity that is its source. The ultimate ground or source must be a pure, self-derived activity. Hence, Fichte frequently contrasts the genetic with the factical. The latter always refers to what is presented merely as given, but the former moves beyond what is given to the process from which it has arisen. Further, the process in question is not usually so much a factical origination within time as it is a transcendental origination from higher level principles, and ultimately from the one.

Einsicht and *einsehen* are other common cognates that play major roles in Fichte's lectures. The first literally means insight, and the second means "to look, or see, into something." For the latter, dictionaries also list "look over, examine, perceive, comprehend, understand, realize, and conceive" as equivalents. Thinking only of the Latin roots, one might be tempted to select "intuit" as a good equivalent. It connotes the right sort of direct knowing, one that resembles visual acuity. On the other hand, one could plausibly translate several other German terms with "intuition," and adding another would simply confuse that issue further. Alternatively, "realize" and "realization" could fill the bill. They share the same relation in English that *einsehen* and *Einsicht* do in German. Unfortunately for that possibility, in this series of lectures Fichte also uses *realizieren* and *Realisation,* which ought to be rendered by their natural English equivalents. For Fichte, *Einsicht* and *einsehen* connote a strong cognitive achievement. He believes that we *sehen etwas ein* when we call up in our own consciousness a constructive process that we follow through to conclusion in the target "seen into." In doing so, we create a state within ourselves that is the resolution of the genetically developmental process. The resulting cognitive state is the authentic permeation of the object to be known, and it yields genuine knowing. The presence of this state is strong warrant for the content that it presents. When understood in this unusually strong sense, "insight" and "see into" seem the least confusing translations. I generally use them. Whenever some other term seems more appropriate, I add the German term parenthetically so the reader can follow the occurrences of these important items.

Evidenz presents similar problems. Like *Genesis* it too has an obvious English analogue, in this case "evidence." However, unlike *Genesis,* this German word has rather different connotations than does its English homonym. In English, "evidence" usually names an object, fact, or observation that has logical bearing on the truth of some proposition. Its predominant meanings are legal (a document, object, or oral statement admissible as testimony in a court of law) and scientific (the results of observation and experiment that bear on some hypothesis). In contrast, Fichte uses *Evidenz* to name a particular *way* in which contents can be present in mind. Specifically, it names the clarity of an immediate mental grasp, certain of its contents. I translate it here as "manifestness."

Nothing in the 1804 *Science of Knowing* reveals the strains that Fichte's quest to express his transcendental insights imposes on the German language more clearly than do his neologisms. Among these, the most striking has to be his treatment of simple prepositions. Consider, for example, what he does with *durch* (meaning "through," "across," or "by means of"). Fichte first calls up a noun which has this preposition as a prefix, namely *Durcheinander.* Although this word usually means "confusion," Fichte takes it literally as meaning "through-one-another." Almost immediately, he shortens it to the invented noun *Durch*, thereby transposing the preposition into an abstract noun. By "the through" Fichte means the inner essence of the concept, as mediative. I take his point in all this to be that, as Kant already had seen, because concepts are inherently abstract, general, and discursive, they involve a synthetic transition. This transition unifies otherwise discrete elements, taking one "by means of" or "through" another. By featuring this linguistic innovation, Fichte emphasizes the central role of activity and process in conceiving. In Lecture XI, Fichte introduces the idea that "reason," as the living "through," is the absolute. This conception identifies active transition and mediation, not just as central to reason, but as what is absolute. Later, in Lecture XVIII, the "through" is identified with the five-fold synthesis, which is one hallmark of the later science of knowing. Clearly, this term stands near the center of Fichte's project. When it occurs as a noun, I translate *Durch* simply as "through," always in quotation marks.

Prinzipiieren is another important neologism. It appears first in Lecture XVII, and it occurs regularly in the later lectures. It names the self-grounding moment in the immanent, self-enclosed life of light (which Fichte has identified in Lecture XVI as his "fundamental principle"). This self-enclosed living unity lacks any ground other than itself, and yet it requires a principle, which it itself provides by seeing itself as the reconstruction (or image) of absolute inconceivable being. Fichte calls this activity *Prinzipiieren*, which I translate as "principle-providing" or "principle-izing."

Despite the general strangeness of his diction, Fichte's meaning can usually be made out if one will enter into the thinking process Fichte is presenting and, as much as possible, make it one's own. Of course, this is just what Fichte consistently advises us to do. In that sense, the mere fact that one *can* enter into these lectures in such a way might be taken as providing some partial confirmation for Fichte's view of philosophy's performative character. At the same time, however, such entry does not necessarily signal unconditional agreement with Fichte's system. Although Fichte himself occasionally seems to suggest other wise, *understanding* his philosophical program need not entail *accepting* the science of knowing in all its aspects. In fact, one might equally consistently point out that attaining the identity of unconditional agreement would itself violate Fichte's insight that consciousness is always penultimate and "downstream from the source."

Syntax and Punctuation

Fichte's syntax and punctuation are also both idiosyncratic and difficult. In order to create some semblance of normal English grammar, I have frequently had to deviate from his literal text. This has happened in several ways.

First, I have frequently altered his divisions of the text. Fichte regularly constructs long, complex sentences, which are creatively punctuated by dashes, colons, or semicolons. Apart from the matter of his basic style, I attribute the form of these sentences to the fact that Fichte never prepared this work for publication. Instead, it remains a text designed for oral delivery as lectures. In addressing a group, a lecturer can negotiate long sentences by modulating the cadence and expression of the speaking voice. Although I have left a number of these very long sentences intact as examples of his style (some readers may say that I have left too many), more frequently I have broken them into smaller pieces. I have noted some of these changes to remind the reader that in this text we are always trying to hear Fichte's voice. Likewise, Fichte does not base his paragraph divisions on any simple principle. In fact, the two extant texts of these lectures frequently locate paragraph breaks in completely different places. With all such divergences, I have followed the version that made the best sense of the text, as I understand it.

Further, Fichte's text is frequently telegraphic, leaving connecting words and phrases implicit. When necessary, I have inserted additional words and phrases, which are consistent with a passage's meaning and which help to make that meaning more evident. Such insertions occur enclosed in square brackets.

Finally, Fichte sometimes includes numbered points within longer paragraphs. His numbering systems can be overlapping and inconsistent. To make them clearer, these imbedded points are printed here as indented lists.

Fichte's punctuation also has many peculiarities. Two particularly frequent examples are his uses of the "=" sign and of the colon. In some places, Fichte uses the "=" sign to indicate the identity of two terms or propositions. When doing so seemed most natural in English, I have translated it by "is" or "equals." In other cases, Fichte seems to use the "=" sign more like a hyphen. For example, he sometimes writes W. = L. as an abbreviation for *Wissenschaftslehre*. Another important instance is his phrase *Vernunft = Effekt* (reason = effect or power).[18] In this case, I take Fichte to be expressing the complex idea

1. that reason intrinsically manifests effects;
2. that appearance occurs as an effect of reason;
3. that this co-occurrence of reason/effect is unitary.

I usually translate this phrase as the "effect of reason," or "reason's effect." Generally, I have attempted to understand the occurrences of "=" contextually and to find some appropriate equivalent in English, without striving particularly to preserve Fichte's orthography. As regards the colon, Fichte deploys this punctuation mark frequently, unusually, and inventively. I regularly substitute occurrences of a semicolon or a full stop for Fichte's ubiquitous colons. These substitutions are not generally marked.

Another oddity of Fichte's punctuation is his use of long dashes to indicate shifts of subject. These often occur in places that violate our now standard rules for using the "—" in prose. I suspect that these marks are yet another reflection of this text's origins as an oral presentation. Perhaps Fichte used them to indicate where he would pause or change his manner of speech to indicate a shift in the flow of meaning. We cannot know for sure. Often, these marks occur in one of the extant versions of the text, but not in both. When they occur in both *SW* and *Copia*, and when they also make some sense of the meaning, I have tried to preserve them.

Although these examples can illustrate Fichte's idiosyncratic approach to syntax and punctuation, they do not exhaust the oddities in orthography and punctuation contained in his manuscript. I have attempted in every case to produce a text that remains—at least approximately—faithful to the standards of contemporary written English and that nevertheless preserves something of the flavor of Fichte's approach. In such a venture it is, of course, impossible to be entirely successful.

One final feature of Fichte's text must be mentioned. At a number of crucial points, both editions of the text reproduce diagrams representing those that Fichte apparently drew during his talks. Usually, Fichte provides some elaboration and explanation for each diagram's elements. There can be considerable variation between diagrams in the two versions; indeed, some diagrams are entirely absent from one or the other version. For this translation, I have reconstructed all of these diagrams somewhat freely, incorporating the elements that seemed to me most illuminative of Fichte's point. Readers wishing to see what other editors have made of these images can consult the original sources.

Five-Fold Synthesis

In thinking about how Fichte structures his lectures, one must say a word about the five-fold synthesis. References to such a synthesis occur regularly in the 1804 *Wissenschaftslehre*, both directly and indirectly. Fichte mentions the concept of five-foldness as early as the end of Lecture IV. In other passages he alludes to it indirectly, or seems to be applying it in some way. The grand conclusion of Lecture XXVIII constructs a five by five matrix of dialectical moments. It articulates four fundamental principles that govern the distinct domains of reason's appearance, each of which in turn contains five basic factors (itself, the other three principles, and the unifying principle). This yields twenty "primordial, fundamental determinations of knowing." Adding these to "the science of knowing's indicated five-fold synthesis which we have just completed" yields a set of twenty-five moments. According to Fichte, this set coincides with the most basic structure of experience. Clearly, Fichte regards the five-fold synthetic process as central to his new science. Indeed, one could plausibly see it as his answer to Kant's "metaphysical deduction" of the categories. Although Fichte never quite says so, he sometimes seems to be suggesting that it is the structural framework for the understanding the development of his system as a whole.

Nevertheless, the exact nature of the five-fold synthesis is frustratingly obscure. Fichte claims that it is the rule by which "multiplicity . . . arises out of . . . reflection on oneness." Yet one can still ask, what exactly is this five-fold synthesis? How does it occur? And in respect to what objects does it occur? Is it a methodological heuristic as well as a necessary rule for reflection on reason? Nowhere within these lectures does Fichte satisfactorily clarify just what he understands this five-fold synthesis to be. However, there are two passages that provide significant clues. The first appears at the end of Lecture XV when he says:

> Therefore, the unity of understanding, which reason presupposes here, cannot merely be a simple self-determined oneness; instead it must be a unity-in-relation, meaningless without *two* terms which arise within it in two different connections: in part as positing one another and in part as negating one another, thus the well-known "through" and the five-foldness recognized in it. (p. 122)

The location of this passage at the end of Lecture XV is particularly significant, because Lecture XV contains Fichte's first invocation of the "basic proposition" *(Grundsatz)* for his science (a "proposition" which, not surprisingly, is less a declarative sentence than an enactment). The passage suggests that five-foldness belongs essentially to reason's activity. To reflect on oneness, is to see it already not as pure oneness, but as unity-in-relation. When reflected on, oneness appears to take the form of a unity composed of two terms together with the double relatedness of these terms. We may look at the situation in different ways. Taken statically, it is a triad, composed of the three terms: unity ($=X$) and the subordinate component terms (a and b). Understood dynamically, however, the process uniting these three components can be seen as a five-fold synthetic process. That is, it is the process of

1. a positing b;
2. a negating b;
3. b positing a;
4. b negating a;
5. this entire interaction composing a unity $= X$.

At the end of Lecture IV, Fichte expresses these two possible viewpoints by referring to a "three or five-fold synthesis." He goes on to say that this synthesis does not arise in common thinking. Instead, it can arise only "from another standpoint, which [the science of knowing] alone oversees."

The second passage occurs in his grand, concluding chapter:

> *Result:* reason, as an immediate, internal, self-intuiting *making*,—and to that extent an absolute oneness of its effects—breaks down within the *living* of this making into being and making: into the *making of being* as made and not made, and into the *[making of] making* as likewise primordial, existing, and not primordial, i.e., copied. This disjunction, expressed just as we have expressed it, is what is absolutely original. (p. 217)

This condensed description of the internal essence of reason is itself three-fold and five-fold. It is three-fold as the terms unity = X, being, and making. As a process it contains five moments:

1. reason as self-making;
2. being as made;
3. being as not made;
4. making as primordial;
5. making as copied.

Fichte calls this five-fold disjunction "what is absolutely original." To understand this passage adequately, one would need to work through all of these lectures in detail. However, it is evident at once that Fichte here is claiming that reason, as absolute oneness, divides itself into a five-fold division. If primordial reason actually did necessarily divide in this way, that fact would provide some warrant for the claim that five-foldness constitutes the structural dialectic for studying the a priori structure of experience.

Although these two characterizations of five-foldness may raise as many questions as they answer, perhaps they can point us in the direction Fichte intends this conception to lead us. I believe—but will not attempt to show here—that the whole course of Fichte's dialectic can best be understood from that perspective. I suggest that one fruitful strategy for readers would be to adopt the working assumption that Fichte builds his series of lectures on the principle of five-foldness as an architectonic foundation.

The Double Path

The full text of the second set of Fichte's lectures from 1804 is devoted to "presenting oneness properly." It divides into two parts: a doctrine of truth or reason, and a doctrine of appearance. The first progresses by discovering increasingly subtle distinctions and resolving them genetically to disclose the ultimate oneness from which they derive. The process leads up to—and consists in—a single insight "into the certainty of pure, self-contained living Being." This insight cannot be had at once, or without careful preparation. We must rise up to it by resolving to awaken the science of knowing. Fichte conducts this process of establishing and enacting this central insight in the first sixteen lectures. In the second part of this course, he seeks to derive the principle of appearance as the basis for the various disjunctions that we encountered and discarded in our ascent. Fichte planned to reinstate these rejected disjunctions as the structure of appearing. However, the second part stops once it has derived the basic form of appearance, leaving the further development as a form sketched in the roughest outline. Despite this incompleteness, these lectures contain one of our tradition's most fundamental and wide-ranging statements of the transcendental program in philosophy. Richly suggestive and deeply fertile, it deserves renewed attention.

Near the end of June 1804, a few weeks after ending the lecture series presented here, Fichte sent a letter to his friend P.J. Appia. This letter contained another brief document called "Aphorisms on the Essence of Philosophy as a Science," together with some further explanatory comments. In these "Aphorisms," Fichte distinguishes transcendental philosophy, which always locates the object of philosophy in the unity of being and consciousness, from all previous philosophical reflection, which has understood philosophy as an investigation of being. He then asserts that for an individual to have "presented this oneness properly" (which of course requires the individual to realize it personally and directly) means understanding why oneness first divides itself into being and consciousness. It further means understanding why, once oneness has divided itself into these two spheres, they each follow the lead of consciousness and divide themselves mutually into such domains as nature, the judicial sphere, morality, and religion. In these brief words, Fichte describes his science and delineates its form. Together, these two documents are in fact an excellent précis of, and introduction to, the conception of philosophy at work in this second course of lectures on the *Wissenschaftslehre*. I have included them at the end as the Appendix.

CHAPTER 1

First Lecture

Monday, April 16, 1804

Honorable Guests:[1]

Nothing about the venture which we now jointly begin is as difficult as the beginning; indeed, even the escape route which I just started to take by beginning with a consideration of the difficulty of beginning has its own difficulties. No means remain except to cut the knot boldly and to ask you to accept that what I am about to say is aimed at the wide world generally and applies to it but not at all to you.[2]

Namely: in my view the chief characteristic of our time[3] is that in it life has become merely *historical* and *symbolic*, while *real* living is scarcely ever found. One not insignificant aspect of life is *thinking*. Where all life has degenerated into a strange tale, the same must also happen to thinking. Of course one will have heard and made a note of the fact that, among other things, human beings can think; indeed that many of them have thought, the first in this way, the second differently, and the third and fourth each in yet another way and that all have failed in some fashion. It is not easy to decide to undertake this thought process again for oneself. One who assumes responsibility for arousing an era like ours to this decision must face this discomfort among others: he[4] doesn't know where he might look for, and find, the people who need arousing. Whomever he accuses has a ready answer, "Yes, that is certainly true of others, but not of us"; and they are right to the extent that, as well as knowing the criticized form of thought they are also familiar historically with the opposite schools, so that if someone attacks them on one side, they are ready to flee to the very position they currently reject. So, for example, if one speaks in the way I did just now, rebuking our historical superficiality, dispersion into the

---

The lecture begins at GA II, 8, pp. 2–3. Double numbers in square brackets refer to corresponding pages in GA II, 8. In that volume the two existing texts are printed on facing pages. Because translation sometimes alters word order, and page breaks in *SW* and *Copia* can differ, these page-break markers are sometimes only approximate. Throughout, I have worked primarily from *SW* and follow it as closely as is practicable.

21

most multifarious and contradictory opinions, indecisiveness about everything altogether, and absolute indifference to truth [4–5] in the way I have just rebuked these things, then everyone will be sure that he does not recognize himself in this picture, that he knows very well that only one thing can be true and that all contradictions must necessarily be false. If we accused him of dogmatic rigidity and one-sidedness for his adherence to the one, the very same person would praise his all-around skepticism.[5]

In such a state of affairs there is nothing for it but to assert briefly and sweetly at a single stroke that I presuppose here in all seriousness that there is a truth which alone is true and everything apart from this is unconditionally false; further, that this truth can actually be found and be immediately evident as unconditionally true; but that not even the least spark of it can be grasped or communicated historically as an appropriation from someone else's mind. Rather, whomever would have it must produce it entirely out of himself. The presenter can only provide the terms for insight; each individual must fulfill these terms in himself, applying his living spirit to it with all his might, and then the insight will happen of itself without any further ado. There is no question here of an object which is already well known from other contexts, but of something completely new, unheard of, and totally unknown to anyone who has not already studied the science of knowing[6] thoroughly. No one can arrive at this unknown unless it produces itself in him, but it does this only under the condition that *this very person*[7] produces something, namely the conditions for insight's self-production. Whoever does not do this will never obtain the object about which we will speak here. And since our whole discourse will be about this object, he will have *no object at all*; for him our entire discourse will be words about pure, bare nothingness, an empty vessel, word breath, the mere movement of air, and nothing more. And so let this, taken rigorously and literally, serve as the first prolegomenon.

I have still more to add, which however first presupposes the following. From now on, honorable guests, *I*[8] wish to be considered silenced and erased, and you yourselves must come forward and stand in my place. From now on, everything which is to be thought in this assembly should be thought and be true only to the extent that you yourselves have thought it and seen it to be true.[9]

I said that I have more to add by way of introduction, and I will devote this week's four lectures to this task. Repeated experience compels me to remind you explicitly that these introductory remarks should not be viewed as most are, that is, as a simple [6–7] approach which the lecturer takes and whose content has no very great significance. The introductory remarks I will present have meaning, and what follows will be entirely lost without them. They are designed to call your spiritual eye away from the objects over which it has heretofore glided to and fro, directing it to the point which we must consider here, and indeed to give this point its existence for the very first time.

They are designed to initiate you into the art which we will subsequently practice together, the art of philosophy. They should simultaneously acquaint you,
and make you fluent, with a system of rules and maxims of thinking whose
employment will recur in every lecture.[10]

I hope the matters which are to be handled in the introduction will
become easily comprehensible to everyone of even moderate attention; but
past experience requires that I add a word about just this comprehending.
First, one must not assume that the standard of comprehensibility for the science of knowing in general is comparable to the standard of study and attention which the introduction requires; since anyone assuming this will be
unpleasantly disappointed later on. Thus, whomever has heard and understood the introductory remarks has acquired a true and fitting concept of the
science of knowing sanctioned by the very originator of this science, but the
listener has not thereby acquired the tiniest spark of the science itself. This
universally applicable distinction between the mere concept and the real, true
substance has particular bearing here. Possessing the concept has its uses; for
example, it protects us from the absurdity of underestimating and misjudging
what we do not possess; only no one should believe that by this possession,
which is not in any case all that rare, one has become a philosopher. One is
and remains a sophist, only to be sure less superficial than those who do not
even possess the concept.

Following these prefatory remarks about the prefatory remarks, let's get
to work.

I have promised a discourse on the science of knowing, and science of
knowing you expect. What is the science of knowing?

First, in order to start with what everyone would admit, and to speak of
it as others would: without doubt it is one of the possible philosophical systems, one of the philosophies. So much as an initially stated genus, according
to the rules of definition.

[8–9] So what generally is philosophy and what is it commonly taken to
be; or, as one could more easily say, what should it be according to what is generally required of it?[11]

Without doubt: philosophy should present the *truth*. But what is *truth*,[12]
and what do we actually search for when we search for it? Let's just consider
what we will not allow to count as truth: namely when things can be this way
or equally well the other; for example the multiplicity and variability of opinion. Thus, truth is absolute oneness and invariability of opinion. So that I can
let go of the supplemental term "opinion," since it will take us too far afield, let
me say that the essence of philosophy would consist in this: *to trace all multiplicity* (which presses itself upon us in the usual view of life) *back to absolute oneness*. I have stated this point briefly; and now the main thing is not to take it
superficially, but energetically and as something which ought in all seriousness

to hold good. *All multiplicity*—whatever can even be distinguished, or has its antithesis, or counterpart[13]—absolutely without *exception*. Wherever even the possibility of a distinction remains, whether explicitly or tacitly, the task is not completed. Whoever can point out the smallest distinction in or with regard to what some philosophical system has posited as its highest principle has refuted that system.

As is obvious from this, *absolute oneness* is what is true and in itself unchangeable, its opposite purely contained within itself.[14] *"To trace back"*— precisely in the continuing insight of the philosopher himself as follows: that he reciprocally conceives multiplicity through oneness and oneness through multiplicity. That is, that, as a principle, Oneness = A illuminates such multiplicity for him;[15] and conversely, that multiplicity in its ontological ground can be grasped only as proceeding from A.

The science of knowing has this task in common with all philosophy. All philosophers have intended this consciously or unconsciously; and if one could show historically that some philosophers didn't have this objective, then one can offer a philosophical proof that, to the extent they wished to *exist* (as philosophers), they must have intended it. Because merely apprehending multiplicity, as such in its factical occurrence, is history. Whoever wants this alone as the absolute one intends that nothing should exist except history. If this person now says that there is something in addition to history, which he wants to designate by the name "philosophy," then he contradicts himself and thereby destroys his entire statement.

[10–11] Since, as a result, absolutely all philosophical systems must agree, to the extent that they wish to exist on their own apart from history, the difference between them, taken initially in a superficial and historical manner, can only reside in what they propose as oneness, the one true self-contained in-itself (e.g., the absolute; therefore one could say in passing that the task of philosophy could be expressed as the presentation of the absolute).

In this way, I say, various philosophies could be differentiated if one looked at them superficially and historically. But let's go further. I claim that, to the extent that general agreement is possible among actually living individuals in regard to any manifold, to that extent the oneness of principle is in truth and in fact *one*. For *divergent principles* become divergent results, and consequently yield thoroughly divergent and mutually incoherent worlds, so that no sort of agreement about anything is possible. But if one principle alone is right and true, it follows that only one philosophy is true, namely the one which makes this one principle its own, and all others are necessarily false. Therefore, in case there are several philosophies simultaneously presenting different absolutes, either all, or all except one, are false.[16]

Further, this significant consequence also follows: since there is only one absolute, a philosophy which has not made this one true absolute its own simply doesn't have the absolute at all but only something relative, a product of an unperceived disjunction which for this very reason must have an opposing term. Such a philosophy leads all multiplicity back, not to absolute oneness as the task requires, but only to a subordinate, relative oneness; and thus it is refuted and shown in its insufficiency not just by the true philosophy but even by itself, if only one is acquainted with philosophy's true task and reflects it more prudently than this system does. Therefore the entire differentiation of philosophies according to their principles of oneness is only provisional and historical, but cannot in any way be adequate by itself. However, since we must start here with provisional and historical knowledge, let's return to this *principle of classification*. Again, the science of knowing may be one of the possible philosophies. Therefore, if it makes the claim, as it already has, that it resembles no previous system but is completely distinct from them all, new, and self-sufficient, then it must have a different principle of oneness from all the rest. What did these have as a principle of oneness? In passing, let me note that it is not my intention here to discuss the history of philosophy and to let myself in for all the controversies which would be aroused for me in this way, instead I simply intend to progress gradually in developing my own concept. For this purpose, what I will say could serve as well if it were assumed arbitrarily and were not historically grounded, as if it were historically true. This can be abundantly demonstrated if such demonstration is necessary and [if] there are people concerned about this. I claim that this much is evident from all philosophies prior to Kant, the absolute was located in *being*, that is, in the dead thing as thing. The thing should be the in-itself. (In passing: [12–13] I can add that, except for the science of knowing, *since* Kant, philosophers everywhere without exception, the supposed Kantians as well as the supposed commentators on and improvers of the science of knowing, have stayed with the same absolute being, and Kant has not been understood in his true, but never clearly articulated principle. Because it is not a matter of what one calls being, but of how one grasps and holds it inwardly. For all that one names it [i.e., the absolute] "I," if one fundamentally objectifies it, and separates it from oneself, then it is the same old thing-in-itself).—But surely everyone who is willing to reflect can perceive that absolutely all being posits a *thinking* or *consciousness* of itself;[17] and that therefore mere being is always only one half of a whole together with the thought of it, and is therefore one term of an original and more general disjunction, a fact which is lost only on the unreflective and superficial. Thus, absolute oneness can no more reside in being than in its correlative consciousness; [14–15] it can as little be posited in the thing as in the representation of the thing. Rather, it resides in the principle, which we have just discovered, of the absolute *oneness* and *indivisibility* of both, which is equally, as we have seen, the principle of their disjunction. We will name this principle *pure knowing*, knowing in itself, and, thus, completely objectless knowing, because otherwise it would not be knowing in itself but would require objectivity for its being. It is distinct from consciousness, which posits a being and is therefore only a half. This is Kant's discovery, and is what makes him the founder of *Transcendental Philosophy*. Like Kantian philosophy, the science of knowing is transcendental philosophy, and thus it resembles Kant's philosophy in that it does not posit the absolute in the thing, as previously, or in subjective knowing—which is simply impossible, because whomever reflects on this second term already has the first—but in the *oneness* of both.

But now, how does the science of knowing differentiate itself from Kantianism? Before I answer, let me say this. Whoever has caught a genuine inner glimpse of just this higher *oneness* has already achieved in this first hour an insight into the true home for the principle of the sole true philosophy, which is nearly entirely lacking in this philosophical era; and he has acquired a conception of the science of knowing and an introduction to understanding it, which has also been wholly lacking. [16–17] Namely, as soon as one has heard that the science of knowing presents itself as idealism, one immediately infers that it locates the absolute in what I have been calling *thinking* or *consciousness* which stands over against being as its other half and which therefore can no more be the absolute than can its opposite. Nevertheless, this view of the science of knowing is accepted equally by friends and enemies and there is no way to dissuade them from it.

In order to find a place for their superiority at improving things, the improvers have switched the absolute from the term in which, according to their view, it resides in the science of knowing to the other term to which they append in addition the little word "I" which may well be the single net result of Kant's life and, if I may name myself after him, of my life as well, which has also been devoted to science.

CHAPTER 2

Second Lecture

Wednesday, April 18, 1804

Honorable Guests:

We will begin today's lecture with a brief review of the previous one. In conducting this review I have an ulterior motive, namely to adduce what in general can be said about the technique of fixing lectures like this in memory and of reproducing them for oneself, and to discuss the extent to which transcribing is or is not useful. "In general," I say, because in what concerns memory and the possibility of directing the attention simultaneously to a number of objects, one finds a great discrepancy among people; and I in particular am among the least fortunate in this regard, since I am utterly lacking in what is usually called memory, and my attention is capable of taking up no more than one thing at a time. For this reason my recommendations are all the less authoritative, and each of you must decide for yourselves how far they apply to you and how you might employ them.

For me, the proper and favorite listener would be the one who is able to reproduce the lecture for himself at home, not literally *{unmittlebar}* for that would be mechanical memory, but by pondering and reflection; and indeed following the course of the argument absolutely freely, moving backwards from the results with which we concluded to the premises, forwards from the premises with which we started deducing the result, and moving both ways at once *from the center.* Further, this listener should be able to do so in absolute independence from specific modes of speech; and, since we propose to conduct what is really only one whole, self-contained presentation of the science of knowing in many lectures separated by hours and days, and with the single lecture periods composing the integrative parts of this whole, just as the single minutes of the lecture hour make up its parts, once again my favorite listener will be the one who is able to present all the single lecture sessions comprehensively as a whole, whether beginning with the first, or with the last he has heard, or with any of those in the middle. This is the first point.[1]

This lecture begins at GA II, 8, pp. 18–19.

Now, in the second place, what is most noteworthy in each lesson for each person, and therefore what each grasps most surely, is whatever new element that person learns and clearly understands. What we genuinely comprehend becomes part of ourselves, and if it is a genuinely new insight, it produces a personal transformation. It is impossible that one not be, or that one cease to be, what one has genuinely become, and for exactly this reason the science of knowing can, [20–21] more than any other philosophy, commit itself to reactivate the dormant instinct for thinking, because it introduces new concepts and insights.[2]

What was new in the last hour for those who are not familiar with the science of knowing, and which may have appeared in a new light for those already acquainted with it, was this: if one reflects properly, absolutely all being presupposes a thought or consciousness having that being as its object; that consequently being is a term of a disjunction, the other half of which is thinking; and that for this reason oneness is not to be found in the one or the other but in the connection of both.[3] Oneness thus is the same as pure knowing in and for itself, and therefore it is knowledge of nothing; or in case you find the following expression easier to remember, it (oneness) is found in *truth* and *certainty*, which is not certainty about any particular thing, since in that case the disjunction of being and knowing is already posited. So if, in the effort to reproduce the first lecture from within, someone had clearly and vividly hit upon just this single point, then it would have been possible with a little logical reflection to develop all the rest from it. For example, the listener might inquire: How did we get to the point of proving that being had a correlative term? Did this arise in a polemical context? Was being taken to be absolute oneness rather than a correlative term? Then each would have recalled that this was the case up until Kant. He could then have asked himself: But how generally did we come to investigate what might or might not be *absolute* oneness? Thus each would recall just from knowing why he attended this lecture series that we were supposed to be doing philosophy and that the essence of philosophy was said to be the assertion of absolute oneness and the reduction of all multiplicity to it, and so the whole thought process can be laid out without any problem: what is the science of knowing, etc.[4]

But this restoration must not lack depth and thoroughness. For example, *"reducing multiplicity to oneness"* is a brief formula, easy to remember, and it is comfortable to use it in answering the common question "What is philosophy?" which is a question to which one usually doesn't quite know how to respond. "But," one asks oneself, "do you really know what you are saying: can you clarify it to yourself to the extent of providing a lucid and transparent construction of it? Has it been described? [22–23] How has it been described? With such and such words. All right, the lecturer said this: and these are *words!*[5] I will construct it." Or—this thing which is neither being nor consciousness but rather the oneness of both, which has been presented as the absolute oneness of the transcendental philosophy, can be indicated with these words. But this cannot yet be completely clear and transparent to you, because all philosophy is contained in the transparency of this oneness, and from here on we will do nothing else but work on heightening the clarity of this one concept, in which at one stroke I have given you the whole. If it were already completely clear to you, you would not need me any longer. Nevertheless,[6] I would add that everyone must possess more than the bare empty formula. One must also have a living *image of this oneness* which is firmly fixed and which never leaves him. With my lectures I attend to this, your fixed image; we will extend and clarify it together. If someone does not have this image, there is no way for me to address them, and for this person my whole discourse becomes talk about nothing, since in fact I will discuss nothing except this image.

And so that I finally say directly what it all comes down to—*without this free, personal re-creation of the exposition of the science of knowing in its living profundity, which I have just mentioned,* one will have no possible use for these lectures. "The subject cannot remain simply in *the form* in which I express myself here"; even though you of course can *recall* it by, and out of, yourselves in just this form. In short, a middle term must come between my act of exposition and your active mastery of what has been expounded, and that term is *your own rediscovery;* otherwise, everything ends with the act of exposition and you never attain active mastery.[7]

It is quite unimportant whether one undertakes this re-creation with pen in hand (as I, for example, would do it because I have no memory but rather an imagination, which can only be held in check by written letters) or whether someone with more memory and a tamer imagination does it in *free* thought. It is essential only that each one *does* it in the individually appropriate way; and, in no case can re-creating it in writing cause harm.[8]

In the light of what has been said, whatever is noted down during the lecture cannot take the place of a proper re-creation; instead it can only serve as resource for the act, which must be undertaken with or without this [24–25] assistance. With the deliberate speech, considerable pauses after important paragraphs, and the repetitions of significant phrases which I am using, it must certainly be possible for your pens to catch in passing the main points of the lecture for the required task. For my part, if I had to attend lectures like these, I would not even begin to try to note down more than such main points, since while writing I cannot listen energetically, and while listening energetically I cannot write; for me it would be more a matter of the whole living lecture rather than the isolated, dead words, and more especially a matter of the seldom noticed, but very genuine and real, physical/spiritual action of keen thinking carried out in my presence. Yet I am completely certain that it can be quite different with others and that more easily activated spirits could indeed do two things at the same time equally well.

So much once and for all on this topic!—Now let's carry on with the investigation begun last time, that is, with provisionally answering the question: *What is the science of knowing?*[9]

All transcendental philosophy, such as Kant's (and in this respect the science of knowing is not yet different from his philosophy), posits the absolute neither in being nor in consciousness but in the union of both. Truth and certainty in and for itself = A. Thus it follows (and this is another point[10] through which today's talk links up with the previous one and by means of which in the general reproduction of all the lectures, the previous one is to be produced from it and it from the previous one) . . . it follows, I say, that for this kind of philosophy the difference between *being* and *thinking*, as valid in itself, totally disappears. Indeed, everything that can arise in such a philosophy is contained in the *epiphany*[11] which we already consummated in ourselves during the last lecture; in the insight that no being is possible without thinking, and vice versa—wholly being and thinking *at the same time*,[12] and nothing can occur in the manifest sphere of being without simultaneously occurring in the manifest sphere of thinking, if one just considers rightly rather than simply dreaming, and vice versa. Thus in *the vision*,[13] which is given and granted, there is nothing primarily of concern for us as transcendental philosophers.[14] But according to our insight that the absolute is not a half but indivisible oneness, an insight which reaches beyond all appearance, it is absolutely and in itself neither being nor thinking, but rather:[15]

If now (in order [26–27] to apply what has just been said and to make it even clearer it is assumed that, in addition to its absolute, fundamental division into B and T, A also divides itself into x, y, z, then it follows:

1. that everything together in and for itself, including absolute A, and x, etc., is only just a modification of A; from this follows directly
2. that it all must occur in B as well as in T.[16]

Assume also that there is a philosophical system that has no doubts that the dichotomy of B and T, which arises from A, is mere appearance, and that therefore it would be a genuine transcendental philosophy; but assume further that this philosophy remained caught in such an absolute division of A into x, y, z, just as we proposed. Thus, this system, for all its transcendentalism, would still not have penetrated through to pure oneness, nor would it have completed the task of philosophy. Having eluded one disjunction, it would have fallen into another; and despite all the admiration one must show it for first discovering the primordial illusion, nevertheless with the discovery of this new disjunction, it is refuted as the true, fully accomplished, philosophy.

The Kantian system is exactly this very one, precisely characterized by the outline I have just given. If Kant is studied, not as the Kantians without exception have studied him (holding on to the literal text, which is often clear as the heavens, but is also often clumsy, even at important times), but rather on the basis of what he actually says, raising oneself to what he does not say but which he must assume in order to be able to say what he does, then no doubt can remain about his *Transcendentalism*, understanding the word in the exact sense I have just explained. Kant conceived A as the indivisible union of being and thinking.

But he did not conceive it in its pure self-sufficiency in and for itself, as the science of knowing presents it, but rather only as a common *basic determination* or *accident* of its three primordial modes, x, y, z—these expressions are meaningful; it cannot be said more precisely—as a result of which for him there are actually three absolutes and the true unitary absolute fades to their common property.

The way his decisive and only truly meaningful works, the three critiques, come before us, Kant has made three starts. In *The Critique of Pure Reason*, his absolute (x) is *sensible experience*, and [28–29] in that text he actually speaks in a very uncomplimentary way about Ideas and the higher, purely spiritual world. From earlier writings and a few casual hints in this *Critique* itself, one might conclude that in his own view the matter didn't end there. But I would commit myself to showing that these hints are only one more inconsistency, since if we correctly follow the implications of the premises stated in that text, then the supersensible world must totally disappear, leaving behind a mere noumenon which has its complete realization in the empirical world. Moreover, he has the correct concept of the noumenon, and by no means the confused Lockean notion which his followers have imposed on him. The high inner morality of the man corrected the philosopher, and he published the *Critique of Practical Reason*. In this text the I comes to light as something in itself through the inherent categorical concept as [30–31] it could not possibly do in the *Critique of Pure Reason*, which is solely based on, and drawn from, what *is* empirically; and thus we get the second absolute, a moral world = z. Still, not all the phenomena that are undeniably present in self-observation have been accounted for; there still remains the notions of the beautiful, the sublime, and the purposive, which are evidently neither theoretical cognitions nor moral concepts. Further, and more significantly, with the recent introduction of the moral world as the one world in itself, the empirical world is lost, as revenge for the fact that the latter had initially excluded the moral world. And so the *Critique of Judgment* appears, and in its Introduction, the most important part of this very important book, we find the confession that the sensible and super-sensible worlds must come together in a common but wholly unknown root, which would be the third absolute = y. I say *a third* absolute, separate from the other two and self-sufficient, despite the fact that it is supposed to be the connection of both other terms; and I do not thereby treat Kant [32–33] unjustly. Because if this y is inscrutable, then while it may indeed always contain the *connection*,[17] I at least can neither comprehend it as such, nor collaterally conceive the two terms as originating from it. If I am to grasp it, I must grasp it immediately as absolute, and I remain trapped forever, now as before, in the (for me and my understanding) three absolutes. Therefore, with this final decisive addition to his system, Kant did not in any way improve that which we owe to him, he only generously admitted and disclosed it himself.

Let me now characterize the science of knowing in this historical movement, from which, to be sure, my speculations, which are independent from Kant, take their origin. Its essence consists first in discovering the root (indiscernible for Kant) in which the sensible and supersensible worlds come together and then in providing the actual conceptual derivation of both worlds from a single principle. The maxims which Kant so often repeated orally and in writing, which his followers parroted (we must stop short again[18] and cannot go farther), and which pre-Kantian dogmatists, too, could have used to answer Kant (we must stand by our dogmatism and cannot go farther), are here completely rejected as maxims of weakness or inertia, which are then taken to apply to everyone. The science of knowing's own maxim is to admit absolutely nothing inconceivable and to leave nothing unconceived; and it is satisfied to wish not to exist if something is pointed out to it which it hasn't grasped, since it will be everything or nothing at all. To avoid all misunderstanding let me add that if it too must finally admit something inconceivable, then at least it will conceive it as just what it is, i.e., absolutely inconceivable, [34–35] and as nothing more; and thus too it will conceive the point at which absolute conceiving is able to begin. Let this much suffice as an historical characterization of the science of knowing vis-à-vis the sole neighbor against which it is immediately juxtaposed and to which it can be compared: Kantian philosophy. It cannot be directly compared to any earlier philosophies or recent afterbirths, since it shares nothing with them and is totally different. It shares the common genus of transcendentalism with Kantianism alone, and to that extent must demarcate itself from it, a demarcation which has to do simply with the clarity of this property but not at all with its vain reputation.

Let me give this characterization in pure concepts, higher than, and independently of, historical setting, and present its schema: A is admitted; it divides itself both into B and T and simultaneously into x, y, z. Both divisions are equally absolute; one is not possible without the other. Therefore, the insight with which the science of knowing begins and which constitutes its distinction from Kantianism is not at all to be found in the insight into the division into B and T which we already also completed in the last lecture, nor in the insight into the division of x, y, z which we have still not finished but have problematically presupposed; rather it is to be found in the insight into the immediate *inseparability* of these two modes of division. Therefore the two divisions cannot be seen into *{eingesehen}* immediately, as it seemed from the outset until now; instead they can be seen into only mediately through the higher insight into their oneness.

I call the attention, especially of the returning listeners, to this most important clue; there you have in its full simplicity a characterization of our speculation much earlier and right from the beginning which did not come into our first lecture series until the middle of our work.[19]

(This schema is a summary of the whole lecture. How to re-create the whole out of it is indicated above.)

CHAPTER 3

Third Lecture

Thursday, April 19, 1804

Honorable Guests:

First let me clarify a point raised at the end of the last lecture, which might occasion misunderstanding. Absolute A is divided into B and T and into x, y, z; all at one stroke. As into x, y, z, so into B and T; as into B and T, so into x, y, z. But how have I expressed myself just now? Once commencing with x and the other time commencing with B. This is just a perspective, a bias in my speaking. I certainly know—and even expressly assert—that implicitly, beyond the possibilities of my mode of expression and my discursive construction, both are totally identical, completely comprehended in one self-contained stroke. Therefore, I am constructing what cannot be constructed, with full awareness that it cannot be constructed.

Let me continue now to characterize the science of knowing on the basis of the indicators found in comparing it with Kantian transcendentalism—among other things, I said that Kant very well understood A as the link between B and T, but that he did not grasp it in its absolute autonomy. Instead, he made it the basic common property and accident of three absolutes. In this the science of knowing distinguishes itself from him. Therefore this science must hold that knowing (or certainty), as soon as we have characterized it as A, must actually be a *purely self-sustaining substance*; that we can realize it as such for ourselves; and it is in just this realization that the genuine realization of the science consists. (A *"genuine* realization," I say, with which we aren't yet concerned here, since we are still occupied with stating the simple concept, which is not the thing itself.) This constitutes today's thesis.[1]

To begin with, we can demonstrate immediately that knowing can actually appear as something standing on its own. I ask you to look sequentially at your own inner experience:[2] if you remember it accurately, you will find the object and its representation, with all their modifications. But now I ask further: Do you not *know* in all these modifications; and is not your knowing, as

---

This lecture begins at GA II, 8, pp. 36–37.

knowing, the same self-identical knowing in all variations of the object? As surely as you say, "Yes," to this inquiry (which you will certainly do if you have carried out the given task), so surely will knowledge manifest and present itself to you (as = A) whatever the variation of its objects (and hence [38–39] in total abstraction from objectivity); remaining as (= A); and thus as a substantive, as staying the same as itself through all change in its object; and thus as oneness, qualitatively changeless in itself. This was the first point.[3]

Thus it presents itself to you with impressive, absolutely irrefutable manifestness. You understand it so certainly that you say: "It is absolutely thus, I cannot conceive it differently." And if you were asked for reasons, you could refuse the request and still not give up this contention. It is manifest to you as absolutely certain. During all possible variation in the object, you have said, knowing always remains self-identical. Have you then run through and exhausted all possible changes in object, testing in each case whether knowing remains the same? I do not think so, because how could you have done it? Therefore, this knowing manifests itself independently of such experiments and completely a priori as self-sustaining and self-identical independent from all subjectivity and objectivity.

1. Now, note what actually belongs to this substantial knowing, so conceived, and do so with the deepest sincerity of self-consciousness, so that the erroneous view of the science of knowing which was criticized at the end of our first lecture, namely that it locates the Absolute in the knowing which stands over against its object, doesn't arise again here. It is true that in our experiment we have started with this consciousness or presentation of an object. T.B.–T.B.[4] and so on. In this part of the experiment, B made the T different in every new moment, because the T was altogether nothing else than the T for this B, and disappears with it. Now when we raised ourselves to the second part by asking, "Is not knowing one and the same throughout?" and finding it to be so, we raised ourselves above all differences of T as well as of B. Therefore we could express ourselves much more accurately and precisely: knowing,[5] which for this reason is not subjective, is absolutely unalterable and self-identical not just independently from all variability of the object, but also independently from all variability of the subject without which the object doesn't exist. The changeable is nothing further, neither the object nor the subject, [40–41] but just the mere pure changeable, and nothing else. Now this changeable in its continuing changeability, which is itself unchangeable, divides itself into subject and object; and the purely unchangeable, in which the division of subject and object falls away, as does change, opposes itself to the changeable.

2. Here has been disclosed a splendid example of an insight that comes from exhaustive, continuous searching, which cannot be derived from experience,

but which rather is absolutely a priori. And so past experiences obligate me to entreat everyone here to whom this insight has really been evident (which I think is the case with all of you given the simplicity of the task) to keep this very example in mind, to hold on to it, and, if the old empiricist demon shows up, to attack it and send it away promptly, until we succeed in completely exterminating it. I would very much like to be spared the eternal struggle about whether in general there is manifestness or something a priori (for both are the same). Individuals come to the conclusion that this is the case only by producing it somehow or other in themselves. This has happened here today and I simply ask that you not forget it.

Result: knowing, in the mentioned meaning as A, has actually appeared to us as self-sufficient, as independent of all changeability, and as self-same and self-contained oneness, as was presupposed by previous historical reports of the science of knowing. We therefore already seem to have realized the principle of the science of knowing in ourselves and to have penetrated into it.

The second advance in today's lecture is this.[6] We only *seem* to have done this, but this is an *empty* seeming. We see merely *{sehen bloss ein}* *that* it is so, but we do not see into what it authentically is as this qualitative oneness. Precisely because we see into only such a *that*, we are trapped in a disjunction and thus in two absolutes, changeability and unchangingness, to which we might possibly append a third, the undiscoverable root of both, and thus end up in the same shape as Kant's philosophy. The ground of this duality, insurmountable in this way, is as follows: the *that* must seem self-creating, just as our recent insight seemed to be. But this appearance is possible only under the condition that a point of origin *{terminus a quo}* appears, which seems (as opposed to this self-creation) to be produced by us, just as the [42–43] first part of our previously conducted experiment actually and in fact appeared to be. In a word, we grasp both changeability and unchangingness equally, and are inwardly torn into two or three immediate terms. How then is this to be? Obviously, it is clear without any further steps both that one of the two would have to be grasped mediately, and that this term which is grasped mediately cannot be unchangingness, which as the absolute can only be realized absolutely, but rather must be changeability. The unchangeable would have to be intuited not only in its being, which we have already done, but instead it would have to be penetrated in its essence, its one absolute quality. It (the unchangeable) would have to be worked through in such a way that changeability would be seen as necessarily proceeding from it and as mediately graspable only by means of it.

Briefly, clearly, and to fix the point easily in memory: the insight that knowing is a self-sustaining qualitative oneness (an insight which is purely provisional and belongs to a theory of the science of knowing) leads to the question, "*What* is it [i.e., knowing] in this qualitative oneness?" The true nature of the science of knowing resides in answering this question. In order to analyze this even further, it is clear that for this purpose one must inwardly construct this essence of knowing. Or, as in this case is exactly the same thing, this essence must construct itself. In this constructive act, it *is* without any doubt and is what it is as existing; and, as existing, it is what it is. Therefore it is clear that the science of knowing and the knowing that presents itself in its essential oneness are entirely one and the same; that the science of knowing and primordially essential knowing merge reciprocally into one another and permeate each other; that in themselves they are not different; and that the difference which we still make here is only a verbal difference of the exact kind mentioned at the start of this lecture. The primordially essential knowing is constructive, thus intrinsically genetic; this would be the original knowing or certainty in itself. Manifestness in itself is therefore genetic.

And with this we have specified the deepest characteristic difference demarcating the science of knowing from all other philosophies, particularly from the most similar, the Kantian. All philosophy should terminate in knowing in and for itself. Knowing, or manifestness in and for itself, is actively genetic. The highest appearance of knowing, which no longer expresses its inner essence but instead just its external existence, is factical; and since it is still the appearance of *knowing*, factical manifestness. All factical manifestness, even if it is the [44–45] absolute, remains something *objective*, alien, self-constructing but not constructed of knowing, and therefore something inwardly unexplained, which an exhausted speculation, skeptical of its own power, calls inexplicable. Kantian speculation ends at its highest point with factical manifestness: the insight *that* at the basis of both the sensible and supersensible worlds, there must be a principle of connection, thus a thoroughly genetic principle which creates and determines both worlds absolutely. This insight, which is completely right in itself, could occur to Kant only as a result of his reason's absolute, but unconsciously operative law: that it [that is, his reason] come to a stop only with absolute oneness, recognize only this as absolutely substantial, and derive everything changeable from this one. This basic law of oneness remains only factical for him, and therefore its object is unexamined, because he allows it to work on him only mechanically; but he does not bring this action itself and its law into his awareness anew. If he did so, pure light would dawn on him and he would come to the science of knowing. Kantian factical manifestness is not even the highest kind, because he lets its object emerge from two related terms and does not grasp it as we have grasped the highest factical object, namely as pure knowing; instead he grasps it with the qualification that it is the link between the sensible and supersensible worlds. That is, he does not grasp it inwardly and in itself as oneness, but as duality; his highest principle is a synthesis *post factum*.[7] Namely, this means a case when by self-observation one discovers in one's consciousness two terms of a disjunction and, compelled by reason, sees that they must intrinsically be one, disregarding the fact that one cannot say how, given this oneness, they can likewise become two. Briefly, this is exactly the same procedure by which in our first lecture we rose from the discovery of the duality of being and thinking to A as their required necessary connection, in order initially to construct for ourselves the transcendentalism common to the science of knowing and Kantianism, but the matter was not to rest there. Additionally there should be a synthesis a priori which is equally an analysis, since it simultaneously provides the basis for both oneness and duality.—Kant's highest manifestness, I said, is factical, and not even the highest factical kind. The highest factical manifestness has been presented today: the insight into knowing's absolute self-sufficiency, without any determination by anything outside itself, anything changeable. This is contrary to the Kantian absolute, which [46–47] is determined by the transition between the sensible and supersensible. Since now this presently factical element in science is itself to become actively genetic and developing, then, change in general will be grounded in it as a genesis pure and simple. But by no means will any particular change be so grounded. It seems that absolute facticity could be discovered only by those who have raised themselves above all facticity, as I have actually *{in der That}* discovered it and consistently made use of it only after discovering the true inner principle of the science of knowing, and as I am using it now to lead the audience from that point forward in the genetic process *{in die Genesis}*.

Kant's manifestness is factical, we ourselves are presently also standing in facticity; and I add that everywhere in the scientific world there is no other kind of manifestness except the factical (namely in the first principles), except in the science of knowing. As far as philosophy is concerned, after conducting the demonstration with Kant, we can safely omit tests on other systems. After philosophy, mathematics makes claims to manifestness, indeed in some of its representatives it takes on airs by elevating itself above philosophy, an error which can be excused in the light of today's philosophical eclecticism. Now abstracting here completely from the fact that things are not so wonderful for mathematics—not even in regard to how it can and should be—this science must confess that its principles admit nothing more than factical manifestness, regardless of the fact that they will become actively genetic as we proceed. For let the arithmetician *qua* arithmetician simply tell me how he is able to elicit a solid and permanent number one; or let [48–49] the geometer explain what fixes and holds his space for him while he draws his continuous lines through it; and whether these and ever so many other ingredients which he needs for the possibility of his derivations are given in any other way than through factical intuition. Of course this does not in any way constitute an objection to mathematics; as mathematics it can and should be nothing else.

It is certainly not our business to obscure the boundaries of the sciences; but one should simply recognize, and this science, like all the others, should know that it is neither the first nor self-sufficient but rather that the principles of its possibility lie in another, higher science.

Now, since in the actual sciences generally no other principles are available than those that are factically manifest, and since by contrast the science of knowing intends to introduce entirely genetic manifestness and then to deduce the factical from it, it is clear that essentially in its spirit and life the science of knowing is wholly different from all previous scientific employment of reason. It is clear that it is not known to anyone who has not studied it directly and that nothing can take the place of such study. It is equally clear that there is no perspective or premise which has appeared in previous life or science from which it can be seen as true, attacked, or refuted, because whatever this perspective or premise is, and however certain it might be, still it is nonetheless surely only factically manifest, and this science accepts nothing of this kind *unconditionally*, but does so only under conditions which it determines in its genetic analysis. But whoever wants to argue against the science of knowing using such a perspective as its principle, wants *unconditional* agreement which is already once and for all ruled out in advance. Therefore he is arguing from a premise that has not been accepted {ex non concessis} and makes himself ridiculous. The science of knowing can only be judged internally, it could be attacked and refuted only internally, by pointing out an internal contradiction, an inner inconsistency or insufficiency. Therefore such activity must be preceded by study and comprehension and must begin with that. Until now to be sure the opposite order has been tried; first judging and refuting and after that, God willing, understanding. As a result nothing has ensued except that the blows have [50–51] completely missed the science of knowing, which has remained hidden from view like an invisible spirit, and they have struck instead the chimeras which these men have created with their own hands. Following this, they have gone so far astray with these fantasies and have spread confusion so extensively that today it can be expected that they would at least understand that they are confused!

CHAPTER 4

Fourth Lecture

Friday, April 20, 1804

Honorable Guests:

It seems to me that we have succeeded, even in the prolegomenon, in gaining a very clear and deep insight into the scientific form of the science that we wish to pursue here. Let us continue the observations with which we have achieved this insight.

Here are the results so far: that we have certainly grasped knowing as unchangeable, self-same and self-sustaining, beyond all *change* and beyond the *subjectivity-objectivity*, which is inseparable from change. But this insight was not yet the science of knowing itself, but rather only its premise. The science of knowing must still actually construct this inner, qualitatively unchangeable being, and as soon as it does this, it will simultaneously create change, the second term, as well.

The true authentic meaning of this simultaneous double construction of the changeable and the unchangeable will become completely clear only when we actually and immediately carry out the construction, something that belongs within the sphere of the science of knowing itself, certainly not in preliminary reports. Misunderstandings about this are unavoidable at the beginning. In order to come as close as possible to complete accuracy right from the start, I venture on a question that has already been raised.

On introducing the schema:[1]

$$A$$
$$x\,y\,z \bullet B\!-\!T$$

I said that the science of knowing stood in the point.[2] I have been asked whether it doesn't rather go in A. The most exact answer is that actually and strictly it doesn't belong in either of these but rather in the oneness of both. By itself A is objective and therefore inwardly dead; it should not remain so,

---

This lecture begins at GA II, 8, pp. 52–53.

indeed it should *become* actively genetic.[3] The point, on the other hand, is merely genetic. *Mere*[4] genesis is nothing at all; but this is not just mere genesis but the *determinate* genesis that is required by the absolute qualitative A; [it is] *a point of oneness*. Now to be sure this point of oneness can be realized *immediately, oscillating and expending itself* in this point; and we, as scientists of knowing,[5] *are*[6] this realization inwardly (I say inwardly and concealed from ourselves). But this point can neither be expressed nor reconstructed in its immediacy, since all expression or reconstruction is conceiving and is intrinsically *mediated*. It is expressed and reconstructed [54–55] just as we have expressed it at this moment: namely, that one begins from A and, indicating that it cannot persist alone, links it to the point; *or* one begins with the point and, indicating that it cannot persist alone, links it to A, *all the while*, to be sure, knowing, saying, and meaning that neither A nor the point can exist *by itself* and that all our talk could not express the implicit truth, but instead that the implicitly unreconstructible something which can only be pictured in an empty and objective image is the organic *oneness* of both. Thus, since reconstruction is conceiving, and since this very conceiving explicitly abandons its own *intrinsic validity*, this is precisely a case of conceiving the inconceivable *as inconceivable*. Therefore—and I put this here first as a clarification—this is a question of the organic split into B–T and x, y, z, as I explained at the beginning of the last lecture; because when I speak, I must always put one before the other. But is it actually so? No, instead it is exactly the same stroke; and let me add this as well: *this deeper connection must indeed itself be a result and a lower expression of the higher one just now described.* Finally, in order to say this in its full meaning and thereby to make your insight into the science of knowing, and into knowing as such, much clearer: secondary knowing, or *consciousness*, with its whole lawful play by means of fixed change and the manifold (within it or outside it), of sensible and supersensible, and of time and space, comes to be, in principle, through this recently noted and demonstrated *division*, taken merely as a division and nothing else. Everything we attribute to the subject, as originating from it, derives from this. Because it is clear without further ado that from a particular perspective, namely the science of knowing's synthetic perspective, the disjunction must be just as absolute as oneness; otherwise we would be stuck in oneness and would never get outside it to changeability. (Let me note in passing that this is an important characteristic of the science of knowing and distinguishes it, e.g., from Spinoza's system, which also wants absolute oneness but does not know how to make a bridge from it to the manifold; and, on the other hand, if it has the manifold, cannot get from there to oneness.)

[56–57] As scientists of knowing, we never escape the principle of division inwardly and empirically (i.e., by means of what we do and promote); but we certainly escape it intellectually with regard to what is valid in itself, in which very regard the principle of division surrenders and negates itself.

Or, so that I make the point at which we have arrived even clearer: since we actually reason as we have just been doing, where does our reasoning stand, if we remain *exclusively {nur recht}* in consciousness *{Besinnung}*? ("If we remain exclusively in consciousness," I say, because we can also lose ourselves in the intelligible realm, and there is even, in its place, an art of consciously losing one-self in it.) Manifestly in our construction by means of the principle of division, it stands in the place not of that which is to be valid *to the extent it is constructed* but of that which is *intrinsically* valid; thus it stands wholly autonomously, as has been said, between the two principles of oneness and separation, simultaneously annulling both and positing both. Thus, the standpoint of the science of know-ing, which stands still in consciousness, is by no means a synthesis *post factum*; but instead a synthesis a priori, taking neither division nor oneness as given, but *creating* both at one stroke. Once again to adduce an even higher perspective what is the absolute oneness of the science of knowing? Neither A nor the point, but instead the inner *organic oneness* of both. Besides this given description of the point of oneness is there also another? None at all, we have seen. Therefore, this description is the original and absolutely authentic one. What are its con-stituents? The organic oneness of both is a construction or a concept, and indeed the single absolute concept, abstracted from nothing existing, since even its own separate existence, and hence the existence of everything conceptual, is denied. Further, the construction as such is denied by the manifestness of what exists autonomously; thus even the inconceivable, as the inconceivable and nothing more, is posited by this manifestness, posited through the negation of the absolute concept, which must be posited just so that it can be annulled.[7]

And so:

1. the necessary unification and indivisibility of the concept and the incon-ceivable is clearly seen into *{eingesehen}*, and the result may be expressed thus: if the absolutely inconceivable is to be manifest as solely self-sustain-ing, then the concept must be annulled, but to be annulled, it must be posited, because the inconceivable becomes manifest only with the nega-tion of the concept. Supplement: hence inconceivable = unchangeable; con-cept = [58–59] change. Therefore along with the foregoing it is evident that if the unchangeable is to appear, there must be change.
2. Now to be sure inconceivability is only the negation of the concept, an expression of its annulment. Therefore it is something which originates from both the concept and knowing themselves; it is a quality transferred by means of absolute manifestness. Noting this, and therefore abstracting from this quality, nothing remains for oneness except absoluteness or pure self-sufficiency in itself.

3. The following consideration makes this particularly important and relevant: *What* is pure self-sufficient knowing in itself? The science of knowing has to answer this question, or, as we put it more precisely, it has to construct the presupposed inner quality of knowing. We are undertaking this construction here: negating the concept by means of manifestness, and thus the self-creation of inconceivability is this living construction of knowing's inner quality. This inconceivability itself originates in the concept and in pure immediate manifestness; likewise the whole quality of the absolute, as well as the fact that a quality can be applied to it at all, originates in the concept.[8] The absolute is not intrinsically *inconceivable*, since this makes no sense; it is inconceivable only when the concept itself tries for it, and this inconceivability is its only property. Having recognized this inconceivability as an alien quality introduced by knowing, I said before, only pure self-sufficiency, or substantiality, remains in the absolute; and it is quite true that at best this self-sufficiency does not originate in the concept, since it enters only with the latter's annulling. But it is clear that this quality enters only within immediate manifestness, within intuition, and thus is only the representative and correlate of pure light. This latter is its genetic principle by which, first of all, according to our hypothesis all manifestness opens up into genetic manifestness, since pure light manifests itself implicitly as genesis. Secondly, the previously presented relationship of concept to being and vice versa is further determined as follows: If there is to be an expression and realization of the absolute light, then the concept must be posited, so that it can be negated by the immediate light, since the expression of pure light consists just in this negation. But the result of this expression is being in itself, period. [This result] is inconceivable precisely because pure light is simultaneously destruction of the concept. Thus, pure light has prevailed as the one focus and the sole principle of both being and the concept.

4. From the preceding it follows that this inconceivable, as the bearer of all reality in knowing, which we grasp[9] in its principle, is absolute only as inconceivable, and cannot be thought in any other way. No other [60–61] additional hidden qualities are attributable to it. Just as little can any quality be added to light, beyond the previously mentioned characteristic, namely that it annuls the concept and remains absolute being. If we made such additions, we would, as Kant has been criticized for doing, run up against something unexplained and perhaps inexplicable. As support for this contention, notice that we have understood it as inconceivable purely in its form and nothing more. We have no right to assert anything before we have seen into it.[10] So if we posit some other hidden quality, we have either invented it, or better, since pure invention from nothing is completely impossible, we have manufactured it by trying to supply a principle

for some facticity. This happened with Kant when he first factically discovered the distinction between the sensible and supersensible worlds and then added to his absolute the additional inexplicable quality of linking the two worlds, a move which pushed us back from genetic manifestness into merely factical manifestness, completely contravening the inner spirit of the science of knowing. Therefore, it is important to note that whatever yet to be determined characteristics the reality appearing in our knowing may carry in itself, besides the common basic property of inconceivability, such characteristics by no means require any new absolute grounding principle besides the one principle of pure light, since this would multiply the number of absolutes. Rather, the multiplicity and change of these various traits is to be deduced purely from the interaction of the light with itself, in its multifarious relations to concepts, and to inconceivable being.

I invite you to the following reflections so that I can offer a hint about this last point, raise what has been said today to a higher level, give the new listeners a unified perspective for viewing everything that they can learn here, and give the returning listeners the same perspective from which they can again gather and reproduce everything they have heard up to now.

The focus of everything is pure light. To truly come to this requires that the concept be posited and annulled and that an intrinsically inconceivable being be posited. If it is granted that the light should exist, then in this judgment everything else mentioned is possible as well. We have now seen {*eingesehen*} this; it is true; it remains true forever; and it expresses the basic principle of all knowing. We can so designate it for ourselves.

[62–63] Now, however, I want to completely ignore the content of this insight and reflect on its form, on our actual situation of insight. I also think that *we*, those of us present here who have actually seen it, are the ones who had the insight. As I remember it and as I think we all do, the process was that we freely constructed the concepts and premises with which we began, that we held them up to each other freely, and that in holding them together we were gripped by the conviction that they belonged together absolutely and formed an indivisible oneness. Thus we created at least the conditions for the self-manifesting insight, and so we likewise appeared to ourselves unconditionally.

But let us not go to work with too much haste; rather let us consider things a little more deeply. Did we create what we created because we wished to do so, and therefore as the result of some earlier knowledge, which we would have created because we wished to create it as the result of an even earlier knowledge, and so on to infinity, so that we might never arrive at a first creation? Somewhere, if the concept is created it must absolutely and thoroughly create itself, without anything antecedent and without any necessity of a "we"; because this "we," as has been shown, always and everywhere requires some previous knowing and cannot achieve immediate knowing. Therefore we cannot create the conditions, they must emerge spontaneously. Reason must create itself, independent from any volition or freedom, or self. But this proposition, disclosed through analysis, [contradicts][11] the first which is given reflexively, and so immediately. Which one is true, and on which should we rely? Before trying to answer, let us return again to the matter of the insight which has become controversial in regard to its principle, in order to grasp its meaning and true worth clearly. We realized that *if light is to be*,[12] then the concept must be posited and negated. Therefore, the light itself is not immediately present in this insight, and the insight does not dissolve into light and coincide with it; instead it is only an insight in relation to the light, an insight which objectifies it, grasping it by its inner quality only. Thus, whatever the principle and true bearer of this insight might be, whether *we* ourselves, as it seems to be, or pure self-creating reason, as it also seems to be, the light is not *immediately* present in this bearer, instead it is present merely mediately in a representative and likeness of itself. First of all, [64–65] that this light occurs merely mediately applies not just in the science of knowing but in any possible consciousness that has to posit a concept so it can annul it; and the science of knowing rests on a completely different point than the one on which many may have assumed it to rest after the last lecture, because undoubtedly knowing was understood too simply.

And now to answer the question: both are clear, therefore both are equally true; and so, as was said at the start on another occasion, manifestness rests neither in one nor in the other, but entirely between both. We arrive here, and this is the first important and significant result, at the *principle of division*, not as before a division between two terms, which in that case are to be intrinsically *distinct* like A and the point, but instead a division of something which remains always inwardly self-same through all division. In a word, we have to do with constructing and creating the very same primal concepts which appear one time as *immanent*, in the unconditionally evident final being, the I; and appear the other time as *emanent*,[13] in reason, absolute and in itself, which nevertheless is completely objectified. Thus, it is a division pure and in itself, without any result or alteration in the object.

Further, manifestness oscillates between these two perspectives: if it is to be really constructed, then it must be constructed in that way. Thus, it must be constructed as oscillating from *a* to *b* and again from *b* to *a* and as completely creating both; thus as oscillating between the twofold oscillation, which was the first point, and which gives rise to a three or fivefold synthesis.

What is the common element in all these determinations? The very same representative of the light, seen in its familiar inner quality. Here it stays. Therefore everything is the same one common consciousness of light. This consciousness, which is held in common and therefore cannot be really constructed but instead can only be thought[14] by means of the science of knowing, can be regarded or represented in the three or fivefold modifications only from another standpoint, which this science alone oversees.

So much for now.

CHAPTER 5

Fifth Lecture

Monday, April 23, 1804

Honored Guests:

It might be appropriate to cancel the lecture this Wednesday, because of the general day of prayer.[1] I would have taken up preliminary matters again today had I not also seen the necessity, because of this, for sparing you the strongest nourishment.

Indeed, I have already adduced and shared with you everything which is conducive for understanding these lectures and which helps one enter their standpoint except for two things: first, what really cannot be imparted, namely the knack for grasping them; and second, some observations which tend not to be received well and which I had hoped to be able to omit this time.

As far as concerns the first item, the knack for grasping these lectures is the knack of full, complete attention. This should be acquired and exercised before one enters on the study of the science of knowing. For this reason, in the written prospectus for these lectures—available at the place of subscription—I have established as the sole, but serious precondition for understanding this science the requirement that participants should have experience with fundamental scientific inquiry. Not, of course, for the sake of the specific information so gained, since none of that is presupposed or even accepted here without qualification; rather, I did so because this study also awakens and exercises full, complete attention. Collaterally, one gains a knowledge of scientific terminology, which we are using freely here. *Full, complete attention*, I have said, which throws itself into the present object with all its spiritual power, puts itself there and is completely absorbed in it, so that no other thought or fancy can occur; since there is no room for anything strange in a spirit totally absorbed in its object: full, complete attention as distinct from that partial attention which hears with half an ear and thinks with half its thinking power, interrupted and criss-crossed by all kinds of fugitive thoughts

---

This lecture begins at GA II, 8, pp. 66–67. It could have possibly been given on Tuesday, April 24, 1804.

47

and fantasies, which eventually succeed in totally overwhelming the mind so that the person gradually falls into a dreamy fog with eyes wide open. And if he should chance to come back to awareness, he will wonder where he is and what he has heard. This full, complete attention of which I speak, and which only those who possess can recognize, has no degrees. It is distinguished from that scattered attention, which is capable of many degrees [68–69], not merely quantitatively; but is totally different and even logically contradictory to it. It fills the spirit completely, while incomplete attention does not.

For understanding these lectures everything depends on one's possessing this kind of attention; everything which makes understanding difficult or impossible follows solely from its absence; if one is freed from this lack, then all these things are ripped out by the roots. So, for example, if this lack is removed, the phenomenon of believing one cannot intuit the particular theorems presented in the lecture because one is too quickly confused will fall away. As I like to repeat frequently so no one will lose heart, in the nature of our science *the same thing* is constantly repeated in the most various terms and for the most diverse purposes, so that an insight which is missed on one occasion can be produced or made good on another occasion. But strictly speaking it should be, and is actually, demanded of everyone that they see into each theorem when it is initially presented. So those for whom things don't happen as we expect have not used these lectures as they should be used; and if things don't flow smoothly, they have only themselves to blame. To give the most decisive proof that what I demand is possible under conditions of complete attentiveness—any distinction between faster or slower mental capacity has no place in the science of knowing, and the presentation of this science aims neither at good nor slow minds but at minds *as such*, if only they can pay attention. For this is our procedure as it has gone up to now and as it will remain: first we are required to construct a specific concept internally. This is not difficult: anyone just paying attention to the description can do it; and we construct it in front of him. Next, hold *together* what has been constructed; and then, without any assistance from us, an insight will spring up *by itself*, like a lightning flash. The slowness or speed of one's mind has nothing more to do in this final event, because the mind in general has no role in it. For *we* do not create the truth, and things would be badly arranged if we had to do so; rather, truth creates itself by its own power, and it does so wherever the conditions of its creation are present, in the same way and at the same rate. And in case the ensuing manifestness did not arise for someone who had really carried out the construction which we postulated, this would only mean that he did not sustain the construction in all clarity and power, but instead that it faded because some distraction intervened. That is [70–71], he did not place his total attention on the present operation.

Or, if this lack is removed, another equally common phenomenon would be destroyed at its root: namely, that an illusion which we have already revealed as an illusion, nevertheless can return and deceive us again, as if it had truth and meaning, or at least confuse us and make us uncertain about insights that we had otherwise already achieved. For example, if you have really seen that in intuiting the one, eternally self-same knowing, all differentiation into subjective and objective completely disappears as arising only in what is changeable, then how can you ever again allow yourself to be deceived by the illusion (which, to be sure, as an illusion, can always recur) that you yourself are the very thing that objectively posits {objectiviert} this one knowing (that you therefore are the subject with it as your object)? Because you indeed have seen once and for all that this disjunction is always and everywhere the same illusion and never the truth, no matter in what form or in what place it might be manifest. If you have seen this, then you have attained this insight and dissolved into it. How then could you possibly cease being what you are, unless, because you have not really entirely become it but only entered half way, you never threw yourself into, and rooted yourself in, this insight which now remains wavering and deceptive for you. In this case the old illusion returns at the first opportunity. But note well the sequence: the insight does not leave you because the illusion steps in, rather the illusion enters because the insight has left you! So much as regards the talent of total attentiveness as the sure and unerring means of correctly grasping the science of knowing. Second, I want to mention a few more things that block apprehension of the science of knowing, because they do not allow proper attention to arise. I take these things up collectively in their oneness, as is my custom (as will likely be the custom of anyone who becomes familiar with the science). They arise together from a lack in one's love of science, which is either a *simple* lack: a weak, powerless, and distracted love; or a secret hatred of knowledge because of some other love already present in the mind.

Let us first take up the last: the other love which leads to a secret hatred of knowledge is the same one from which hatred arises against every good, namely, a perverted self-love for the empirically arisen self instead of for the self which is immersed in the good, the true and the beautiful. This love is either that of self-valuation, which therefore becomes pride, or that of self-enjoyment, which therefore becomes spiritual lasciviousness {Wohllustigkeit}.

[72–73] The first of these is unwilling to admit that anything could occur in the domain of knowing that it had not itself discovered, and long been aware of. Whether it explicitly says so or not, to such a one, the science of knowing's claim to absolute novelty seems to be a statement of contempt for itself. It would very much like to humiliate this arrogance on the part of this science—for this is how things must seem to it. Therefore, instead of giving itself freely and with complete attention from the start, it focuses on whether it can possibly catch this science in some failing; and ambivalence of purpose distracts it so that it misses the right idea, does not enter into the true subject matter, but rather finds just what it was looking for in the confused concepts which it obtains of the enterprise, weaknesses in its "science of knowing."[2]

The other mode of thought, love for the empirical self's self-enjoyment, loves the free play of its mental capacities (which it partially becomes) with the objects of knowing (which it in the same manner partially becomes). I think it can best be characterized in the following way: it calls making something up "thinking" and it names the invention of a truth for oneself in one's own body "thinking for oneself." A science which brings all thinking without exception under the most stringent rules and annuls all freedom of spirit in the one, eternal, self-sustaining truth can hardly please such a disposition, and it must also incite this later mode of thought to the same secret polemic against itself, producing the very consequences we have just described. Moreover—just to take this opportunity to make the point decisively—I do not warn each of you against this secret inner polemic for my own sake, but rather for yours, because one cannot achieve correct attention, let alone understanding, while doing it. If one will only first understand and master the science of knowing and then feel a desire to argue against it, I will have nothing more to say against this.

Or again it could be a ruling passion for the merely empirical and for the absolute impossibility of feeling and enjoying one's spirit in any way except as trained memory. These personified memories are not capable of such secret hate; but they necessarily become very ill-tempered in this setting. They want what they call results: namely what can be observed and can be reproduced in similar circumstances; "[that is] a sufficient statement and one that says something." Now when they think they have grasped something of this kind, the next lecture arrives further qualified, differently arranged, [74–75][3] symbols and expressions change, so that not much remains from the hard-won treasure. "What eccentricity! Why couldn't the man just say what he meant from the start?" For people like that the most extreme confusion and contradiction must arise from what has the purest oneness and strongest coherence, simply because it is the true inner coherence and not the merely external schematic coherence, which is all they really want.[4]

Originally, I first mentioned cold, weak love of science (which is not exactly hate) as an obstacle to attention. Namely, whoever seeks, desires, or wishes in science for something besides science itself does not love it as it ought to be loved and will never enjoy its complete love and favor in return. Even the most beautiful of all purposes (that of moral improvement) is too lowly in this case; what should I say of other, obviously inferior ones! Love of the absolute (or God) is the rational spirit's true element, in which alone it finds peace and blessedness; but science is the absolute's sweet expression; and, like the absolute, this can be loved only for its own sake. It is self-evident that there is no room for anything common or ignoble in a soul given over to this love, and that its purification and healing are intrinsic to it.

This love, like every absolute, recognizes only the one who has it. To those who are not yet possessed by it, it can give only the negative advice to remove all false loves and subordinate purposes, and to allow nothing of that kind to arise in them so that the right will spontaneously manifest itself without any assistance from them. This much should be remembered once and for all on this subject.

Now to the topic set for today. When I presented it, I already suspected that my last talk might seem too rigorous and deep for a fourth lecture [76–77], and it was made so in part to help me discover what mode of presentation I would need to follow with this new audience. Now I will repeat it in a suitable form:

1. First, a remark that is valid for all previous and subsequent lectures, and that will be very useful in order to reproduce and review them. Our procedure is almost always this:
   a. we perform something, undoubtedly led in this process by a rule of reason which operates immediately in us. What in this case we really *are* in our highest peak, and that in which we culminate, is still only *facticity*.
   b. we then search out and reveal the law which guided us mechanically in the initial action. Hence, we see *mediately* into what we previously had seen into immediately, on the basis of its principle and the ground of its being as it is; and we penetrate it in the origin *{Genesis}* of its determinateness. In this way we will ascend from factical terms to genetic ones. These genetic elements can themselves become factical in *another* perspective, in which case we would be compelled again in connection with this new *facticity* to ascend genetically, until we arrive at the *absolute source*, the source of the science of knowing. This is now noted and can be clarified in reference to the consequences: x is nothing but the developmental link to y, and y in turn to z.[5]

Now, whoever either has not comprehended z from the start, or has lost and forgotten this understanding in the process, for that person neither x nor y exists and the entire lecture has become an oration about nothing, through no fault of the lecturer. This, I say, has been and will continue to be our procedure for some time. It was so in the last lecture. Whoever may have recognized this process—it was obvious for everyone to see, and the earlier distinction between factical and genetic manifestness should have led right to it—could have reproduced the entire lecture and made it intrinsically clear by simply asking: Was any such factical term presented, and which one was it? Which could it be after the earlier ones? Did the presentation succeed in presenting the genetic term after the factical one? Assume that I may have completely forgotten this second step or perhaps never heard of it. Then I will have to discover it for myself just as it was discovered in the talk, because the rule of reason is unitary, and all reason which simply collects itself is self-same.

So what was the factical term? It was not in A and not in the point, but unconditionally in both. We have now grasped {*eingesehen*} this, it has made itself evident, and so it is. Analyze [78–79] it however you wish: it contains A, the point, and, in the background, a union of both. With the first two terms denied as the true point of oneness, the other one is thereby posited, and in this fashion you will not arrive at any other term. It *is* so, factically. But now I ask on another level: How have we brought it about that this insight has arisen for us? We did not reflect further on the content, which we completely abandoned; but focused instead on the *procedure*, asking about the origin {*Genesis*}. In this way, as I indicated earlier, the initial, materially constituted, *immediacy*[6] becomes *mediately* visible: once such an origination is posited, this factical insight is posited, but solely by means of our establishment of the origin.

How did we do it? Apparently we made a *division* in something which on the other hand ought to be a *oneness*.[7] I say division and disjunction in a general way, because one can ignore the fact that the terms separated are "A" and the point, when it is a question of the act *qua* act.[8] This division shows itself to be invalid in an immediate insight {*Einleuchten*}. We did not produce this insight because we wished to, instead it produced itself absolutely (not from any ground or premise) in an absolutely self-generating and self-presenting manifestness, or pure light. The distinction, in the sense that it should be valid by itself, would therefore be annulled by the [one's] manifestness. On the contrary, the same manifestness posits a self-same, intrinsically valid oneness which is incapable of any inner disjunction. The principle of division equals the principle of construction, and thus of the concept as well. [Now, consider] this principle in its *absoluteness*[9] (and by that I mean, the principle as *dividing* the wholly and intrinsically one, which is seen into as one, [working] wholly and absolutely by itself without other ground and doing so rather in contradiction to the truth)—this principle is negated in its absoluteness, i.e., in its intrinsic validity.[10] It is seen unconditionally as negated, and therefore it is negated in and through the absolute light. Thus, in this annulling of the absolute concept in relation to intrinsic being {*das Wesen an sich*}, this being is inconceivable. Without this relation it is not even *inconceivable* but rather *is only* absolute self-sufficiency. But further even this predicate "is" derives from manifestness. Hence the sole remaining ground and midpoint is the *pure light*, and so on.

This was by far the greatest part of the earlier talk's content. That this all has intrinsic clarity and incomparable manifestness is obvious to anyone who sees it at all. [80–81] I am convinced that it could not be presented with greater order, distinctness, clarity, and precision than in this case. Whomever doesn't see it now must be lacking in the undivided attention required here.

The part still to be added, which I will repeat now, is another developmental analysis {Genetisieren} of the insight we have achieved: I said that *we* saw into [the fact] that the light was the sole midpoint. In this reflexion, the process we initially unfolded itself becomes *factical*. Now, since in this case we have produced nothing, and [since] rather the insight as insight has produced itself, we cannot ask as we did before *how* we did this, but we can rise to greater clarity. It is clear; if only we see {sehen wir nur ein} that it is the *light*, then we are not immediately consumed in this light, instead we have the light present through its agent or representative, that is, through an insight into the light, into its originality or absolute quality. We must disregard the fact that we cannot now ask without contradiction how the light itself is produced; since it is recognized as the principle of absolute creation, the question would deny the insight again. We can certainly still ask how the *insight* into light (which we called not light itself but rather its agent and representative) has been produced; that is a different question. Therefore we only need to pay attention to how the production of this insight has taken place. 1. *We* have put ourselves in the condition; 2. how could we do this?—Both are true:—not the light and not even the insight into light, but the insight into the insight into the light stands between both. [The *emanence* and the *immanence*: these are matters with which we must concern ourselves.

Regarding the entire distinction between the immanence and emanence of the production of an insight into light, one must not forget that the same thing extends to the insight and to *the light* itself. As before, the objective light *qua* objective neither is, nor can become, the one true light. Instead pure light enters insight under this aspect. But here we have won this: that the highest object is no longer substance for itself, but light. Substance is only the form of light as self-sufficient. On the other hand, insight (subjectivity), actually the inner expression and life of light, disengages itself from the negation of the concept, and of *division*. Can you penetrate into the true midpoint more deeply in any other way? Into the entirely unique concept that is nevertheless required here? 1. It is clear "that its being is not grasped except in *immediate doing*." 2. It can be made clear [82–83] here that *immediate* doing is a *dissolving* into immanence (the initially uncovered making of his being, as this sort of making). First of all, *doing* deposes *being* and *being* deposes *doing*—or stated otherwise: here is the fundamental reversal; and this must *be understood*: doing replaces *actual* being—*being beyond* all being (not actual or material being) deposes doing. Now it is also *very clear* that—to posit it without any *actuality* (just in barely hypothetical form and in a "should") and thereby to deduce and materialize doing itself, thus also to intellectualize and idealize—being negates itself in the other as a result of its own doing. Thus we once again come back to the previous point, and we find the previous principle again in this *self-negation*. Perhaps this is just the *concept of being*, dead in-itself: clearly there is a *division* in it between being (what endures) and doing: and indeed *as* a division this is intrinsic to constructing non-separation or oneness. Thus this negation would be true in a certain respect. It is right since *primordially* the division into being and doing is *nothing at all*.][11]

Sixth Lecture

Thursday, April 26, 1804

Honorable Guests:

In today's and tomorrow's talks I will continue with the further development of what has already been presented. In doing so I aim at an end useful to both sorts of listeners. That is, since, like all philosophy, the science of knowing has the task of *tracing* all multiplicity *back* to absolute oneness (and, correlatively, to *deduce* all multiplicity *from*[1] oneness), it is clear that it itself stands neither in oneness nor in multiplicity, but rather stays persistently between both. It never descends into *absolute* multiplicity, which must after all exist and indeed does exist (as mere empirical givenness), but rather it maintains the perspective from above, from the standpoint of its origin. Therefore, in the science of knowing we will be very busy with multiplicity and disjunctions.

Now, these disjunctions, or differences and distinctions, which the science of knowing has to make are new and previously unrecognized. Therefore, in the usual modes of representation and speech from which we begin, these differences collapse unnoticed into oneness, and when we are required to draw them, they seem *very minute.* (*It is hairsplitting,*[2] as the literary rabble has put it; and it is necessary that it be so, since if a science that is to trace everything that is multiple—that is, everything in which a distinction can be constructed—back to oneness allows any distinction that the science could possibly make to remain *hidden*, then it has failed in its purpose.) Therefore one of main problems for the science of knowing consists in just this: making its very precise distinctions visible and distinct; so that when this problem is finally solved, these distinctions will be fixed and established in the *mind* of those studying it, so that they will never again confuse them. I think that both difficulties will be significantly reduced if I lay out for you in advance (so far as this is possible) the general schema and basic rule in terms of which these divisions will come about—although in an empty and purely formal way. And, so that this schema can be correctly understood and

---

This lecture begins at GA II, 8, pp. 84–85.

noticed, I will *deduce* it *in its unity and from its principles*, to the extent that this can be done with what we know so far.

To begin I mention in general the following:

[86–87] 1. Since, according to the nature of our science, we must stand neither in oneness nor in multiplicity but instead between the two, it is clear—and I focus on this because I believe I have detected several of you making this error—that no oneness at all that appears to us as a simple oneness, or that will appear to us as such in what follows, can be the true oneness. Rather, the true and proper oneness can only be the principle simultaneously of both the apparent oneness and the apparent multiplicity. And it cannot be this as something *external*, such that it merely projects oneness and the principle of multiplicity, throwing off an objective appearance; rather it must be so *inwardly and organically*, so that it cannot be a principle of oneness without at the same moment being a principle of disjunction, and vice versa; and it must be comprehended as such. Oneness consists in just this absolute, inwardly living, active and powerful, and utterly irrepressible essence.—To put it simply, oneness cannot in any way consist in what we *see* or *conceive* as the science of knowing, because that would be something objective; rather it consists in what we are, and pursue, and live.—Let this be introduced once and for all to characterize the oneness which we seek and to eliminate all the errors about this central point which, if they continued, would necessarily be very confusing in what follows. And be warned, not only so that you don't content yourself merely with that sort of oneness, taken just relatively and one-sidedly, as if it was the absolute, but also so that if I in this lecture, or any other philosopher, remain content with such a oneness, you will know and state strongly that this philosopher has stopped half way and has not made things clear.

2. *In consequence:* Since the true oneness is the principle simultaneously of the (apparent) oneness and of disjunction, and not one without the other, it therefore makes no difference whether we regard what we will present provisionally as our highest principle at each juncture in the progress of our lectures as a *principle of oneness* or of disjunction. Both perspectives are one-sided, merely our necessary point of view, but not true in themselves. Implicitly the principle is *neither one nor the other*, rather it is both as an organic oneness and is itself their organic oneness.

Therefore, so that I can say it even more clearly—*first of all* only principles can enter the circle of our science. Whatever is not in any possible [88–89] respect a principle, but is instead only a principled result *{Principiat}* and phenomenal, falls to the empirical level, which, of course, we understand on the basis of its principle, but which we never scientifically construct, as this cannot ever be done. *Then*, every *principle* that enters our science (and indeed every principle *qua* principle) is simultaneously a principle of oneness and multiplicity, and it is truly understood only insofar as it is conceived in those terms. Our own scientific life and activity, therefore, to the extent that it is a process of penetrating and merging with the principle, never enters into that oneness which is opposed to multiplicity nor into multiplicity; rather it maintains itself undisturbed between both, just like the principle. *Finally* each principle in which we stand (and we never stand anywhere but in a principle) yields an absolutely self-differentiating *oneness*:[3]

$$a = \alpha\!\!-\!\!\begin{array}{c} x \\ y \\ z \end{array}$$

The only question is whether this oneness is the *highest*. If not, and there are several such a's ($a^1, a^2, a^3, \ldots$), then not just in the former case but in the latter as well, "α" is still in this regard a principle of disjunction for unities, which to be sure would be unities in relation to

$$\begin{array}{c} x \\ y \\ z \end{array}$$

but in connection to one another, they would by no means be so. For these α's we need a new a, until we have uncovered the highest oneness, which would be the absolute disjunction, just as we have described it in relation to the absolute oneness. This gives us the first general model for the procedure of the science of knowing.

One comment here: the interchangeability of direction from α to x, y, z and vice versa is evident, and this greatly aids their linkage.

3. Now the same point, from another side and deeper. As regards the explanation we have been pursuing up to now in this hour (not about the *principle of disjunction*, since strictly speaking there is no such thing, but rather our *view* of the one implicit principle *as* a principle of disjunction, a one-sided view that we undoubtedly must start with since the science of knowing finds us completely trapped in this one-sidedness and starts from there), we find ourselves trapped in the familiar, frequently cited inexpressibility: that the oneness is to separate itself at one stroke into being and thinking and [90–91] into x, y, z, both equally immediately. In expressing this verbally and in diagrams, we were compelled to make one of the two the immediate term, though our inner insight contradicted this, negating the intrinsic adequacy of the construction of our mode of expression. Expressing this curious relation in its logical form will help us to speak precisely: in this actual disjunction there are two distinguishing grounds *{fundamenta divisionis}* neither of which can occur without the other. Therefore, expressing the matter just in the way we

have done is probably an empirically discovered turn of phrase, since we found it on the occasion of explaining Kant's philosophy and in adding a disjunction, which has been demonstrated neither by *Kant*[4] nor yet by us,[5] not only between being and thinking, but between sensible and supersensible being and thinking. And the claim that both distinguishing grounds are absolutely inseparable would therefore be grounded simply on this: If what is evident in empirical self-observation *is to be explained,* then we *must* assume that the distinguishing grounds are inseparable. This *"must"* grounds itself directly on a law of reason which operates in us mechanically and without our awareness [of it] *{eigene Einsicht}.* Thus at bottom we had only an empirical basis on top of which we postulated a supersensible one;[6] that is, we began a synthesis *post factum.* This cannot be blamed on the science of knowing as long as it is the science of knowing; it is not permitted simply to report this inseparability of the distinguishing grounds, instead it must *grasp* this ground *conceptually* in its principle and from its principle as necessary. It must therefore see into it genetically and mediately. "It grasps this ground conceptually" means it sees the distinguishing grounds (and by no means just the actual factically evident distinctions—whoever remains with these has simply not finished the climb we have just completed) as themselves disjunctive terms of a higher oneness, in which they are one and *inseparable* as they are when enacted *{im Akte},* so that, as we have said, it remains one and the same stroke. But they are separable and conceptually distinguishable, as we may provisionally think in order thereby to have something to think. "Separable" so that, for example, the ground for distinguishing being and thinking can appear as a further determination and modification of the ground for distinguishing sensible and supersensible, and so that likewise from another point of view [92–93] the latter can appear vice versa as a further determination and modification of the former. As has been said, *when it is enacted,* this disjunction in the oneness of the mere *concept* concresces *{concresciert}* into a factical oneness which is not further distinguishable, and in this concrete union, every eye that remains factical is entirely closed to the higher world of the conceptual beyond.

(And now a number of additional remarks. I ask that you not allow yourself to be distracted while I state them):

1. I have now specified the boundary point between absolutely all factical insight and truly philosophical and genetic insight entirely and exactly, and I have opened up the sources of the entirely new world in concepts which appear only in the science of knowing. The creation and essence of this new world is found just here, in the negation of the primordial disjunctive act as immediate and in the insight into this primordial act's principle—materially, that it is *thus,* and formally, that it is at all.

2. I have here explained the essence of the final scientific form of the science of knowing from a single point more precisely than I have been able to do previously. The main point of this scientific form resides in seeing into the oneness of the distinguishing ground—of being and thinking as *one* and of sensible and supersensible (as I will say in the meantime) as one. Whoever has understood this—as it is to be understood up to now, namely as an empty form—and holds on to it firmly, can scarcely make any further errors in the subsequent actual employment of this form.

3. In order to assist both your memories and repeated reproduction: in the last hour I said that the path of our lectures was, and would for a long time continue to be, that we first present something in factical manifestness and then would ascend to a genetic insight into this object on the basis of its principles. This is exactly what we have done in the just-completed explanation. Already since the second lecture, we had developed the inseparability of both recognized distinguishing grounds historically out of Kant's own statement, and we admitted the factical correctness of this statement. Now we raise ourselves—to be sure not to a genetic insight into the principle of this inseparability (since we do not yet actually know this inseparability itself, nor its terms, but have only assumed all this temporarily and for the time being—but to the *genetic* insight, which must be the form of this principle, if such inseparability and such a genetic principle are to exist).

Now back to our project. It is also not at all our intention to see directly into this inseparability and its principle, since these do not allow themselves to be "seen into" directly. And in fact:

4. to take the process further—by our beginning we have already jumped past this principle, which was discussed here in its form simply for the intelligibility of what really concerns us, in order to derive it deductively; and [94–95] indeed we have already uncovered good preliminaries for this derivation. Namely, you recall that we have already presented a point of oneness and difference, which covers the oneness of these distinguishing grounds: the one between A and the point, and, in connection with the deeper distinguishing grounds which are materially different from oneness and difference, we have said that this might be only a profounder view of this same higher principle, disregarding the fact that we could not yet prove this contention.[7]

[Let me] repeat a third time this oneness which has already been constructed twice before our eyes. To that end I recall only that an absolute dividing principle was evident there—not A and the mentioned disjunctive point, since these are *principled results {Principiate}* of absolute division, which disappear when one looks to the principle; but rather the *living absolute* separation within us. I stress again what I said before about this essential point, which is designed to tear our eyes away from facticity and to lead them into the world of the pure concept, if I can succeed in making it clearer. I hope nobody assumes here that the act of thinking the distinction between A and . is actually grounded in an original distinction in these things, independent of our thinking. Or, in case someone is led to this conclusion by the previous factical ascent with which we had to begin, he will recover from this idea if he considers that in A and . he thinks only the oneness which, according to him, should be unconditionally one containing no distinction within itself; that he himself thus makes clear that the distinction is not based in the object itself, since he could not think the object except by virtue of this distinction; that he thus expressly makes his own thinking as thinking into the distinguishing principle. But the validity and result of this product of thought expressly surrenders and dies in relation to the thing itself. With it as the root, its products A and . are also doubtlessly uprooted and destroyed as intrinsically valid. Thus away with all words and signs! Nothing remains except our living thinking and insight, which can't be shown on a blackboard nor be represented in any way but can only be surrendered to nature.

[We *intuit*, I say, that it rests neither in A nor in . but rather in the absolute oneness of both; we intuit it unconditionally without sources or premises. *Absolute insight* therefore presents itself here. Pure intuition, pure light, from nothing out of nothing, going nowhere. To be sure bringing oneness with it, but in no way based on it.][8]

[96–97] Here everything depends on this: that each person correctly identify with this insight, in this pure light; if each one does, then nothing will happen to extinguish this light again and to separate it from yourself. Each will see that the light exists only insofar as it intuits vitally in him, even intuits what has been established. The light exists only in living self-presentation as absolute insight, and whomever it does not thus grasp, hold, and fix in the place where we now stand, that one never arrives at the living light, no matter what apparent substitute for it he may have.

5. Consideration of the light in its inner quality, and what follows from it, to which we will proceed after this step, is entirely different from this surrender and disappearance into the living light. This consideration as such will inwardly objectify and kill the light, as we will soon see more precisely. But first we said: only the light remains as eternal and absolute; and this [light], through its own inner immediate essence, sets down what is *self-subsistent*, and this latter loses its previously admitted immediacy to the light, whose product it is. But there is no life or expression of this light except through negating the concept, and hence through positing it. As we said, no expres-

sion or life of the light could arise unless we first unconditionally posit and see a life as a necessary determination of the light's being, without which no being is ever reached, except, that is, *in the light* itself—its essence in itself and its being, which can only be a living being. Thereby, however, what matters to us, since we add life to light, is that we have nevertheless divided the two, have therefore, as I said, actually killed the light's inner liveliness by our act of distinction; that is, by the concept. Now, to be sure, we contradict ourselves, *ipso facto* denying that life can be distinguished from light, the very thing we have just accomplished. This is a contradiction which may well be essential and necessary, since it may implicitly in itself be the negation of the concept to which, according to the foregoing, it must someday certainly come. (What I'm saying now is added parenthetically for future use. It is easy to remember; since it connects with our reflections on the objectifying consideration of the light, and allows itself to be reproduced from it for anyone who has paid even a little attention to our proceedings, in case he has otherwise completely forgotten.)

To review: in this consideration of the light, light shows itself through its mere positedness, absolutely and without anything further, as the ground for a self-subsisting being—and at the same time for the *concept*; and, to be sure, for the concept [98–99] in a twofold sense: in part as *negated*, precisely in its intrinsic validity; and in part as posited, *posited* as absolute but *not realized* (though still actual); that is, as *appearance* and as the light's vitality, but in no way an appearance that conditions its inner essence. By the concept's being posited, A and . are also posited—to be sure as *appearance* and certainly not as *primordial appearance*, but rather as conditioning appearance and the inner life of the primordial appearance = β, thus *appearance's appearance*. [In its inner life, appearing should occur again as the unity of the above mentioned distinguishing grounds, its life comes from the livingness of the concept, this in turn stems from the light's livingness, thus an appearance of appearance of appearance. Everything is brought together again when enacted *{im Akte}*. This would be the schema of an established, rule-governed descent, in no way like [the one outlined] yesterday, one equally possible on all sides and therefore very exposed to error.][9]

CHAPTER 7

Seventh Lecture

Friday, April 27, 1804

Honorable Guests:

[Our] purpose [here is] to give a brief account of the rules according to which the disjunction we will have to make proceeds.

1. [It is a disjunction into] principles, with each being equally a principle of unity and of disjunction.
2. [It provides a deduction from this to a general] schema of the total empirical domain according to the form of its *genetic* principle[1]—this will be an entirely new explanation, because I observed to my pleasure that some of you had seen that there is something else even more deeply hidden, despite the fact that you could not assist yourselves [to find it], which, to be sure, was not even required.[2]
3.[3] With the remark that our investigation has already gone beyond this principle to a higher one and that it has already begun to deduce this principle itself, [I repeat] this achieved insight. Neither in A nor .—for us the oneness beyond is nothing in itself, although it is *posited as in itself*; rather it exists only through the light and in the light, and (is) its projection—*light itself*—*contemplation* of light. Now back to our former topic—[4]

[There is] one further step which opens up a whole new side of our investigation; as I said: we have already previously begun to derive the principle of oneness and disjunction of materially different principles of division, only without recognizing that this was what we were doing.[5]

So (dropping what we have done so far until I take it up again) recall with me and consider the following: when we observe the light, the light is objectified, alienated from us and killed as something primordial. We have explained what is attributed materially to the light in this observation of the light, and we have connected this explanation to the *schema under consideration.*[6]

This lecture begins at GA II, 8, pp. 100–101.

Now we will explain this observing itself⁷ in its inner form, that is, no longer asking what it contains and leads to, but rather how it itself inwardly occurs, while also rising to its principle and viewing it genetically to some extent. It is immediately clear that: 1. the light is in us (that is, in what we ourselves are and do in observing it) not immediately but rather through a *representative or proxy*,⁸ which objectifies it as such, and so kills it. So then, where does the highest oneness and the true principle now rest? No longer, as above, in the light itself, since we, as living, dissolve in the light. Neither [is it] in the representative and image of the light which is to be identified now: because it is clear that a representative without the representation of what is represented or an image without the imaging of what it images, is nothing. In short, an image as such, according to its nature, has no intrinsic self-sufficiency, but rather points toward some external, primordial source. Here, therefore, we have not only, as above, factical manifestness, as [102–103] with A and .; instead [we even have] *conceptual*⁹ manifestness: oneness only with disjunction, and vice versa. "Even conceptual manifestness," I say: something imaged—like the light, in this case—is not thinkable without an *image*, nor likewise an image, *qua* image, without something imaged. Notice this important fact, which will take one deep into the subject matter, if it is properly grasped here. In this case you carry out an *act of thinking {ein Denken}*, which has essence, spirit, and meaning and is fully and completely self-identical and unchangeable in relation to this essence. I cannot share this with you directly, nor can you share it with me; but we can construct it, either from the concept of something imaged which then posits an image, or from the image which then posits something imaged. I ask: apart from the arrangement of the terms, which is irrelevant here, have we then thought two different things in the two concepts thus fulfilled, or have we not rather thought exactly the same thing in both, an issue that genuinely touches the inner content of thinking? The listener must be able to elevate himself to the required abstract level out of the irrelevance of the arrangement to the essential matter of the content, of spirit, and of meaning, and then the insight which is intended will immediately manifest itself to him. Should this indeed be the case, then an *absolute oneness*¹⁰ of content is manifest here that remains unaltered as oneness but that splits itself only in the *vital fulfillment*¹¹ of thinking into an inessential disjunction, which neither spoils the content in any way nor is grounded in it. Either [there is] an *objective* disjunction into *something imaged* and its *image*, or, if you prefer, [there is] a *subjective-objective* disjunction into a *conception* of something imaged on the basis of the directly posited image, and a *conception* of the image on the basis of the directly posited imaged something. I do advise you to prefer the latter, since in that case you have the disjunction first hand.—And thus in this case our principle in the genetically-oriented *{genesirten}* view of the light would be the concealed oneness, which cannot be described further, but which is lived only immediately in this act of seeing, and which, as the primordial concept's content, presents itself as absolute oneness, and as absolute disjunction, in its living fulfillment. Now, the something imaged in the concept's content should be *the light*: therefore our principle (i.e., we, ourselves) rests no longer either in the light or in the light's representative, but rather in the oneness in and between the two, a oneness realized in our act of thinking.[12] Therefore, I have called the concept situated here *the primordial concept {Urbegriff}*. [I call it this] because what up to now we have taken as the source of the absolutely self-sufficient, and which therefore appeared as the original and was original for us, actually first arises in the way it appears, in its objectivity, from this concept as one of its disjunctive terms. Therefore, this concept is [104–105] more original than the light itself; hence, so far as we have yet gone, it is in this sense what is truly original. Thus we have given a deeper genetic explanation of the hint, given only as a fact in the lecture just eight days ago,[13] concerning the representatives of the original light, although, to be sure, we have done so for the particular end we intend here.

Thereby you will see that the concept is determined further and grasped more deeply than it has been heretofore. Until now it was a dividing principle which, as self-sufficient, expired in the light, and which preserved only a bare *factical* existence as an appearance, qualifying the appearance of the original light. Further, it had no contents and acquired no contents except that which pure light added to it in immediate intuition through a higher synthetic unity. Now, however, the concept has its own implicit content, which is self-subsistent, totally unchangeable and undeniable; and the principle of division (which arises again in this case, and as before is negated as intrinsically valid) is no longer essential to it, but instead only conditions its life, i.e., its *appearance*. The concept's content, I say, is self-subsistent; thus it is exactly the same substantial being which was previously projected out of intuition and which manifests here in the concept as *prior to*[14] all intuition and as the principle of the objective and objectifying intuition itself. Previously, the concept qualified both life and the appearance of light, and these conversely qualified the concept's being. Therefore, it was a reciprocal influence, and every [act of] thinking the two terms was qualified externally. Now the same single concept grounds its appearance through its own essential being; therefore, in this concept the image and what it images are posited absolutely, things which are constructed organically only through one another. And, hence, its appearance announces, and is the exponent of, its inner being, as an organic unity of the *through-one-another {Durcheinander}*, which must be presupposed. Its being for itself, permanent and unchanging, and as an inner organization of the *through-one-another*—essential, but in no way externally constructed—are completely one: therefore, in this case, *absolute oneness* is grounded and explained through itself.

We will achieve a great deal if here and now we see fundamentally into what I meant by the inner organic oneness of the primordial concept, which

I mentioned just now; since this oneness is the very thing we will need as we continue. In this regard I ask: Does the image, as image, completely and unconditionally[15] posit something imaged? And if you answer "Yes," does not the something imaged likewise posit such an image? Now [106–107] without further ado I admit that both can be seen (by you) as posited immediately by the other, but only if you posit one of the two as prior. But I ask you for once to abstract from your own insight. This is possible in the way that I will preconstruct for you now, and in ordinary life it happens constantly when it shouldn't. Further, one could not ever enter the science of knowing without this abstraction.[16] That is, I ask about the *truth* in itself, which we recognize as being and remaining true even if no one saw it, and we ask: Is it not true in itself that the image entails something imaged and vice versa? And, in this case, what exactly is true *in itself*? Just reduce what remains as a pure truth to the briefest expression. Perhaps that a posits b and b, a? Do we want to divide the true into two parts and then link these parts by the empty expletive *"and,"* a word which we scarcely understand and which is the least understandable word in all language, a word which is unexplicated by any previous philosophy? (It is indeed the synthesis *post factum*.) How could we, since beyond this it is certainly clear that the determination of the terms derives solely from their place in the sequence—for example, that image is the consequent because something imaged is the antecedent, and vice versa.—Further, if one enters more deeply into the meaning and sense of both terms, it is clear that their meaning simply changes itself into the expression "antecedent" and "consequent," while something imaged is *really* antecedent and so forth: thus all this dissolves into appearance. So then, what common element remains behind as the condition for the whole exchange? Obviously only the *through-one-another* that initially holds together *every* inference[17] however it might have been grasped, and which, as through-one-another, leaves the consequence relation exactly as free in general as it has appeared to be.[18]

[Let me say this in a preliminary way (there is not time today to explain the deeper view which is possible here and which I will go into in the next hour)—. The focal point = the *concept* of a pure enduring through-one-another in living appearance:[19]

a—act and consequence either *ideally,* or [108–109] *really*—I say *either/or,* it always remains *act,* the concept proceeds from it alive, but not finished and complete; whomever wants this must do it.

On the other side, the concept projects the one eternally self-same light as intuition, from which follows (and this is its absolute essence): what stands beneath it are parts of its externalization and thus are further modifications not of the light but of its appearance *{Ansicht}* in the living concept. 1. Only through life to the concept and only through the concept to life and the appearance of the light in itself: but its first modification, never as pure but in one or another variant. 2. Creation of the science of knowing in its possible modifications.]

CHAPTER 8

Eighth Lecture

Monday, April 30, 1804

Honorable Guests:

I believe we have arrived at a focal point in our lectures, a point which more effectively facilitates a clear insight and overview than does any other, and which therefore will permit us greater brevity in what follows. Therefore, let us not economize on time now, and from here on out we will make ourselves more secure. Today we will do this with the contents of the last lecture.

We have seen {eingesehen} actually and in fact, and not just provisionally, that an absolute, self-grounded insight negates an equally absolutely *created division* (that is, one not grounded in things) as invalid, and that this insight posits in the background a self-subsistence, which cannot itself be described more precisely.—Let this be today's first observation: at this point the main thing is that all of us assembled here together have really and actually seen into this just as it has been presented, and that we will never again forget this self-insight or allow it to fade; but rather we will take root in it and flow together with it into one.[1]

Thus—what has been said is not just *my* report or that of any other philosopher, but rather it exists {ist} unconditionally, and it remains always true, before anyone actually sees into it, and even if no one ever does. We, in our own persons, have penetrated to the core and have viewed the truth with our own eyes. Likewise, as has been evident from the first, what has been said is in no way proposed as a hypothetical proposition, which is shown to be true in itself only by way of its usefulness in explaining phenomena, as is the case in the Kantian, and every other philosophy. Instead it is immediately true independently of all phenomena and their explicability. (A good reason for making this more precise!) Therefore, what genuinely follows from this, if only it is itself completely enough determined, is also as unconditionally true as it [i.e., the original insight] is. And everything which contradicts it, or the least of its results, is unconditionally false and should be abandoned as false

---

This lecture begins at GA II, 8, pp. 100–111.

and deceptive. This categorical decisiveness between truth and error [112–113] is the condition for our, and every, science; and it is presupposed. It is far removed from that skeptical paralysis which in our days parades as "wisdom," doubts what is unconditionally manifest, and wants to make the latter clearer and more manifest by the most derivative means.

And as particularly concerns the explanation of phenomena from a principle that is manifest, it is obvious right away that if the principle is sound, and likewise the inferences, then things will go well with the explanation; we need only note that, since the principle first grants us a true insight into the phenomenon's essence as such, it may well happen that in this proof process many things do not even have the honor of being genuine, orderly phenomena, but rather dissolve into deceptions and phantasms, although all ages have held them to be phenomena, or—God forbid—even to be self-subsisting realities. Therefore, it may happen that in this regard science, far from acquiring some law or orientation from the factical apprehension of appearances, on the contrary rather legislates for them. This situation can also be expressed as follows. Only what can be derived from the principle counts as a phenomenon; what cannot be derived from it is an error simply because of its non-derivation, although it may perhaps incidentally also be immediate, if one wants to boast of this direct proof.[2]

This is the second observation—already as a result of this just repeated insight, a new world of light has opened for us, which transcends our entire actual knowledge, and a world of error, in which nearly every mortal without exception finds himself, has perished, especially if we appropriate what follows and is recorded below. If we take up this result directly here, it will be invigorating for the attention and throw a very beneficial light on what comes next.

[114–115] 1. By annihilating the formal concept, which is the condition for its own real appearance and vivacity, the light, as the one true self-sufficiency, posits a self-sufficient being, which is not further determinable and which, as a result of the insufficiency *{Nichtgültigkeit}* of the concept that attempts to grasp it, is inconceivable. The light is simply one, the concept that disappears in the light is one (the division of what is one in-itself), and being is one; it can never be an issue of anything other than these three.[3] The one existence arises[4] in the intuition of what is independent, and in the concept's negation (and it will turn out that whatever genuinely concerns true existence will also rest in this). If, as is customary, you want to call the absolutely independent One, the self consuming being, *God,*[5] then [you could say that] all genuine existence is the intuition of God. But at the same time note well—and already a world of errors will be extinguished—that *this being*, despite the fact that the light posits it as absolutely independent (because the light loses itself in its life), is actually not so, just because it bears within itself the predicate "is," "persistence," *{des Bestehens}* and therefore death. Instead, what is truly absolutely independent is just the light; and thus divinity must be posited in the living light and not in dead being. And not, I certainly hope, in *us*, as the science of knowing has often been misunderstood to say; for however one may try to understand that, it is senseless. This is the difficulty with every philosophy that wants to avoid *dualism*[6] and is instead really serious about the quest for oneness: either we must perish, or God must. We will not, and God ought not! The first brave thinker who saw the light about this must have understood full well that if the negation is to be carried out, we must undergo it ourselves: Spinoza was that thinker. It is clear and undeniable in his system that every separate existence vanishes as [something] independently valid and self-subsistent. But then he kills even this, his absolute or God. Substance = *being* without *life*—because he [116–117] forgets his very own act of insight— the life in which the science of knowing as a transcendental philosophy makes its entrance. ("Atheist or not atheist?" Only those can accuse the science of knowing of atheism—I am not concerned here with real events,[7] because regarding all those the science of knowing is not at issue, since in fact no one knew anything about it—who want a dead God, inwardly dead at the root, notwithstanding that after this it is dressed up with apparent life, temporal existence, will, and even sometimes with blind caprice, whereby neither its life nor ours becomes comprehensible; and nothing is gained except that one more number is added to the crowd of finite beings, of whom there are more than enough in the apparent world: one more that is just as constrained and finite as themselves and that is in no way different from them in kind.—[I mention] this in passing to state clearly and in a timely way a significant basic quality of the science of knowing.)[8]

One term is *being*, the other—the negated concept—is without doubt *subjective* thought, or consciousness. Therefore we now have one of the two basic disjunctions, that into B and T (being and thinking), we have grasped this in its oneness, as we should, and as proceeding completely and simply from its oneness, (L = light); and thereby, so that I can add this, too, parenthetically, we would simultaneously have the schema for the negation of the I in the pure light and even have it *intuitively*.[9] For if, as everyone could easily agree, one posits that the principle of the negated concept is just the I (since *I* indeed appear as freely constructing and sketching out the concept in response to an invitation), then its destruction in the face of what is valid in itself is simultaneously *my* destruction in the same moment, since I as its principle no longer exist. My being grasped and torn apart by the manifestness which *I* do not make, but which creates itself, is the phenomenal image of my being negated and extinguished in the pure light.

2. This, I say, is a result of the light itself and its inward living expression: things must remain here as a consequence of this insight and in case they simply follow it, and we will never get beyond it. But I claim that, if only we

reflect correctly, we are already beyond it: we have certainly considered the light and objectified it: the light therefore—whomever has forgotten this circumstance during the previous explanation should recall it now—[118–119] has a twofold expression and existence, partly its inner expression and existence (conditioned by the negation of the concept, conditioning and positing absolute being), partly an *external* and *objective* expression and existence, in and for our insight.

As concerns the latter,[10] that at first we speak of it alone; we surely remember that we did not possess it, and everything that lies within it, immediately; instead we raised ourselves to it from the beginning of our investigation, initially by abstracting from the whole variety of objective knowings [and rising] to the absolute, self-presenting insight that genuine knowing must always remain self-same in this variation; and then [we continued] by means of deeper, genetic examination of this insight itself. So far this has been our procedure; the new and unknown spiritual world in which we pursue our path has arisen by this procedure alone, and without it we would be speaking of nothing. It now further appears to us that we could very properly have neglected this procedure, just as we have undoubtedly neglected it every day of our lives before we came to the science of knowing. Taking up this appearance now—while not making any further inquiry into its validity or invalidity—[we find that] it contains the following: the light's external existence in an insight directed to it, as the one absolute,[11] eternally self-same in its fundamental division into being and thinking; [it] is conditioned by a series of abstractions and reflections that we have conducted freely, in short by the procedure that we state as the free, artificially created science of knowing; this *external* existence arises only *in this way* and *for it*, and *otherwise not at all*. This the first point here.[12]

But, on the contrary, we assert, as concerns the *inner* existence and expression of the light, that if the light exists unconditionally—and in particular whether we have insight into it or not, and this is the very insight which depends on appearing freedom—it is in and for itself the very same one, eternally self-identical, and thoroughly necessary, if only the light exists. Therefore we assert a meaningful consequence, something I bid you to mark well, that there are *two* different modes of light's life and existence: the one mediately and externally in the *concept*, the other simply immediate *through itself*, even if no one realizes it. Strictly speaking in actual fact no one ever does realize it, but instead this inner life of the light is completely *inconceivable*. This is the second point.[13]

Light is originally divided into being and thinking. That the light lives unconditionally therefore means that it splits itself completely originally, and also inexplicably, into being and concept, which *persists*, even though it is negated *qua* concept. To be sure, insight can follow this very split, just as it is now on our [120–121] side following *reconstructively* the split into concept *qua* concept and being *qua* being; but at the same time insight must leave the inner split standing as impenetrable to it. This yields, in addition to the previously discovered and well-conceived *form* of inconceivability, a material *content of light* that remains ever inconceivable.

(I have just expressed myself on a major point in the science of knowing more clearly than I have previously succeeded in doing. We would accomplish a great deal if this became clear to us right now on the spot.—That the light lives[14] absolutely *through itself* must mean: it splits itself absolutely into B (being) and T (thinking). But "absolutely through itself" also means "independent of any insight [into itself] and absolutely negating the possibility of insight." Nevertheless for the last several lectures we have seen, and had insight into, the fact that light splits itself into B and T: consequently this split as such no longer resides in the light, as we had thought, but in the insight into the light. What then still remains? The inward life of the light itself in pure identity, from itself, out of itself, through itself *without* any split; a life which exists only in immediate living and has itself and nothing else. "It lives"; and thus it will live and appear and otherwise no path leads to it.—"Good, but can you not provide me with a description of it?" Very good, and I have given it to you; it is precisely what cannot be realized, what remains behind after the completely fulfilled insight which penetrates to the root, and therefore what should exist through itself. "How then do you arrive at these predicates of what cannot be realized—i.e., is not to be constructed from *disjunctively*[15] related terms as being is from thinking and vice versa—predicates such as that it is "what remains behind after the insight," "that which ought to exist through itself," qualities which are the content or the reality you have claimed to deduce fundamentally? Manifestly only by *negation* of the insight: hence all these predicates, leading with the most powerful—absolute substance—are only negative criteria, in themselves null and void. "Then your system begins with negation and death?" By no means; rather it pursues death all the way to its last resort in order to arrive at life. This lies in the *light* that is one with reality, and reality opens up in it. And the whole of reality as such according to its form is nothing more than the graveyard of the concept, which tries to find itself in the light.)[16]

It is obvious that our entire enterprise has achieved[17] a new standpoint and that we have penetrated more deeply into its core. The light, which up to now has been understood *{eingsehen}* only in its form as self-creating manifestness [122–123], and hence assigned only a merely formal being, has transformed itself into one *living* being without any disjunctive terms. What we have so far assumed to be the original light has now changed itself into mere insight and representation of the light; and we have not merely negated the concept that has been recognized as a concept, but even light and being as well. Previously only the *mere being* of the concept was to have been negated;

but how were we supposed to have arrived at this being even though it is empty? It was to be negated by something that itself was nothing. How could that be possible? Now we have an absolute reality in the light itself, out of which perhaps the being *that appears*, as well as its nonexistence in the face of the absolute, might be made comprehensible.

I now explicitly mention in addition what direct experience teaches in any case, that this reality in the original light, as it has been described, is unconditionally and completely one and self same, and that no insight is allowed into how it might arrive inwardly at a division and at multiplicity. Observe: the division into being and thinking—as well as what might, following previously given hints, depend on this—resides in the concept which perishes in the presence of reality and so has nothing at all to do with reality and the light. Now, according to the testimony of appearance in life to which our system has provisionally granted phenomenological truth, another disjunction ought to arise which stands either higher, or at least on the same level with being and thinking, since it ranges across both of the latter; and this is taken for a disjunction in reality. Since this last contradicts our previous insight it is thus certainly false; hence this new grounds for disjunction must lie in a determination of the *concept* that has not yet been recognized or is not yet sufficiently explored. The concept, as a concept, must itself be conceivable, and so no new inconceivability can appear here. But if this determination of the concept is grasped conceptually, then everything that it contains can be derived conceptually from it. Whatever range of differences may come forward in appearing reality now and for all time, yet it is once and for all clear a priori that they are B—T + C + L;[18] one-and-the-same, remaining eternally self-identical, and only different in the concept. Therefore, it is clear that, since everything true must begin with it and that falsity and illusion must be turned away, *reality* (with which alone true philosophy can be concerned), not only is generally completely deduced and made comprehensible, but also divided and analyzed a priori into all its possible parts. "Into its parts," I say, excluding from this L (= the light). For in fact this is not a part, but the one true essence.—It is hereby likewise clear how far the deduction and re-construction of true [124–125] knowing goes in the science of knowing: insight can have insight into *itself*, the concept can conceive itself; as far as one reaches, the other reaches. The concept finds its limits; conceives itself as limited, and its completed self-conceiving is the conceiving of this limit. The limit, which no one will transgress, even without any request or command from us, it recognizes exactly; and beyond it lies the one, pure living light; insight points therefore beyond itself to life, or experience, but not to that miserable assembly of empty and null appearances in which the honor of existing has no part: but rather to that experience which alone contains something new: to a divine life.

CHAPTER 9

Ninth Lecture

Wednesday, May 2, 1804

Honored Guests:

In the next three lectures I am about to enter into a deeper investigation than has been made so far. This investigation will, as it happens, set out to secure a stable focus and, leading from it, a permanent guide for our science, even before we possess this guide. So, in order not to get confused, a lot depends on our holding on to what we have laid down provisionally; therefore:

1. Formally, i.e., in relation to the material which we are investigating and to the manner in which we take it, we are already located beyond the prolegomenon and actually inside the science of knowing; because (the previous lecture began by recalling this) we have already actually created insights in ourselves, which have transposed us into an entirely new world belonging to the science of knowing and raised above all factical manifestness, in whose realm the prolegomenon always remains. We have passed unnoticed out of the prolegomenon and into science; and indeed the transition started as follows: we had to elucidate the procedure of the science of knowing by examples, and, since I found that the state of the audience[1] made it possible, we made use of the actual thing as the original example. Let us now drop this as a mere example and take things up earnestly and for real; thus we are inside the science. Just as this has so far happened tacitly, let us now proceed conscientiously and explicitly.

2. Here is how things stood in the hour before last: I—L—B. a (a = our insight into the matter). I (Image), positing something imaged in it, = B (being) and vice versa; united in the oneness of the light (L). Thus—on the one side, the connection of I—L—B, the *essential element* of all light without exception: on the other side, the *modifications*[2] without which it does not exist. This effectively indicates the way in general, but nothing is still specially known thereby. It is only the prolegomenon to our investigation.[3]

Additionally, this gives a good hint concerning an important point which is not to be handled without difficulty as to its form. Knowing should

---

This lecture begins at GA II, 8, pp. 126–127.

divide itself entirely at one stroke according to two distinct principles of division: B–T / oneness, and x, y, z / oneness. Here we see that the light, in itself eternally one and self-identical [128–129], does not divide itself *in itself,* but rather divides itself, in its insight and as being seen, into this multiplicity, whatever x, y, z may be; the [same] light, which, in itself and in its eternal identity independent from insight into it (at least as we have posited this more deeply), divides itself into *being* and *thinking.* Therefore, if the light does not even *exist* except in being the object of insight, this again divided; likewise the light does not exist in itself without dividing itself into being and thinking, so this disjunction is absolutely one and indivisible according to both distinguishing grounds. At present things must remain here, and this proposition, together with all further qualifications which it may yet receive, true in itself and remaining true, will never be permitted to fall. (Just by virtue of the fact that one has fixed termini in the conduct of the investigation, one is able to follow the investigation's most divergent turns without confusion, and to orient oneself in it as long as the point at which everything ties together remains; while otherwise one would very quickly be led into confusion.)

Now, in regard to the concept—which lies neither in the light, as what is imaged for the concept, nor in the insight, as the image itself, but rather between these two—we realize that formally in itself this concept is a mere *through-one-another {Durcheinander},* without any external consequences, i.e., without antecedent and without consequent, which two, and all their shifting relations, arise only out of the living exhibition of this concept. This insight, which, if I am not mistaken, has been presented with the highest clarity, is presupposed and here only recalled for you. If I wished to add something here to sharpen this insight, then it could only be this: since the concept, as absolute relation of the imaged to the image and vice versa, is only *this relationship,* it makes no difference to it that the thing imaged should be self-sufficient light and that the image should be *this* image. Something imaged and the image, simply as such, are sufficient. Further, *the imaged thing* and the *image* are also of little concern to the concept's *inner essence,* the latter presupposed as absolutely self-sufficient; instead this inner essence is evidently a mere *through-one-another.* That this *through-one-another,* as simply existing, manifests in the image and the thing imaged has shown itself empirically. But who then authorizes us to say, on the one hand either that this *through-one-another must* manifest itself or exist, or, on the other hand in case the former should be true, that it must construct itself directly in the image and the thing imaged rather than, say, construct itself for another and under other conditions in an endless variety of ways? Through this consideration we lose the subordinate terms, and their distinguishing grounds, for a system of genetic knowing. [130–131] On the other hand, in case someone is willing to grant us this, who would then authorize us to assume that the thing imaged could only be the light, and that therefore necessarily the image of the light, which arises in the concept as its imaged object and by means of it, must thereby bring in *the other distinguishing ground*? Thereby we also lose the second half in any system which does not rest content with factical manifestness, and rejects everything that is not seen genetically as necessary.

Of course, this result comes out the only way it could, as soon as we think seriously. If we posit the concept, the absolute *through-one-another*, as an independent self-subsisting being, then everything external to it disappears and no possibility of escaping it is to be found; just as things happened previously with the light when we likewise posited it. That is obvious. Any independent being annuls any other being external to it. Whenever you might wish to posit a being of this sort, it will always similarly have this result, which resides in its form.

This observation provides exactly the right task for our further procedure; and I wish that we could come to know this procedure in its unity right now in advance, so that we would not go astray among the various forms and changes which it may assume as we go along, would easily recognize the same pathway in every possible circumstance only with this or that modification, and would know which modification it was and from whence it comes.—The genetic relation whose interruption has come to light must be completed. This cannot simply be done by inserting new terms and thereby filling the gap, for where would we get them? We are scarcely capable of adding something in thought where nothing exists. Therefore, the genetic relation which is currently absent must be found in the terms already available; we have not yet considered them correctly, i.e., completely genetically, but so far still only considered them in part factically. "In the terms already available," I say; thus, if the only important thing were to arrive at our goal by this path, it would not matter with which available term we began. If we worked through only one of these to its implicit, creative life, then the flood of light which simultaneously overcomes and connects everything would of necessity dawn in us. But beyond this we also have the task of following the shortest way; and so it is quite natural for us to hold on to what has shown itself to us as the most immediate, those terms in which we alternatingly have placed the absolute, and in regard to which we now find ourselves in doubt as to which is the true absolute, namely *light* and *concept*. [132–133] If we work through both so that *each*[4] shows itself as the principle of the other, then it is clear that

a. in each we have grasped *mediately* the distinguishing ground which is *immediately* present in the other, and that
b. beginning from both, we, in our scientific procedure, have obtained a yet higher common principle of distinction and oneness for both on essential grounds.

Therefore, both of these lose their absolute character and retain only relative validity. Thus, our knowledge of the emerging science of knowing transcends them as something absolutely presupposed; and according to its external form this is a synthesis *post factum*. But since this transcendence is itself genetic in its inner essence—and it is not simply as Kant, and indeed we ourselves speaking preliminarily, have said, that "there must surely be some yet higher oneness," but rather this oneness in its inner essence is actually constructed—it is a *genetic*[5] synthesis. But again, the science of knowing, which is genetic in its principles and which permeates the higher oneness, is permeated by it, and is therefore itself identical with it, steps down into multiplicity and is simultaneously *analytic* and *synthetic*, i.e., truly, livingly genetic. Our task is discovering this oneness of L [light] and C [concept], and discovering it in this briefly but precisely prescribed way; this discovery is the common point to which the whole of our next stage refers. This procedure's modifications and various turnings are grounded in the necessity now of properly permeating C by genetically permeating L, and then again the other way. Thus, [it grounds itself] on constant shifts in standpoint and being tossed from one to the other.[6] I will not conceal[7] the fact that this procedure is not without difficulty and that it demands a particularly high degree of attention; instead I announce this explicitly. But I am overwhelmingly convinced that whoever has actually seen into what has been presented so far, and holds fast to the present schema and the just asserted common point for our investigation, orienting himself in terms of these from time to time, will not be led astray. On the other hand, this is the only truly difficult part of our science. The other part, deducing the mediate and secondary disjunctions, is a brief and easy affair for those who have properly achieved the first, no matter how monstrous and mad it may appear to those who know nothing of the first. This second part namely, as is evident from the foregoing and, which I mention here only redundantly, has the task of deducing all possible modifications of apparent reality. The individual who has so far remained trapped in factical manifestness wonders at this because it is the only difficulty which is accessible and apparent [134–135] to him. But until it has its own openly declared principle, this deduction (of the manifold of apparent reality) is nothing more than a clever discovery, which has recourse to the reader's genius and sense of truth, but can never justify itself before rigorous reason, if it does not have, and declare, its own principle. Now to discover and clarify this principle may certainly be the right work: for one who possesses it, the application will thus surely be simple, and—since the most complete clarity and distinctness is to be found here—it will be even simpler than the application of principles in other cases. Indeed, one could, if necessary, simply rest satisfied to have shown this application through a few examples.—Since I would gladly dispose of this once and for all, let me take it down to specific cases: the deduction of time and space with which the *Kantian*[8] philosophy exhausts itself and in which a certain group of Kantians remain imprisoned for life as if in genuine wisdom, or of the material world in its various levels of organization, or of the world of the understanding in universal concepts, or of the realm of reason in moral or religious ideas, or even the world of minds, presents no difficulty and is certainly not the masterpiece of philosophy. Because all these things, together with whatever one might wish to add to them, are actually and in fact nonexistent; instead, in case you have only just understood their nonexistence, each one is the very easily grasped appearance of the truly existing One. To be sure, up until now, some have freely believed in the existence of bodies (i.e., truthfully, in the nothing which is presented as nothing) and—at the most—in the existence of souls (i.e., truthfully, in ghosts), and perhaps they have even conducted deep researches into the relation of body and soul or into the soul's immortality. Let me add that not for one moment do I support skepticism about the latter or wish to wound faith. The science of knowing legislates nothing about the immortality of the soul, since in its terms there is neither soul, nor dying, nor mortality, and hence there is likewise no immortality; instead there is only life, and this is eternal in itself. Whatever exists, is in life, and is as eternal as life is. Thus, the science of knowing holds with Jesus that "whoever believes in me shall never die," but it is given him to have life in himself. But I say, picking up the thread, whoever has believed something like this [136–137] and is used to philosophical questions of this kind demands that a science, which says the things ours does, address this point with him and free him from error, if only by an induction on what he has so far taken as reality. This is what *Kant*[9] *for instance*, did; but it did not help at all. Nothing could help that did not address the problem at its roots. The science of knowing does even better than they wish, according to rigorous methods and in the shortest possible way. It does not cut off errors individually, since it is evident that in this work as soon as error is removed on one side it springs up on the other; rather it insists on cutting off the single root for all the various branches. For now, the science of knowing asks for patience and that one not sympathize with the individual appearances of disease, which [our science] has no wish to heal: if only the inner man is first healed, then these individual appearances will take care of themselves.

What must be built up in us today is this declaration of our proper standpoint, and to consider the unity of our following proceedings, its coherence as a first part, with a later piece that can be seen as the second part; and in relation with this you can view everything previous as a condition of clear insight into today's material. Nothing is thereby gained for material insight into our investigation's object; there is indeed a very important point in this insight which we found last time while doing something else *{aliud agendo}*, dropped today as not relevant to our purpose, and which we will investigate again tomorrow for the purpose we have announced clearly today. As concerns the form, however, a general perspective and orientation has been achieved which will guard us from any future confusions. The schema serves as provisionally valid and it will endure only those revisions grounded in our growing insight and no capricious ones.

In conclusion, in order to point out to those who have attended my previous course[10] where they find themselves in the process and thereby to put them in a position [138–139] to view the science of knowing with the complexity that repeatedly pursuing it allows: what I am now calling *concept* was named in the first series "inner essence of knowing," what is called here "light" was there called "knowing's formal being," the former [was called] simply the intelligible, the latter intuition. For it is clear that the inner essence of knowing can only be manifested in the concept, and indeed in the original concept; likewise, [it is clear that] that this concept, as implicitly insight, must posit insight, or light. Therefore, it is clear that the task here expressed as "finding the oneness of C and L" is the same one expressed there by the sentence: "The essence of knowing [is] not without its being, and vice versa, nor intellectual knowing without intuition and vice versa, which are to be understood *{eingesehen}* so that the disjunction that lies within them must become one in the oneness of the insight." Recall that we have concerned ourselves with this insight for a long time, and that it has returned under various guises and in various relations, but always according to synthetic rules. Certainly it could not happen any differently in this case, and it was this something, surrendering itself even then, which I meant when I spoke previously about the manifold shifts and modifications of the one selfsame process. The difference from before—and it seems to me also an advantage of the present path—is this: that already from the start, even before we plunge into the labyrinth of appearance, we can recognize our various future observations in their spiritual oneness. It is to be hoped—and this hope does not really concern my own knowledge and procedure in lecturing but rather the capacity of this audience to follow the presentation—that an ordering principle for these various shifts will soon be available, by means of which the process will be further facilitated. And so it will not be difficult for this part of the audience to recognize in what is now expressed in a particular way what was said in a different way before and vice versa. In being liberated from my two different literal presentations *{Buchstaben}* they may free themselves from any literal presentation, which would mean nothing and would be better not existing if it were possible to hold a lecture without one. And in freeing themselves, [they] build realization for themselves in their own spirit, free from any formulas and with independent control in every direction.

Let me add the following while we still have time, although it is not essential and has relevance only to the smallest circle of those gathered here:

except for the fact that one [140–141] possesses as one's own genuine property only that which one possesses independently of the form in which one received it, one can intentionally present it afresh and share it only under such conditions. Only what is received living in the moment, or not far removed from it, strikes living minds; not those forms which have been deadened by being passed from hand to hand or by a long interval. If I had needed to hold these lectures on the science of knowing immediately after the previous series to the same audience, who had all known the science for a long time and had no need for further instruction in it, and who simply wanted to prepare themselves further for their own oral presentation of philosophy, yet I still believe that I would have been required to take almost as diverging a path as I have taken this time, and I would have had to advise these future teachers of philosophy about the utility of this divergence in just about the same way I have advised you, for whom it is relevant.

CHAPTER 10

Tenth Lecture

Thursday, May 3, 1804

Honored Guests:

Our next task is now clearly determined: to see into L (light) as the genetic principle of C (concept) and vice versa, and thus to find the oneness and disjunction of the two. (Let me add yet another parenthetical remark. Who among you, prior to studying the science of knowing, has known L or C, not *in general* and with *confusion*—since any sort of philosophy distinguishes an *immediate presentation* of an actual object and a *concept*, which is usually an abstract one—but true L and C in the purity and simplicity with which they have been presented here? Our task concerns itself with doing this; and, with the *resolution* of this task, the science of knowing is completed *in its essentials*. Accordingly, the science answers a question that it itself must pose, and dissolves a doubt that it has first raised. It should not seem strange to anyone that there is no bridge to it from the usual point of view and that one must first learn everything about it from within it.) Something has happened for the *resolution* of this task on Monday,[1] which we will now briefly review to confirm our grasp of it.

As factical manifestness makes clear, light plainly arises in a dual relation: in part as inwardly living—and through this inner life of its own it must divide itself into *concept* and *being*—and in part in an external insight,[2] which is freely created and which objectifies this light along with its inner life.[3] Let us take up the first. What makes this inward life *inward*? Obviously that it is not external. But it becomes external in [being seen by] the insight. Thus, what follows immediately and is synonymous: it is an [inward] life because in this regard it is outside any insight, is inaccessible to it, and *negates* it. Therefore *light's absolute, inner life* is posited; it exists only in living itself and not otherwise; therefore it can be encountered only immediately in living and nowhere else. I said that the genuinely, truly *real {Reale}* in knowing rests here. But we *ourselves* have just now spoken of this inner life and therefore in some-

---

This lecture begins at GA II, 8, pp. 142–153.

way conceived it. Yes, but how? As absolutely inaccessible to insight; so we have conceived and determined it only negatively. It is not conceivable in any other way. The concept of *reality*, of the inner material content of knowing, etc., which we have introduced is only the *negation* of insight and arises only from it; and this should not just be honestly admitted, rather, a philosophy which truly understands its own advantage should carefully enjoin this idea. In truth it is no negation, but rather the highest [144–145] affirmation *{Position}*, which indeed is once again a concept; but in truth we in no way *conceive* it, but rather we *have* it and *are* it.[4]

Let this be completed and determined by us right now, and in this act it will have its application uninterruptedly. And don't let the truly crucial point of the matter escape: [there are] two ways for the light to live absolutely: internally and externally; *externally* in the insight, *internally*, therefore, absolutely not in the insight, and not for it, but instead turning it away.—By this means, our system is protected against the greatest offense with which one can charge a philosophical system, and without exception nearly always justly: namely *vacuity*. Reality, as genuine true reality, has been deduced. No one will confuse this reality with being (objectivity); the latter is *subsistence-for-self* and *dependence-on-self* which is closed in on itself and therefore dead. The former exists only in living, and living exists only in it; it can do nothing else than live. Therefore, because our system has taken life itself as its root, it is secured against death, which in the end grasps every [other] system without exception somewhere in its root. Finally, we have seen *{eingesehen}* and enjoined that, since light and life too are absolutely one, this reality [and the insight, through the negation of which it becomes reality,][5] can altogether be only one and eternally self-same. [146–147] Thereby our system has won enduring *oneness* and has secured itself from the charge that there may still be some duality in its root.

Insight, I assert, is completely negated in living light.[6] But then we *see*, and *see into*, the disjunction into C and B. Therefore, this disjunction, which we previously ascribed to the inner light itself, should not be ascribed to this, but instead to the insight that takes its place, or to the original concept of light. The concept reaches higher, the true light withdraws itself. The absolute negation of the concept may well remain a nothing[7] for the science of knowing, which has its essence in concepts, and only become an affirmation in living.[8] With this, two further comments which belong to philosophy's art and method.

1. Here we retract an error in which we have so far hovered. How did we arrive at this error, or at the proposition that we now take back as erroneous? Let us recall the process. Driven by a mechanically applied law of reason (therefore, *factically*), we realized immediately that it [i.e., the absolute] cannot reside in A (the oneness of B and T) nor in the disjunction point, but

rather in the oneness of both; this was the first step. Then, as the second step, we raised ourselves to the *apprehension of the general law for this event*, which naturally we could apprehend only as follows: in an immediately self-presenting insight, a disjunction is *negated* as intrinsically valid and a oneness, which cannot be any more exactly described, is *absolutely posited.*[9] What then did we finally do? In fact we did nothing new, apart from the fact that we relinquished the *specificity* of the disjunctive terms "A" and "." and likewise the specificity of their unity, and posited disjunction, and also self-sufficient oneness, *generally* and *unconditionally*, in which case the possibility of the procedure could arouse wonder and give rise to a question. Besides this, I say, we simply grasped the rules of the event historically, always led by the event, and, if that were removed from us,[10] [we] lacked all support for our assertion. Therefore, although this, our second insight, appears to possess a certain genetic character in the first mentioned part *{Ingredienz}*, in the second part it is something merely factical; and so what we advanced yesterday as the ground for the uninterrupted connection between the disjunctive terms is confirmed here at a genuinely central point: [148–149] that our whole insight might not yet be *purely* genetic, but is instead still partially factical. To get back to the point[11]—this insight, arising in concrete cases and led to its general rule in the second step, we now named *pure, absolute light*, simply in this respect, that in terms of content it arises immediately, without any premises or conditions. But in its form it remains factical and is dependent on the prior completion in concrete cases. We might have inferred from the following that it cannot possibly have its application here: although dividing the concept into "A" and "." was given up as inadequate, there yet remained a new disjunction in what was taken as absolute, since it was simultaneously *negating* and *positing*, the former through its formal being, and the latter through its essence. But *no* disjunction can be absolute and merely factical, rather, as surely as it is a disjunction, it must become genetic, since disjunction is genetic in its root. (Remarks of the kind just made bring no progress in the *subject matter*, but they elevate the freedom of self-possession and reproduction for everyone and facilitate the comprehension of what follows.)[12] *Result:* since our initial supposition grounded itself partially on factical insight, we must give it up.

Further, how then have we arrived at this insight of giving something up, as well as at the higher [term] for which we give it up? If you recall, we did so by means (i)[13] of the distinction between two ways the light exists and lives: *inwardly* and *outwardly*, a distinction admittedly given only with factical manifestness;[14] (ii) by genetic insight into this distinction and by the question how something absolutely inward might arise as inward; and (iii) by elevating into a genetic perspective something that had been thought previously only in faded, factical terms. Moreover, I admitted, as is indeed evident and as everyone will remember, that this entire disjunction between inner and outer arises {*liegt*} only in a factical point of view. Here, too, this observation: that in our present investigation as well, the facticity, which is erased on one side, pops up again on the other, and that we will not be entirely and purely relieved of it until the present task is completed.[15] (For returning listeners this as well: the distinction drawn here between the light's inner and outer life is the same as the distinction between *immanent* and *emanent forms of existence* that was so important and meaningful in the previous series.)

[150–151] Second remark:[16] C and L are both only concepts: the first is purely disjunction in general, a disjunction which can give no further account of itself; i.e., from our current point of view, it has simply *two* terms which are not further distinguishable. L, on the other hand, is not a disjunction in general, but is rather the specific disjunction into being and concept.[17] The latter, as the *principle* of disjunction in general, consequently has enduring inner content, as does B [Being], the principle of oneness. Therefore, the terms of this second disjunction are not just two terms in general, they also have an *internal* difference. From our standpoint, therefore, L is still by no means negated, nor can it be from that perspective. If nevertheless it must be negated, as it evidently must be a priori, since otherwise it could not come to the zero state[18] in which no further disjunction truly remains, then completely different means will have to be employed from the ones now available to us.[19]

Now to characterize (in relation to our task) the point I have just repeated, a point which fits our system in every aspect, of which I said last time that it already belonged to our process, and which we need to apply in solving our next and primary task: C and L are to be reduced to oneness, just as they were before this point of ours; and this will have to be done so that C is so rigorously mastered that we see into it as the genetic principle of light, and vice versa. With which of the terms to begin is left either to our *caprice* or our philosophical *skill*, which is unable to give any account of its maxims before applying them. In the previously discussed point, L was taken up as a starting point, as things stood then; [152–153] if so, the concept proceeds genetically from this L, since L has transformed itself into the concept. Or said more exactly: our own observing—which was not then visible, which we lived, and into which we merged—*divided itself* beyond the then regnant L, and in this division negated the L (light) into $0/C$;[20] thus creating both out of itself. Now note well that this shift in viewpoint is in no way merely a change of the *word and the sign*, but rather that it truly is a real change; because what stood here previously, whether called L or C, light or concept, was to be the absolute (which is a real predicate) and should divide itself into C and B[21] (which is also a real predicate). Both predicates combine to form a synthetic sentence that determines the absolute. In its essence—entirely apart from the expressions and signs in which one realizes and presents this essence—this sentence is contradicted by the really opposite sentence: the principle of the disjunction into being and thinking is not absolute but something subordinated (however one may more exactly name and signify this subordinate something); in the absolute the two are not distinguished. From this, another correction must follow first and foremost, not so much regarding our viewpoint as our manner of expression. There were supposed to be two different distinguishing grounds, which of course are to be reunited again, but which would have been held sufficiently far apart from one another by two basic principles that were as distinct as until now *light in itself* and its representative concept have been. Now all disjunction collapses into one and the same concept, and hence this latter could very easily provide the one eternally self-same disjunctive factor, which does not appear in the original appearance, but rather appears as doubled in the secondary appearance, in the appearance *as* appearance.

But let me go back. As things stood previously, the spirit of our task was to realize L as the genetic principle of C and vice versa. We have tried by beginning with L: the attempt had its narrowly circumscribed result and the matter does not stand as it did before but as the schema instructs. The spirit of the task remains the same through all shifts in perspective, just because it is spirit: *L through C and vice versa.* Our true L is now = 0, [154–155] and it is clear that this cannot be approached more closely: it negates all insight. Therefore, this first path is already completed on the initial attempt. Nothing more remains besides taking up C and testing whether through it we can further determine—not 0, since this remains purely unchangeable and indeterminable,—but rather it[22] as the truly highest term that we now are and live. Thus—a new classificatory division, the determination on the basis of C, becomes the second principal part of our present work.

Let me now give some preliminary hints and thereby prepare you for tomorrow's lecture, setting out a rough outline for you.

The concept's inward and completely immutable essence has already been acknowledged in an earlier lecture as a *"through."*[23] Although in its content this insight is in no way factical but is instead a purely intellectual object, still it has an factical support: the construction of the image and the thing imaged, and the indifference of the inference between them. However, we would be permitted to use this basic quality of the concept, if only, in this application, we succeeded in negating its factical origin. If one embraces a *"through"* just a little energetically, it can readily be seen that the same principle is a disjunction. Except the same question must always be repeated which already arose previously on the same occasion: how should a *dead "through,"* defined as we have defined it, come to life—despite all the capability with which it is prepared to meet life, especially by means of the *"throughness"* {*Durchheit*}, or the transition that it makes from one to another, if only it is brought into play—because it has no basis in itself for coming to actualization? How would it be if the internal life of the absolute light (= 0) were *its*[24] life, and therefore the *"through"* was itself first of all deducible from the light by this syllogism:[25]

i.   If there is to be an expression—an outward existence of the immanent life as such—then this is possible only with an absolutely existent *"through."*
ii. But there must be such an expression.
iii. Hence, the absolute *"through"* (i.e., the original concept, or reason) exists absolutely as everyone can easily see for himself.

Further, how would it be if just this *living "through"* (living to be sure by an alien [156–157] life, but still living) as the oneness of the *"through,"* divided itself into *thinking* and *being*, i.e., *in itself*, and in the *origin of its life*? This division, as a division of the enduring "through" *as such*, would be comprehensive for the same reason, and inseparable from it and its life. How would it be if it did not remain trapped in this, its essence as "through," but rather might itself be objectifying and deducing the latter; it would hence certainly have to be able to do just as we ourselves have done—the objectification and deduction can themselves come about according to the law of the "through,"[26] since fundamentally and at base it[27] is nothing but a "through": how would it be if in this objectification and deduction it split itself again in the second way? [Further, how would it be, since a "through" clearly can exist only by means of a "through"—that is, its own being as a "through" can be only mediate—and the first mode of being would scarcely be possible without at least a little of the second, if the first division could not be without some of the second, and vice versa? Since this "through" is our own inner essence, and a "through" dissolves completely into another "through," then absolutely everything based in these terms must be completely conceivable and deducible.][28] In all of these "how would it be if ____" clauses, I have consistently regarded "0" as *life*; but it is not merely this, rather it is something indivisibly joined with life, a thing we grasp by the purely negative concept of *reality*. If it is indivisible from life, and if life lives in a "through,"[29] then it lives as absolute reality, but since it is a "through," it lives it in a "through" and as a "through." Now, consider what follows if the one absolute reality, which can only be lived immediately, occurs in the form of an absolute *"through."* I should think this: that it cannot be grasped anywhere, unless an antecedent arises for what has been grasped, through which it is to be; and, since it is grasped only as a "through," it must also have a consequence that is to follow from it. This must follow unavoidably by absolutely every act of apprehending reality. In short, the infinite divisibility in absolute continuity—in a word, what the science of knowing calls *quantifiability*[30] as the inseparable form of reality's[31] appearance—arises as the basic phenomenon of all knowing.

In this last brief paragraph of my talk I have pulled together the entire content of the science of knowing. Whoever has grasped it and who can see it as necessary—the premises and conditions for this manifestness have already been completely laid out—such a one can learn nothing more here, and he can only [158–159] clarify analytically what has already been seen into. Whoever has not yet seen into it has at least been well prepared for what is to follow. For the one as for the other, we will move forward tomorrow.

CHAPTER **11**

Eleventh Lecture

Friday, May 4, 1804

Honored Guests:

Yesterday, I succeeded in presenting the essence and entire contents of the science of knowing in a few brief strokes. [Losing time at the right place means gaining it; therefore, against my initial purpose, I will apply today's hour to presenting further observations about this brief sketch. The more certain we are in advance about the form, the easier the actual working out of the contents within this form will be.][1]

C^2 = "through," in which resides disjunction. "If only this "through" could be brought to life," I said; it has nearly all the natural tendencies of life, nevertheless in itself it is only death. It would be useful to reflect further about this expression, since the *"through"* can be more clearly understood in it, than it has yet been understood:[3] this "through," which according to the preceding represents the central point in our entire investigation. Indeed, it is immediately clear what it means to say: " a "through" actually arises,"[4] "a 'through' has *taken place*," or "there is an existing 'through.'" I further believe it will be clear to anyone who considers the possibility of this existence that, considered *formally, something* else belongs to it besides the pure *"through."* In the "through" we find only the bare formal duality of the terms; if this is to find completion, then it needs a transition from one to the other, thus it needs a *living* oneness for the duality. From this it is clear that life *as* life cannot lie in the "through," although the form which life assumes here, as a transition from one to the other, does lie in the "through":—so life generally comes entirely from itself and cannot be derived from death.—

Result: the existence of a *"through"* presupposes an original *life,*[5] grounded not in the "through" but entirely in itself.[6]

We see into this at once:[7] but what is contained in this insight? Evidently the insight formed in positing the "through's" existence (and the question about the possibility of this existence) brings life with it, that is in the image

---

This lecture begins at GA II, 8, pp. 160–161.

and concept. Therefore, in *this insight* life is grasped in the form of a "through," i.e., only mediately. The *explanation* of the "through" is itself a "through." The first of these posits its terms at one stroke; and, in the resulting insight, it is itself posited as positing them in one stroke by the explanatory "through" (horizontally arranged):[8]

$$\frac{a}{a \times b}$$

So too, in the same way, with regard to the inner meaning,[9] sense, or content, the first "through" does not posit its terms at one stroke; rather, life should be the condition and the "through's" existence [162–163] should be what is conditioned; thus it [i.e., life] should be in the concept as a concept—in truth and in itself—the antecedent, and the latter should be the consequent. [This is the] *perpendicular arrangement*. Both obviously [exist] only in connection with each other, and [are] only distinguishable in this context.

The concept remains the focus of everything. (To *re*construct: here in a certain respect to *pre*construct.)[10] [The concept] *constructs* a *living "through,"* and, to be sure, does so hypothetically. *Should* this latter be, then the *existence* of living follows from it. It is immediately clear that a hypothetical *"should"* is not grounded on any existing thing, but is rather purely *in* the *concept*, and collapses if the concept collapses; and that, therefore, the concept announces itself in this "should" as pure, as existing in itself, and as creator and sustainer from itself, of itself, and through itself. The *"should"* is just the immediate expression of its independence; but if its inner form and essence are independent, then so are its contents as well. Hence, the existence of a *"through"* announces itself here as completely absolute and a priori, in no way grounded again on another real existence which precedes it. Therefore, the concept is here the antecedent and absolute *prius* to the hypothetical positing of the "through's" existence: the latter is only the concept's expression, something which depends on it and through which it, as concept, preserves itself as an absolutely inward "through." Which was the first [point].[11]

In this, its vivacity, the concept changes itself into an insight,[12] which, unconditioned, produces itself—insight into a life in and of itself, which must necessarily be presupposed. Ascending, I can therefore say: the absolute concept is the principle of the insight, or intuition, into life in itself, that is to say into [life] in intuition.[13] It seems quite possible, namely in a shallow and faded way, to think the existence of a "through" without any insight arising into the life that it absolutely presupposes. For the latter to happen, this existence must be conceived with full energy and vivacity: Now, I say, (as is clear right away): in this pale imitation the "through" is not really thought as it must be thought:

that is, as a genetic principle. For if it were thought in that way, then what ought to be manifest would be manifest. So the true focus, the genuine ideal *prius* is no longer just the concept, but rather the *inward* life whose outcome *(posterius)* is the concept. And the "should" is not, as I said before, the highest exponent of the independence of reason, [164–165] rather the appearance of inner energy is this highest exponent. (If I ask you to think energetically, I am really demanding that you be fundamentally rational!) The hypothetical "should" is again an exponent of this exponent, and the concept is not, as I said initially, the principle of intuition, but rather the inner immediate life of reason, merely *existing* and never appearing, which appears as energy (energy which obviously is again the expression of a "through" immanent in itself). This inner life, I say, is the principle of concept and intuition at once and in the same stroke:—thus it is the absolute *principle of everything*. This, I say, would be the *idealistic* argument.[14]

Once we have proceeded in this way, let us climb higher in order to get to know the real spirit and root of this mode of argument. Without further ado, it is obvious that we could have expressed our entire procedure thus: there *may be* the intuition of an original and absolute life, but how and from what does it come to be? Just construct this being as I have, or grasp it in its becoming;—now this has happened actually and in fact, and the inner life of reason as a living "through" has been deduced as the genetic principle for this being. Thus, the basic character of the ideal perspective is that it originates from the presupposition of a being which is only hypothetical and therefore based wholly on itself; and it is very natural that it finds just this same being, which it presupposes as absolute, to be absolute again in its genetic deduction, since it certainly does not begin there in order to negate itself, but to produce itself genetically. Thus, the *maxim of the form of outward existence*[15] is the principle and characteristic spirit of the idealistic perspective. By its means, reason, which we already know very well as a living "through," becomes *the absolute*; it becomes this in the genetic process because it already exists absolutely as the constant *presupposition*. Absolute reason, as absolute, is therefore a "through" = the form of outward existence. *Prior* and *absolute being*[16] shows itself to be inwardly static, motionless, and dead at just this [point of going] "through," where it always remains; *the inward life of reason*,[17] which we have already established, shows itself in this being's hypothetical quality.[18] One need only add now what is implicitly clear: that this idealistic perspective does not arise purely in the genetic process, since it assumes a being as given, and that therefore it is not the science of knowing's true standpoint. This is also clear for another reason: in the idealistic perspective, reason exists, or lives, *as* absolute reason. But it lives only *as* absolute (in the image of this "as"); hence it does not live absolutely; its life or [166–167] its absoluteness is itself mediated by a higher *"through,"* so that in this standpoint it is only derivative. So much by way of a sharp, penetrating critique of the idealistic perspective. This is especially important, because beginners are easily tempted to remain one-sidedly trapped in this point of view, since it is the perspective in which their speculative power first develops.

Now let us turn things around and grasp them from the other side. If the "through" is to come to existence, then an absolute life, grounded in itself, is likewise presupposed. Therefore, this life is the true absolute and all being originates in it. With this, intuition itself is obviously negated, though not indeed as empirically given, since if we simply try to remain in an energy state and to consider nothing further, then we will always find that we still grasp [this state] in intuition. Let me mention in passing that this is idealism's stubbornness: not to let one go further, once one has finally arrived at it. Faced with this, since in any case idealism is something absolute, it does not allow itself to be explained away by any machinations of reasoning, but rather yields only to the arrival of what is *primordially absolute*. Among other things, this idealistic stubbornness too has been attributed to the fantasy of the science of knowing which circulates among the German public, disregarding the fact that of course people cannot speak clearly about this charge because they do not know the genuine science; e.g., Reinhold did this for his whole career. It is like this: the non-philosopher or half-philosopher forgets himself, or the absolute intuition, either because he never knew it or, if he knew it, he periodically forgets it again. The one-sided idealist who knows it and holds it fast does not let it develop, because he knows nothing else.—To return: by recognizing the absolute *immanent* life we negate intuition as something that is genetically explicable and [that plays a part] in a system of purely genetic knowledge. [168–169] Because if the immanent life is self-enclosed, and all reality whatsoever is encompassed in it; then not only can one not see how to achieve an objectifying and expressive intuition of it, one can even see that such an intuition could never arise—and, because of its facticity, just this last insight cannot itself be comprehended anew, but simply directly carried out; it is the absolute, self-originating insight. So, however stubbornly one might hold on to his immediate consciousness of this intuition, it does not help things; no one challenges this intuition in its facticity. What has been asserted and demonstrated is just this: not merely that [this consciousness] is inconceivable, but even that it can be conceived to be impossible. Thus, the truth of what it asserts is denied, but in no way its bare appearance.

Let me note in passing that the place for denying ourselves at the root is here, i.e., just in the intuition of the absolute, which of course might very well be our root, and which up to now has played that role. Whoever perishes here will not expect any restoration at some relative, finite, and limited place. But we do not achieve this annulment by an absence of thought and energy, as happens in other cases. Instead, [we do so] through the highest thinking, the thought of the absolute immanent life, and through devotion to the maxims of reason, of genesis or of the absolute "through," which denies its applicability here and thus denies itself through itself. Everything has dissolved into the one = 0.[19]

Reasoning which is conducted and characterized in these terms is *realistic*. There is no progression or multiplicity in it except for pure oneness.— Let me relocate you in the context.[20] The two highest disjunctive terms stand here absolutely opposed to one another, life's inner and outer life, the forms of immanent and emanent existence[21] as well, separated by an impassable gulf and by truly realized contradiction. If one wishes to think of them as united, then they are united exactly by this gulf and this contradiction.—

As we did before with the idealistic perspective, let us now discover[22] the inner spirit and character of the realistic perspective just laid out. Obviously, this whole perspective takes its departure from the maxim: [170–171] do not reflect on the factical self-givenness of our thinking and insight, or on how this occurs in mind, rather reckon only the content of this insight as valid. Thus, in other words: do not pay attention to the external form of thought's existence in ourselves, but only the inner form of that thought. We posit an absolute truth, which manifests itself as the content of thinking, and it alone can be true. As before, it happens for us as we presupposed and wished; since the inner content alone should be valid, so in fact it alone really matters, and it negates what it does not contain. Made genetic by us, it was just so. So much in general.[23]

Now allow us to delineate realism's presupposition of an inner absolute truth more precisely. I believe that there is no way to give a better description, such as is indeed needed, than this: this implicit truth appears as an image {*Bild*}, living, completely determined, and immutable, which holds and bears itself in this immutability. Now this implicit truth reveals itself in *absolute life*,[24] and it is immediately evident {*einzusehen*} that it can only reveal itself in the latter. Because life is just as truth is: the self-grounded, held and sustained by itself. Truth is, therefore, in and through itself only life's image, and likewise only an image of life gives truth, just as we have described it. By means of the truth, as grounded by itself, only the image is added. So we stand at about the same point as before,[25] between life itself and the image of life; as regards this, we saw that they are fully identical in terms of content, which alone matters in realism, and are different only in form, which realism leaves to one side.

Living

Concept Image Being[26]

Now it is noteworthy that the image—which holds and sustains itself—should exist only in the truth as truth, when the former seems, according to its character, to be exactly the same as thought and the latter the same as being; and that therefore in realism (and working from it, if we simply compel it to clarify its fundamental assumption) we are led to a perspective {*Ansicht*}, which is so similar to idealism that it could even be the same.

Without venturing further here into this last hint, which meanwhile could be tossed in to direct our attention to what follows, I will simply conclude[27] today's lecture and pull it together into a whole by means of the following observation. Both idealism and realism grounded themselves on assumptions. Both of these assumptions—that is in their facticity and in the circumstance that one actually arises here and the other there—grounded themselves on an inner maxim [172–173] of the thinking subject. Hence, both rest on an empirical root. This is less remarkable in the case of idealism, which asserts facticity, than of realism, which, in its effects and contents, denies and contradicts what it itself fundamentally is. As we have seen, both are equally possible, and, if only one grants their premise, they are equally consistent in their development. Each contradicts the other in the same way: absolute idealism denies the possibility of realism, and realism denies the possibility of being's conceivability and derivability. It is clear that this conflict, as a conflict in maxims, can be alleviated only by setting out a law of maxims, and that therefore we need to search out such a law.

We can get a rough idea in advance about how a settlement to the conflict will work out. All the expressions of the science of knowing so far show a predilection for the realistic perspective. The justifiability of this preference follows from this, among other things: that idealism renders impossible even the being of its opposite, and thus it is decidedly *one-sided*. On the other hand, realism at least leaves the being of its opposite undisputed. It only makes it into an *inconceivable* being, and thereby brings into the light of day its inadequacy as the principle for a science in which everything must be conceived genetically. Perhaps a simple misunderstanding underlies the proof, given earlier in the name of realism, that an expressive intuition of absolute life can in no wise arise. In that case, what is proven and needs to be asserted is only that such an intuition, as valid for itself and self-supporting, can never arise. This assertion very conveniently leaves room for an interpolation: this intuition might well arise, and must arise under certain conditions, simply as a phenomenon not grounded in itself. Insight into this interpolation could thus provide the standpoint for the science of knowing and the true unification of idealism and realism;—so that the very intuition, purely as such, which we previously called "*our selves* at root," would be the first appearance and the ground of all other appearances; and because this would not be any error but instead genuine truth, it and all its modifications, which must also be intuited as necessary, would be valid as appearances. On the other side, however, seeming and error enter where appearance is taken for being itself. This seeming and [174–175] error arise necessarily from [truth's] absence, and hence can themselves be derived as necessary in their basis and form, from the assumption that this absence itself is necessary. Some have either discovered or thought they discovered, I know not which, that in measuring the brow they could measure people's mental capacity on the basis of their skulls.[28] The science of knowing could easily claim to possess a similar measure of inner mental capacity, if only it could be applied. In every case the rule is this: tell me exactly what you do not know and do not understand, and I will list with total precision all errors and illusions in which you believe, and it will prove correct.

CHAPTER **12**

Twelfth Lecture

Monday, May 7, 1804

Honored Guests:

In the last discussion period,[1] it was obvious from those who attended and allowed themselves to converse about things not only that you have followed me well even in the most recent deep investigations, but that, as is ever so much more important, a comprehensive vision of the inner spirit and outer method of the science we here pursue has grown in you. Consequently, I assume that this is even truer with the rest of you who did not speak; and I [will] abstract from everything that does not arise for me on this path, with no misgivings about carrying the investigation forward in the strength and depth with which we have begun.

A brief review in four parts: 1. production of an insight, which may have many genetic aspects in its content, but which at its root can only be factical, since otherwise we would not have been able to go higher. If there really is to be a "through," then—as a condition of its possibility—we must presuppose an inner life, independent in itself from the "through," and resting on itself. 2. We then made this insight, produced within ourselves, into an object, in order to analyze it and consider it in its form. There we proposed initially (in the whole of the second part) that we saw into our concept of an *actual* *"through,"*[2] which appears freely created; or rather, since everything depends on this, [we proposed] that this concept was energetic and living, that the *inward life* of this concept was the principle of the energetic insight into a life *beyond*, which grasped us, and which was *intuited* in this insight as self-sufficient. Thus, it[3] was the principle of intuition and of life in the intuition. This latter need not arise except in intuition, and its characterization as life in and for itself is not intrinsically valid. Instead, it can be fully explained from the mere *form* of intuition as projecting something self-sufficient in the form of external existence. In case another perspective is also possible, and since it

---

This lecture begins at GA II, 8, pp. 176–177. It may have possible taken place on Tuesday, May 8, 1804.

94

begins with the energy of reflection and makes it a principle, this way of looking at the insight can conveniently be labelled the *idealistic* perspective, in the
terminology already provisionally adopted and explained.

3. But this *other* view, posited as the basis for the insight, also proved to
be possible, and was realized as well. The presupposed life in itself [178–179]
should be entirely and unconditionally *in-itself*;[4] and it is intuited as such.
Therefore, all being and life originates with it, and apart from it there can be
nothing. The reported subjective condition of this perspective and insight was
this: that one not stubbornly hold on to the principle of idealism, the energy
of reflection, but rather yield patiently to this opposite insight. The *realistic*
perspective.[5]

With this a warning!—not as if I detected traces of this misunderstanding in someone speaking about the matter, but rather because falling into
this error is very easy, as nearly all the philosophical public has done in regard
to the published science of knowing.[6] Do not think of "idealism" and "realism"
here as artificial philosophical systems which the science of knowing wants to
oppose: having arrived in the circle of science, we have nothing more to do
with the criticism of systems. Instead, it is the natural idealism and realism
that arise without any conscious effort on our part in common knowing, at
least in its derived expressions and appearances: and notwithstanding [the
fact] that both can certainly be understood {*eingesehen*} in this depth and so
on the basis of their principles, they nevertheless arise only in philosophy and
especially in the science of knowing. It is still the latter's intention to derive
them as wholly natural disjunctions and partialities of common knowing, arising from themselves.

4. Both these perspectives were more closely specified in their inner
nature and character. Thus, just as at the start, we elevated ourselves *above*[7]
both (we are not enclosed within them, since we can move from one to the
other), [and we moved] from their facticity to the *genesis* of both, out of their
relative and mutual principles. Hence, the insight which in this fourth part we
lived and were, was their genesis, just as they were the genesis for the previously created [terms], in which both came together. Thus, according to the
basic law of our science, we are constantly rising to a higher genesis until we
finally lose ourselves completely in it.[8]

We characterized them in this way: through its mere being, the *idealistic* mode of thinking locates itself in the standpoint of reflection, makes this
standpoint absolute *by itself*, and its further development is nothing more than
the genesis of that which it already was without *any* genesis other than its own
absolute origin. In its root, therefore, it is *factical*, not just in relation to something [180–181] outside itself (as is, e.g., Kant's highest principle[9]) but rather
in relation to *itself*. It just posits itself unconditionally, and everything else follows of itself; and it frees itself from any further accounting for its absolute

positing. The *realistic* mode of thinking proceeds no differently. Abstracting entirely from [the facticity of][10] its thinking, it presupposes the bare content of its thought as solely valid and unconditionally true, and completely consistently it denies any other truth which is not contained in this content, or, as would actually be the case here, which contradicts it. But this residing in the content is itself an *absolutely given fact*,[11] which makes itself absolute without wanting to give any further account of itself, just like idealism. Therefore, both are at their root *factical*;[12] and even ignoring that they are presented one-sidedly, each annulling the other, in this facticity each bears in itself the mark of its insufficiency as a *highest*[13] principle for the science of knowing.[14]

Let me describe it again with this formula: at this highest point of contradiction between the two terms absolutely demanding unification, we find these: 0 and C,[15] or the *form* and the *content*, or the forms of *outer* and *inner* existence, or [as] in the previous lectures, *essence* and *existence*. We appear to have obtained the absolute disjunction; its unification promises to bring with it absolute oneness and so to resolve our task fundamentally.

Today we will present considerations regarding this solution which still remain preliminary[16]—preliminary because we must advance even further just to get to the point:—in order to prepare ourselves soundly for the highest oneness.

First, it must be clear that the problem cannot be resolved simply by combining, rearranging, etc., what we know so far. In relation to our next aim, everything up to now is only preparation and strengthening our spirit for the highest insight; and if the preceding should have some further significance beyond this, this significance can arise only by deduction from the highest principle. Now we must bring up something entirely new, i.e., according to the insight adduced just above, it is certain that something has remained to some extent empirical and concrete for us. We must investigate this and master it genetically. The rule, therefore, is[17] to investigate this facticity. We have demonstrated the factical principles of the perspectives in which we recently spent ourselves, one after the other (and which therefore undoubtedly contain the highest [form of being] that we, the scientists of knowing, have ourselves so far attained). One of the two must be developed. Which shall it be?

[182–183] If one grasps hold of it first, the principle of idealism is admitted to be absolutely incontrovertible. Realism attacks this immediately as idealistic stubbornness and a false maxim, which it repudiates. Thus, [realism] denies the principle and cannot reason with idealism in any way. On the other hand, idealism in turn makes even the beginnings of realism impossible; it ignores realism completely, and hence can not have anything against it, since, for idealism, [realism] does not exist. Now realism obviously takes itself to be superior just because of its denial of idealism's principle and by its origin from this denial; thus in realism at least a negative relationship to idealism remains, whereas even the possibility of such relatedness is extirpated in idealism. We must therefore attend to realism, temporarily abstracting in every way from idealism; since, as said before, we cannot let realism be absolutely valid, but rather want to correct it, and since we cannot combat it from the perspective of idealism, we must fight against it on its own grounds: catch it in self-contradiction. Through *this very contradiction*, which indeed brings a disjunction with it, realism's empirical principle would become *genetic*, and in this genesis, perhaps it will become the principle of a higher realism and idealism *[united] into one*. We have solved the first task, finding which factical principle to develop. This is where we grasp[18] realism in its strength. Its crucial point was life's *in-itself {Ansich}* and *within-itself {Insich}*. For now, we hold to this feature alone, and in the mean time we could let go of life. From this "in-itself" realism infers the negation of everything outside it.

But how does it bring about this very in-itself? Let's reconstruct the process, thinking the in-itself energetically. I assert, and I invite you to consider this yourselves, and see *{einzusehen}* it immediately as true—I assert: the in-itself has meaning only to the extent that it [is] not *what has been constructed*, and completely denies everything constructed, all construction, and all constructability. Consider well: when you say, "thus it is *in itself, unconditionally* in itself," then you are saying [that] it exists thus entirely independently from my asserting and thinking, and from *all* asserting, thinking, and intuiting, and from whatever other things outside the *in-itself* may have a name. This, you say, is how the *in-itself* must explain itself, if it wishes to explain itself. No other explanation yields the *in-itself*. Result: the in-itself is to be described purely as *what negates* thinking.[19]

[This is] the first surprising observation: here for the first time realism—the perspective which, during the last lecture, we made evident only *factically*[20] on the basis of its consequences, [184–185]—is understood genetically. Previously, that is, this insight arose and grasped us, that if this life in itself is posited, nothing apart from it can exist. That is how it was; we saw into it this way and could not do otherwise. Now we see *{einsehen}* that realism, or we ourselves standing in its perspective, act like the *in-itself*,[21] which negates everything outside itself. [We see] that realism therefore to some extent (at least in its effects) is itself the *in-itself*, and collapses into it; and for this implicit reason, in the appearance of our insight, which grasped us in the previous lecture, it annuls everything outside itself. Therefore, we have comprehended genetically something about realism which previously was only factical.

With this out of the way on one side, let's reflect more closely about our own insight, evoked before, and its principle. I call on you to think the in-itself and its meaning exactly and energetically, whereupon you would then see into, etc. You admit that without this exact thinking you would not have seen it; perhaps you even admit that for your whole life you have thought the in-itself, faintly to be sure, and yet this insight has not been produced in you. (It can be shown that things have gone this way for all philosophy without exception: since if this insight opened itself really vividly for anyone, then the discovery of the science of knowing would not have taken so long!) Thus, *your* insight into the negation of thinking in itself presupposes positive thought, and the proposition is as follows: "In thought, thinking annuls itself in the face of the in-itself."

Now, to add even more consequences, with which I only wish to make you acquainted: the negation of thinking over against the in-itself[22] is not thought in free reflection, as the in-itself *ought*[23] to be thought by us, rather it is *immediately* evident. This is what we called *intuition {Intuition}*, and without doubt, since the absolute in itself is found here, this is the absolute intuition. What the absolute intuition projects would therefore be negation, absolute pure nothing—obviously in opposition to the absolute in itself. And thus idealism, which posits an absolute intuition of life, is refuted at its root by a still deeper founding of realism. It may well come up again as an appearance; but, taken as absolute in the way it gave itself out to be before, it is merely illusion. Hence, we do not get past *{es bliebt daher bei}* the previously mentioned fundamental negation of ourselves over against the absolute.

The negation is *intuited*; the in-itself is *thought*. I ask how and in what way it is thought; and I explain this implicitly obscure question by [186–187] the answer itself. That is, we constructed this in-itself, assembling it from parts, just as, for example, at the beginning of our enterprise we constructed oneness in the background as not being empirically manifest identity, and not multiplicity either, but rather as the union of these two. I ought not believe, instead we posit it directly, together with its meaning, in pure simplicity as the genuine construction: thinking's *negation* is directly evident to us, it grasps us as proceeding from it in its simplicity. *We* therefore—this is very important— didn't actually construct it, instead it constructed *itself by means of itself.*

Intuition, the absolute springing forth of light and insight, was bound directly together with this construction.[24] *We*,[25] however, would certainly not have produced this, since it obviously produces itself and draws us forward with it.—Thus, the absolute's absolute self-construction and the original light are completely and entirely one and inseparable, and light arises from this self-construction just as this self-construction comes from absolute light. Hence, nothing at all remains here of a pregiven *us*:[26] and this is the *higher*[27] realistic perspective. But now we still hold on to the requirement, as with right we can, that we should be able to *think* the in-itself, and think it *energetically*,[28] thus that the living self-construction of the in-itself within the light must have yielded to us, and that once again this energy must be the first condition of everything, which results in an *idealism*,[29] which lies even higher.

But on this subject there are once again two things to consider: first, we are also aware of this thinking, of this energy, and apparently our claim that it *exists* (without which general existence it could surely not be a principle) is grounded solely on this awareness. This, however, presupposes the light. But since the light itself, at least in this its objective form, does not exist in itself apart from the absolute (as indeed it cannot, since nothing exists apart from the absolute) but rather has its source in the *in-itself*, we cannot appeal to it: something which itself bears witness against us, if we examine it more closely. If one retains this higher presupposition of the light in all possible deliverances of self-consciousness (as the source of all idealistic assertions), then the constant spirit of idealism in its highest form and the fundamental error which contradicts and destroys it fundamentally would be that it [188–189] remains fixed on facticity, at the *objectifying*[30] light from which one can never begin factically, but only intellectually.

So then (which is surely the same point from another angle), one must reflect in opposition to the idealistic objection: You are not thinking the in-itself, constructing it originally—you are not *thinking it out*; indeed how could you! Nor is it known to you through something else, which is not itself the in-itself, rather it is merely known by you: thus your knowing in and of itself sets it down; or, as the matter may be more accurately put, it sets itself down in your knowing and *as*[31] your knowing. You have been doing this your whole life without your will and without the least effort and in various forms, as often as you expressed the judgment: so and so *exists*. And indeed philosophy has made war with you and bound you in its circle, not because of this procedure itself but because of the thoughtlessness of it. You will not give any credit to your freedom and energy regarding the event itself. Only now that you are aware of this action and its significance does your energy add anything; likewise again with the declaration of that which gives itself to you without any effort: intuition. Therefore, before we listen to you at all, we must inquire more exactly how far the testimony of intuition is valid.[32]

This, additionally, by way of conclusion. Whether it appears in its oneness as the concept of some philosophical system, either killed or never having lived, as it was for us before our realization of its significance, or in a particular determination as the *"is"* of a particular thing, the faded in-itself is always [an object of] intuition and is therefore dead. For us it exists {*ist*} in the *concept*, and is therefore living. Hence for us there is nothing in intuition, since everything is in the concept. This is the most decisive distinguishing ground between the science of knowing and every other possible standpoint for knowing. It grasps the in-itself conceptually: every other mode of thought does not *conceive* it, but only intuits it, and in that way kills it to some extent.

The science of knowing grasps each of these modes of thought from its own perspective as negations of the in-itself. Not as absolute negations, but as privative ones. The things which, as we ascend, we find to be not absolutely valid (for instance, one-sided realism and idealism), or which might be found to be so, the science of knowing will take up again on its descent as similar possible negations of the absolute insight.

CHAPTER 13

Thirteenth Lecture

Wednesday, May 9, 1804

Honored Guests:

Again today and even beyond I will climb on freely. I say "freely" for you, because I cannot provide the foundation for the distinctions that will emerge here before using them, rather I must first acquaint you with them in use, even though a firm rule of ascent may well stand at the basis of what I am doing. If one just grasps my lecture precisely in other respects, there is no danger of confusion despite the former circumstance, because instead of the initially given crucial points L (life) and C (concept) we have the two perspectives: *realism* (= genesis of life) and *idealism*[1] (= genesis of the concept). This should be known from Friday's clear presentation and its review the day before yesterday.[2] (Not generally, [but rather] in relation to the point, as it was grasped there, one had to adhere to life in itself, which was required to animate a "through." We will not move very far away from this now, and it will easily be possible to reproduce from it everything that needs to be presented, or to trace the latter back to it.)[3] In a word, these two perspectives are our present guide, until we find their principle of oneness and can dispense with them *directly*. Here, if anywhere, we need the capacity to hold tight to what is presented firmly and immovably, and to separate from everything that may very well be rationally {*in der Vernunft*} bound to it. Otherwise, one will leap ahead, anticipate the inquiry, and will not grasp the genetic process linking what is taken up first and its higher terms, which is what really matters; instead the two will flow into one another factically.[4] "*One*[5] will anticipate," I said; but it is not actually "one,"[6] not the self to whom this happens, rather it is speculative reason, running along automatically. (Then let me add this remark in passing: speculation, once aroused and brought into play, as I partly know it has truly been brought into play in you, is as active and vital as the empirical association of ideas ever can be, because it is surrounded by a freer, lighter atmosphere: and once one has entered this world, one must be just as watchful

---

This lecture begins at GA II, 8, pp. 190–191.

against leaps of speculation as previously against the stubbornness of empiri-
cism. I want especially to warn those for whom the objects of the present
investigation appear very easily about this danger; I advise you to make them
a little harder for yourself, since this appearance of ease may well arouse the
suspicion that the subject can be grasped more easily by speculative fantasy
than by pure, ever serene, reason.)

[192–193] To work.

The in-itself reveals itself immediately as entirely independent from
knowledge or thought[7] of itself, and therefore as wholly denying the latter in
its own essential effects, in case one assigns such to it. *We* did not construct
the in-itself in this immediately true and clear concept, instead, as was immediately evident to us, it constructed itself just as it was in the constructive
process, as denying thinking;—immediate insight, the absolute light, was
immediately united with this concept and was evident in the same way. Thus,
the absolute in-itself revealed itself as the source of the light; hence the light
was revealed as in no way primordial:—which is now the first point and which
obviously bears in itself the stamp of a higher realism.[8]

Another idealism now tried to raise itself against this realism, proceeding from *this* basis:[9] since we saw into the in-itself as negating vision, we must
ourselves have reflected energetically on it. Thus, although we cannot deny
that it constructed itself, and the *light* as well, all of this was nevertheless qualified by own vigorous reflection, which therefore was the highest term of all.
As basing itself on absolute reflection, this is obviously *idealism*; and, since it
does not depend, as did the previous idealism, on reflection about something
conditioned (actually carrying out a "through") as a means to realize the condition—but instead[10] rests on reflection on the unconditioned *in-itself*—it is a
higher idealism.

We quickly struck down this idealism with the following observation.—
"You then," we address it in personified form—"You *think* the in-itself: that is
your principle. But on what basis do you know this?[11] You cannot answer otherwise, or bring up a different answer than this: 'I just see it, am immediately
aware of it,' and to be sure you do see it, unconditionally objective and intuiting."—(The last point is important and I will analyze it more closely. In realism too we simply had an insight into the self-construction of the in-itself; but
we had an in-sight, i.e., we saw into[12] something living in itself, and this living thing swept insight along with itself, the very same relationship which we
have already frequently found in every manifestness presented genetically.
Now, however, ignoring [the fact] that a purely objectifying intuition[13] seems
to hover above the origin, [194–195] still this intuition is drawn at once
toward, and along with, the genesis. In this insight, therefore, a unification of
the forms of *outer* and *inner* existence, of facticity and genetic development
seems to be hinted at. Things stand completely differently with the seeing of

its thought to which idealism appeals. That is, in that case we will certainly not wish to report that we witness thinking as thinking (i.e., as producing the in-itself) in the act of producing, as we certainly actually and in fact witness the *in-itself* producing its construction; rather intuition accommodates itself immediately only to a thinking which is essentially *opaque* and can be presented only factically. Thus, it remains completely ambiguous whether thinking originates from this intuition, the intuition comes from the thinking, or whether both might be only appearances of a deeper hidden oneness which grounds them.[14]

In case it is necessary to make this clearer.[15] Could you ever think really clearly and energetically, which is what we are discussing here (because faded thoughts and dreaming are completely to be ignored),[16] without being aware of it; and conversely could you possibly be *aware* of such thinking without assuming that you really and in fact were thinking?[17] Would the least doubt remain for you about the truth of this testimony of your consciousness? I think not. It is therefore admittedly clear, and immediately proved by the facts that you cannot distinguish genuine thinking from consciousness of it, and vice versa; and that in this facticity, thinking posits its intuition, and the intuition posits the absolute truth and validity of its testimony.[18] We do not quarrel with you about that. But you cannot provide the genetic middle term for these two disjunctive terms. Hence, you remain stuck in a facticity. But, on the other hand, the genesis which has arisen in the opposite, realistic perspective opposes you; that is to say, in that perspective we know nothing about one term of your synthesis, your so-called thinking. But we recognize that to which you appeal for verification of the latter. Although [we do not do so] immediately, we still do in its principle. I say "not *immediately*"; just as little do we recognize there a simple consciousness, expressing a fact absolutely, as yours does according to our closer analysis. But I also said "in *its principle*": in any event[19] your consciousness presupposes *light* and is only one of its determinations. But light has been realized as itself originating from the in-itself and its absolute self-construction; however, if it originates from the in-itself, then this latter cannot likewise originate from it, as you wish. In your report that you are thinking actually and in fact because you are conscious of yourself doing so,[20] you must posit your consciousness as absolute, but the very source of this [196–197] consciousness, *pure* light, is not looked at {angesehen} factically, which would bring us to the same level you occupy; rather (which is more significant) it is *seen into {eingesehen}* genetically as itself *not absolute*. And so this new idealism has been in part determined further; it does not, as first appears, even posit as absolute a reflection which, according to it, belongs simply to thinking, instead, it posits the immediate intuition of this reflection as absolute and is therefore different in kind from the first: in part it is refuted as in truth valid, although as an appearance it is not yet derived. Assuming that it has become entirely clear to you, hold onto this and let go of what is deeper.

By the way: in passing and while doing something else {*aliud agendo*}, I have touched here on the very important distinction between a merely *factical regarding* {*faktischer Ansicht*}, like our thinking of the in-itself, and *genetic insight* {*genetischer Ansicht*}, like that into the in-itself's self-construction. By means of the immediate testimony of our consciousness, we cannot witness our thinking, as thinking, literally as production; we see it only so long as it *exists*, or should exist, and it already is, or should be, while we see it; on the other hand, we see the in-itself as *existing* and as self-constructing, *simultaneously* and reciprocally.[21] This point will have to come up again naturally as the higher point of disjunction for a still higher oneness, and it will be very significant. Meanwhile, let it be impressed [on you], and, as an explanation, let the following historical commentary be added which may have whatever worth it can for admirers. At the same time it may serve as an external test of whether one has understood me.

Reinhold (or, as Reinhold claims, *Bardili*)[22] wishes to make *thinking qua thinking* the principle of being. Therefore, on the most charitable [198–199] interpretation, his system would be situated within the idealism we have just described, and one must assume that by this he means the thinking of the in-itself which we carried out the day before yesterday. Now, first of all, he is very far removed from explaining that this in-itself negates seeing, as we have shown; but then, which is worse, in regard to the in-itself's *real* existence (with which he generally has no dealings and which, to be sure, he would be able to prove only factically from the existence of individual things) he does not appeal to consciousness (a fact of which I reminded him,[23] but which escaped him) because he sees very well that doing so would lead him to an idealism, and he seems to have developed an unconquerable horror of any idealism. Hence, in the first place, his principle stands entirely in the air, and he works to build a realism on absolutely nothing; and he could only be driven to this by despair, following the rule: "since it wouldn't work with anything I tried so far, then it must work with the one thing still left in my field of vision." Second (and I have made this observation especially to make this point), since, according to an absolute law of reason, thinking does not let itself be seen into as producing itself as *thinking*, then naturally Reinhold cannot realize it this way either, nor can he genetically deduce the least thing from it. Hence he can only say, like *Spinoza*: since everything that is lies in it, and since now so-and-so exists, it too must lie in it. Because he was educated in the Kantian school, and later by the science of knowing, he may not now do this. Hence he labors to *deduce*; but since, if one only has a clear concept, this appears to be completely impossible, [200–201] total darkness and obscurity arise in his system, so that nobody grasps what he really wants. If one considers this system from the point of view of the science of knowing, and indeed from the very point from which we have just seen it, then the obscurity of its principles is clear.)

Let's get back to business and draw the conclusion, because in passing we have once again gained a very clear insight into the true essence of the science of knowing, that is, of the *principle* which we are still obliged to present. The refuted idealism makes immediate consciousness into the absolute, the primordial source, the protector of truth; and indeed *absolute* consciousness reveals itself in it as the oneness of all other possible consciousness, as reflection's *self-consciousness*. In the first place, then, this stands firm as one of our basic foundations. Wherever we say "I am conscious of that," our testimony bears the basic formal character of an absolute intuition, which we have just described, and makes a claim for the intrinsic validity of its contents. This consciousness is now realized as *self-consciousness* and *reflection* in its root: all possible disjunctions and modes of consciousness must be deduced from self-consciousness; and we would therewith already have achieved a comprehensive study.

It is clear that this consciousness is completely one in itself and capable of no inner disjunction; because the thinking that arose in it was that of the in-itself which, as in-itself, is entirely one and self-same; thus it too was one, and the consciousness of it was only this one consciousness; and therefore it was also one. The self, or I, which arises here is consequently the absolute *I*—pure eternally self identical, and unchanging—but not the *absolute* as will soon be more precisely evident. A specific disjunctive principle will also have to be identified if:

a. in the course of thinking "the one in-itself" it should appear in a multi-faceted perspective, even though in the background it is to remain perpetually the same single in-itself, or categorical *is*, and

b. as a result there also arises a manifold view of thinking, or reflection, and hence of the reflecting subject, or I (all of which, just like the in-itself, are also to remain the same *one* in the background).[24]

It could well be, and indeed will turn out, that, if we remain trapped in the absolute I and never raise ourselves beyond it, we may never discover this disjunctive principle in proper genetic fashion, and it will have to be disclosed factically.

(An historical note in passing: [202–203] even where things go the best for the science of knowing, it has been taken for this idealistic system we have just described, which presupposes what we have exactly characterized as the absolute I to be *the absolute* and derives everything else from it; and no author known to me, friend or foe, has risen to a higher conception of it. That most have remained at an even lower level than this conception goes without saying.

If a higher understanding is to arise for anyone besides the originator of this science, it could only be among the present listeners, but it would not be written; because what can be understood in writing stands under the previous rule; or it will be hit upon by you. This remark has the consequence that nobody will get a report about the essence of the science of knowing from anyone other than the present one from the originator. It will be immediately evident even from just the clear and decisive letters of what has been published on the topic how false this interpretation is.)[25]

The intrinsic validity of this idealism is refuted; nevertheless, it may preserve its existence as an appearance, and indeed as the foundation of all appearance, which we have to expect: it has been refuted on the grounds that it is factical and that a higher development points to its origin. One calls a fact *{Thatsache}* "factical," *{faktisch}* and since here we are speaking of consciousness, this fact would be a "fact of consciousness"; or, to put it more strongly: according to this idealistic system,[26] consciousness itself is a fact, and since consciousness is for it the absolute, the *absolute*[27] would be a fact. Now, from the first moment of its arising the science of knowing has declared that the primary error[28] of all previous systems has been that they began with something factical and posited the absolute in this. It, on the other hand, lays as its ground and has given evidence for, an *enactment*,[29] which in these lectures I have called by the Greek term *genesis*, since these are often more easily understood rightly than German terms. Therefore from its first arising, the science of knowing has gone beyond the idealism we have described. It has shown this in another equally unambiguous way: particularly regarding its basic point, the I. It has never admitted that this [204–205] I—as *found and perceived*[30]—is its principle. "As found" it is never the *pure* I, but rather the individual personal being of each one, and whoever claims to have *found* it as pure finds himself in a psychological illusion of the kind with which we have been charged by those ignorant of this science's true principle.—So then, the science of knowing has always testified that it recognizes the I as pure only as *produced*, and that, as a science, it never places the I at the pinnacle of its deductions, because the productive process will always stand higher than what is produced. This production of the I, and with it the whole of consciousness, is now our task.

The idealism which has been rejected as intrinsically valid is the same as absolute immediate consciousness. Therefore, so that we now express as forcefully as possible what it comes down to, the science of knowing denies the validity of immediate consciousness's testimony absolutely as such and for this exact reason: that it is this,[31] and it proves this denial. Solely in this way does the science of knowing bring reason in itself to peace and oneness. Only pure reason, which is to be grasped merely by intellect, remains as solely valid. So that no one is confused even for a moment by a fancy which might easily arise here, I immediately add a hint which must be discussed further in what follows.

Namely, someone may say: "But how can I *grasp something in intellect*[32] without being conscious in this intellectualizing?" I answer: "Of course you cannot." But the ground of truth as truth does not rest in consciousness, but only and entirely in truth itself. You must always separate consciousness from truth, as in no way making a difference to it. Consciousness remains only an outer *appearance* of truth, from which you can never escape and whose grounds are to be given to you. But if you believe that the grounds why truth is truth are found in this *consciousness*, you lapse into illusion; and every time something seems true to you because you are conscious of it, you become at the [206–207] root idle illusion and error. Here now it is obvious: 1. how in fact the science of knowing keeps its promise and, as a doctrine of truth and reason, expunges all facticity from itself. The primordial fact and source of everything factical is *consciousness*. It can verify nothing, in light of the science of knowing's proof that whenever truth is at issue, one should turn it aside and abstract from it. To the extent that this science in its second part is a *phenomenology*, a doctrine of appearance and illusion, which is possible only out of the first and on the ground and basis of the latter, to that extent it surely deduces both as existing, but simply as they indeed exist, as *factical*.[33] 2. It has become completely clear why nothing external could be brought up against the science of knowing, but that one always must begin with it to gain entrance into it. The beginning point for a fight against it is either grasped in intellect or not. If it is grasped in intellect, then it is either grasped intellectually immediately—and that is the principle of the science—or it is grasped *mediately* and these must be either deductions of the fundamental phenomenon or phenomena derived from it. One can come to the latter only through the former. In this case, therefore, one would in every circumstance be at one with the science of knowing, be the science of knowing itself, and in no case be in conflict with it. If it were not grasped intellectually but should nevertheless be true, then one must appeal for verification to one's immediate consciousness, since there is no third way to get to the absolute itself or even to an appearance of it. But making this appeal one is straightaway turned aside with the instruction that precisely because you are immediately aware of it and appeal to that fact, it must be false. Of course thoughtlessness and drivel have created a fancy title for themselves, that of "skepticism," and they believe that nothing is so high that it cannot be forced under this rubric. It must stay away from the science of knowing. In pure reason doubt can no longer arise; the former bears and holds itself—and everyone who enters this region—firmly and undisturbedly. But if skepticism wishes to doubt the implicit validity of consciousness—and this is approximately what it wants in some of its representatives—and it does this provisionally in this or that corner, although without having been able to bring about a properly basic general doubt;—[208–209] if it wants this, then with its general doubt it has arrived too late for the science of knowing, since the latter does not just doubt this implicit validity[34] in a provisional way, but rather asserts and proves the invalidity of what the general doubt only puts in question. Just the possessor of this science (who surveys all disjunctions in consciousness, disjunctions which, if one assumes the validity of consciousness in itself, become contradictions) could present a skepticism which totally negated everything assumed so far; a skepticism to which those who have been playing with all kinds of skeptical doubts as a pastime might blanch and cry out: "Now the joke goes too far!" Perhaps in this way one might even contribute to arousing the presently stagnating philosophical interests.[35]

CHAPTER 14

Fourteenth Lecture

Thursday, May 10, 1804

Honored Guests:

[Yesterday, an idealism, which made absolute *consciousness* (in its *actuality* that is) into its principle was presented, characterized, and refuted;—"in its actuality" I say, since today we will uncover still a different [idealism] in a place where we do not expect it, one which makes the same thing its principle, only *merely in its possibility*. Now this absolute consciousness was *self-consciousness* in the energy (of reflective thinking, as it later turned out). On this point I will add another remark relating to the outer history of the science of knowing, which naturally is not intended to parade my conflict with this unphilosophical age in front of you, but rather only to provide hints to those who are following this science in my published writings and who want to rediscover it in the form employed there—telling them where they should direct their attention.]¹

[Let me add just this, it is clear that just as the form of outer existence as such perishes, so its opposite as such perishes as well; therefore, realism, or more accurately *objectivism* perishes along with that idealism which, because of language's ambiguity, we might better call *subjectivism*. Reality remains, as *inner* being—as we must express ourselves just in order to talk; but in no way does it remain a term of any relation, since a second term for the relation, and indeed all relations in general, have been given up. Therefore, it is not "objective," since this word has meaning only over against subjectivity, which has no meaning from our standpoint. Only one recent philosophical writer (I mean Schelling) has had a suspicion about this truth, with his so-called system of identity; not, certainly, that he had seen into the absolute negation² of subject and object, but that with his system he aimed at a synthesis *post factum*; and with this operation he believed he had gone beyond the range of the science of knowing. Here is how things stand about that: he had perceived this synthesizing in the science of knowing, which carried it out, and he believed himself to be something more when he *said* what it *did*. This is the first unlucky

---

This lecture begins at GA II, 8, pp. 214–215.

blow that befell him: *saying*, which always stems from subjectivity and by its nature presents a dead object, is not more but less excellent than doing, which stands between both in the midpoint of inwardly living being. Moreover, he does not prove this claim, but lets the science of knowing do it for him,[3] which again seems odd: that a [216–217] system which admittedly contains the grounds for proving our own system's basic principle should be placed *below* it. Now he begins and asserts: reason is the absolute indifference between subject and object. But here must first also be added that it cannot be an absolute point of indifference without also being an absolute point of differentiation. That it is neither one nor the other *absolutely* but both relatively; and that therefore, however one may begin it, no spark of absoluteness may be brought into this reason. So then he says: *reason exists*; in this way he externalizes reason from the start and sets himself apart from it; thus one must congratulate him that with his definition he has not hit the right reason. This objectification of reason is completely the wrong path. The business of philosophy is not to talk around reason from the outside, but really and in all seriousness to conduct rational existence. Nevertheless, this author is the hero of all passionate, and therefore empty and confused heads; and especially of those who do not disavow defects like those reproved above, to which, when possible, they come even more extremely because they think either that the inferences are good, although the principles are false, but that the whole is still excellent, admittedly overlooking that all the individual parts are good for nothing; or finally that although it is neither true, nor good, nor beautiful, it still remains very interesting. For my own person, I have said all this only in the interest of history and to elucidate my own views, but in no way to weaken anyone's respect for their hero or to lead them to myself. Because if anyone wishes to be condemned to error, I have nothing against it.][4]

Further, and to the point; [here is the] chief result:[5]

Consciousness has been rejected in its intrinsic[6] validity, despite the fact that we have admitted we cannot escape it. *We* absolutely, i.e., even here in the science of knowing.[7] Therefore, 1. if we have once seen into this fact, although *factically* we could never negate consciousness, we will not really believe it when judging truth; instead, when judging, we will abstract from it; indeed, on the condition that we want to get to truth, we must do this, but not unconditionally, since it is not necessary that we *see into*[8] the truth. Here for the first time, *we ourselves* have become entwined mediately in science and the circle of its manifestness, and we became the topic without any effort on our part in a new way,[9] because we were speaking of consciousness and we ourselves occur empirically as consciousness, which might serve very well for the genetic deduction of the I, which we seek. Further, we should cultivate here a maxim for ourselves, a rule of judging which can be appropriated only[10] through freedom; and this maxim should become the absolute principle [218–219] in and for us: if never of truth itself, then of this truth's factical appearance. In one respect, this is generally meaningful and may lead to a new idealism, in a region where it alone can have value as the principle of appearance; and in another respect it confirms the opinion expressed previously when we were characterizing and refuting the more deeply placed idealism and realism: that, as grounded on conflicting maxims, both could only be reunited by means of a higher maxim. And so notice this also at the same time: that the present maxim is quite different from that of the previous realism (which allowed truth alone to be unconditionally valid) in that the present one has a *condition* *{bedingt ist}*: "if truth is to *{soll}* be valid, then it must, etc."; at the same time certainly acknowledging that truth need not necessarily be valid. Finally, freedom shows itself here in its most original form, in respect to its actual operation as we have always described it, not as affirmative, *creating* truth, but rather merely as negative, averting *illusion.*[11] All of which, although very significant, are only expositions of this[12] insight: if consciousness in itself has no validity and relation to truth, then we must abstract from all effects of this consciousness in the investigations which lie before us, and whose task is to deliver truth and the absolute purely to the light of day.

2. From what, then, do we actually need to abstract, and what is its unavoidable effect? This is evident from that salient point and nerve, for whose sake consciousness was rejected as insufficient. But, in virtue of our last investigation, the nerve was this, that it projected something *factically*, that is in its highest potency; and in our case [it projected] the energy, which then would become thinking, whose genetic connection with it it could in no way give; thus a thing that it projected purely and through an absolute gap *{per absolutum hiatum}*. Grasp this character exactly, just as it has been given, and to that end remember what was said last time: e.g., you would not presume that you could actually think without being conscious of it, and vice versa; nor that you could be conscious of your thinking, without in fact actually thinking, or that this consciousness was *deceiving* you; but if you were asked to provide an explicable and explanatory ground for the connection of these two terms, you would never be able to provide such a ground. Thus, changing places with you at the site from which you conducted your proof: your consciousness of thinking should contain a thinking process *{Denken}*, actual, true and really present, without you being able to give an accounting of it; [220–221] therefore, this consciousness projects a *true* reality outward, discontinuously: an absolute inconceivability and inexplicability.

This discontinuous projection is evidently the same one that we have previously called, and presently call, the form of outer existence, which shows itself in every categorical *is*. For what this means, as a projection, concerning which no further account can be given and which thus is discontinuous, is the same as what we called "death at the root." The gap, the rupture of intellectual activity in it,[13] is just death's lair. Now we should not admit the validity of this projection, or form of outer existence, although we can never free ourselves from it factically; and we should know that it means nothing; we should know, wherever it arises, that it is indeed only the result and effect of mere consciousness (ignoring that this consciousness remains hidden in its roots) and therefore not let ourselves be led astray by it. This is the sense of our discovered maxim, which is to be ours from now on in every case where we[14] need it. This very *is* is the original appearance: which is closely related to, and may well be the same thing as, the I which we presented previously as the original appearance.

3. Thus it is decreed against the highest idealism, and this maxim imposes the highest realism yet on us. Before we go further under its leadership, though, it may be advisable to test it against the law which it itself has brought forward, thus to draw it directly before its own seat of judgment in order to discover whether it itself is indeed pure realism.—It proceeds from the *in-itself* and proposes this as the absolute. But what is this *in-itself* as such and in its own self? You are invited here to a very deep reflection and abstraction. Although the foregoing brings to an end the thinking[15] of this in-itself, reflected first by consciousness, although, we have likewise already had to admit before that we did not construct this *in-itself* but that it already is found in advance as completely constructed and finished and comprehensible in itself, and thus as constructed by itself, so that we in any case have nothing to do with this; we may still investigate this original construction more closely in terms of its content.

—I have said that I invite you to a very deep reflection and abstraction. What this abstraction is—an abstraction which may be described in words as well as possible—will barely be made clear from what follows; but this will not harm anything, and it is certain in any case that it is already clear, and I impose on myself the task [222–223] of grasping the highest in words, and on you the task of understanding it in a pure form. Thus—once again, as already previously, the topic is the in-itself, and we are called, here as before, to a consideration of its inner meaning and to its re-construction. We will not complete again what has been done before, an act which, holding us in a circle, would not advance us from the spot. But, if we wish [to achieve] something else, how is this to be distinguished from the preceding? Thus, above we presupposed the *in-itself* and considered its meaning while we supplemented it with life, or a primal fantasy, dissolved ourself in the latter, and had our root in it.[16] Of course this life is not supposed to be our life, but rather the very life and self-construction of the in-itself: it was then an inner determination (one which arose immediately in this context) of the original life itself, which still remained dominant in this case. So it was previously.—Now, however, we elevate ourselves for the first time to the *in-itself* that is presupposed in this procedure, [knowing it] as presupposed and unconditionally immediate, independent of this living reconstruction, *determinate*, and comprehensible: and without this original significance the reconstruction, as a *reconstruction* and *clarification*, would have no basis and no guide. For this reason, I said previously that the originally completed construction, the enduring content, should be demonstrated. Therefore, things must proceed in this work so that what is absolutely presupposed remains presupposed,[17] so that as a result the living quality which we bring with us will mean nothing at all—neither as our vivacity, nor as vivacity in general—likewise the very validity of primal fantasy, although it cannot be withheld factically, yet is denied as real, in which denial the true essence of reason may well consist. (Or, more succinctly, if only one will understand it; *what has been made perceptible* resides in this latter construction, and the meaning of the *in-itself grasped purely intellectually* should be found there.[18])

So much in the way of preliminary formal description of this new reconstruction of the *in-itself*. Now to the solution.—However one may wish to take up the *in-itself*, it is still always[19] qualified by the negation of something opposed to it, thereby as *in-itself* it is itself something relative, the oneness of a duality, and vice versa. Certainly, it is genuinely at once a synthetic and analytic principle, as we have all along looked for: but still it is no true self-sufficient oneness; since the oneness lets itself be grasped only through *duality*: although admittedly duality also lets itself be completely grasped and explained through oneness. In a word, the *in-itself*,[20] grasped more profoundly, is no in-itself, no absolute, because it is not a true oneness, and even our realism has not [224–225] pushed through to the absolute. Viewed still more rigorously,[21] in the *oneness*[22] there is in the background a projection of in-itself and not-in-itself, which posit one another reciprocally for explanation and comprehensibility, and which negate one another in reality; and in return, the oneness is a projection of both terms. Further, this projection happens completely immediately, through a gap, without being able to provide the requisite accounting of itself. Because how an in-itself and a not-in-itself follow from oneness as simple, pure oneness cannot be explained. Of course, it can be done if the oneness is already assumed to be the oneness of the in-itself and not-in-itself; but then the inconceivability[23] and inexplicability is in this *determinateness* of oneness, and it itself is only a projection through an irrational gap. This determinateness would have no warrant other than immediate awareness; and actually, if we will think back to how we have arrived at everything so far, it has no other ground. "Think an in-itself" it began, and this thinking, or consciousness was *possible*. And this possibility has shaped our entire investigation to date; thus we have supported ourselves on consciousness, if not quite on its actuality, then certainly on its possibility, and in this quality we have had it for our principle. Hence, our highest realism, i.e., the highest standpoint of our own speculation, is itself revealed here as an idealism, which so far has just remained hidden in its roots; it is fundamentally factical and a discontinuous projection, does not stand up to its own criteria, and, according to the rules it itself established, it is to be given up.

4. Why should it be given up? What was the true source of the error which we discovered in it? Being *in-itself* [was discovered][24] as a negation and a relational term. Hence we must unconditionally let that go, if it, or our entire system, is to survive. But something is still left over for us. I affirm this and instruct you to find it with me: *being*[25] and *existence*[26] and *resting*,[27] taken as absolute,[28] remains—and of course I add: "being and resting on itself," but I already clearly knew that the latter would be a mere supplement for clarification and [226–227] illustration, but would mean nothing at all in and for itself and would add no supplement to the completeness and self-sufficiency of being's inner essence.—If I wish to look back to the previous, already discarded expression, "being *in-itself*" means a being which indeed needs no other being for its existence. Precisely through this not-needing it becomes intrinsically more and more real than it was before; and not-needing this not-needing does not also belong to its absolute not-needing, and so too with the not-needing of this not-needing of not-needing, so that this supplement in its endless repeatability remains always the same and always meaning nothing in relation to the essence taken seriously and inwardly. Thus, I see into [the fact] that (generally, in its core, thus indeed as the point of oneness, which was previously tested and discarded) the entire relation and comparison with the *not-in-itself*—from which the form of the in-itself as such arises—is completely null in comparison to the essence. It is without meaning or effect. Because I see into this, and thereby handle the addition in almost as negative a way as does the essence itself, then I must, as an insight, participate in the essence in some manner still to be developed.

Now, to be sure, if I pay attention to myself, I can always become aware that I objectify and project this pure being: but I already certainly know that this means nothing, alters nothing about being, and adds nothing to it. To be sure, in another shape this projection is the in-itself's supplement, whose nothingness has already been realized: therefore I will never be deceived by it. In brief, the entire outer existential form has perished in this shape, since it is the latter in the highest [element] in which it occurs, the in-itself; we have only the inner essence left with which to deal, in order to work it through: but we truly work it through if we see into it as the genesis for its appearance in the outer existential form; and nothing else can lead us to that except not allowing ourselves to be deceived by this form. If it does deceive us, then we just are it, dissolved and lost in it, and we will never arrive at its origin *{Genesis}*.

I wished at least to attach this last, fourth, point here, in order not to end the lecture with death and destruction, as it does on first appearance. Tomorrow its further development.[29]

CHAPTER 15

Fifteenth Lecture

Friday, May 11, 1804

N.B. Which Contains the Basic Proposition

Honored Guests:

My task for today is this: *first of all* to work out fully and completely the main point discovered last time; then to present a general review of the new material added this week, and thus, as it were, to balance the accounts, since with this lecture we conclude the week's[1] work and a discussion period intervenes *{dazwischen fällt}*.[2]

On the first matter. This much as a reminder in advance. To begin with, the point I must present is the clearest and simultaneously the most hidden of all, in the place where there is *no* clarity.[3] Not much can be said about it, rather it must be conceived at one stroke; even less can anything be said about it or words used to assist comprehension, since *objectivity*, the first basic twist of all language,[4] has already long been abandoned in our maxim, and is to be annulled here within absolute insight. At this point, therefore, I can rely only on the clarity and rapidity of spirit which you have achieved in the previous investigations. So then, on a particular occasion I divided the science of knowing into two main parts; one, that it is a doctrine of reason and truth, and second, that it is a doctrine of appearance and illusion,[5] but one that is *indeed true* and is grounded in truth. The first part consists of a single insight and is begun and completed with the single point which I will now present. To work! After the problem of absolute relation, which appeared in the original *in-itself*, which itself pointed to a *not-in-itself*,[6] nothing remained for us except the pure, bare being by which, following the maxim, our objectivizing intuition must be rejected as inadequate.—What then is this pure being in its abstraction from relatedness? Could we make it even clearer to ourselves and reconstruct it? I say

---

This lecture begins at GAII, 8, pp. 228–229. The subtitle here occurs only in the *Copia*. The *GA* editors observe that "N.B." abbreviates either *nota bene* or *NebenBemerkung*. I prefer the former.

yes: the very abstraction imposed on us helps. Being is entirely *of itself, in itself, and through itself*; this *self* is not to be taken as an antithesis, but grasped with the requisite abstraction purely inwardly, as it very well can be grasped, and as I for example am most fervently conscious of grasping it. Therefore, to express ourselves scholastically, it has been constructed as a being in pure act *{esse in mero actu}*, so that both being and living, and living and being completely inter-penetrate, dissolve into one another, and are the same, and this self-same inwardness is the one completely unified being, which was the first point.

[230–231] This sole being and life can not exist, or be looked for, out-side itself, and nothing at all can exist outside it. Briefly and in a word: dual-ity or multiplicity does not occur at all or under any conditions, only oneness; because by its own agency being itself carries self-enclosed oneness with itself, and its essence consists in this. Being—understood by language as a noun—cannot literally be[7] actively[8] except immediately in living; but it ["being" understood as a noun] *is* only verbally; because completely noun-like being is objectivity, which in no way suffices: and it is only by surrendering this sub-stantiality and objectivity, not merely in pretense but in the fact and truth of insight, that one arrives at reason.

On the other side,[9] what lives immediately is the *"esse,"*[10] since only the "to be" lives, and then it, as an indivisible oneness, which cannot exist outside itself and cannot go out of itself into duality, is something to which the things we have demonstrated immediately apply.

But *we live*[11] immediately in the act of living itself, therefore we are the one undivided being itself, in itself, of itself, through itself, which can never go outside itself to duality.

"We," I say—[12] to be sure, we are immediately conscious that, insofar as we speak of it, we again objectify this "We" itself with its inward life: but we already know that this objectification means as little in this case as in any other. And surely we know that we are not talking about this We-in-itself, separated by an irrational discontinuity from the other We which ought to be conscious;[13] rather [we are talking] purely about the one We-in-itself,[14] living purely in itself, which we conceive merely through our own energetic negation of the conceiving which obtrudes on us empirically here.—This We, in *imme-diate*[15] living itself; this *We*,[16] not qualified or characterizable by anything that might occur to someone, but rather characterizable purely by immediately actual life itself.[17]

This was the surprising insight to which I wished to elevate you, in which reason and truth emerge purely. If anyone should need it, I will point to it briefly from yet another aspect. If being is occupied with its own absolute living, and can never emerge out from it, then it is a self-enclosed I, and can be nothing else besides this; and likewise a self-enclosed I is being:[18] which "I" we could now [232–233] call "We" in anticipation of a division in it. Hence, we *in no way*[19] depend here *on an empirical perception* of our life, which would need to be completely rejected as a modification of consciousness; rather we are depending on the genetic insight into life and the I, which emerges from the construction of the one being, and vice versa. We already know, and abstract completely from, the fact, that this very *insight* as such, together with its *reversal*, is irrelevant and vanishes; we will need to look back to it again only in deducing phenomena.[20]

As it has been presented now, this intrinsically cannot be made clearer by *anything else*; since it itself is the original source and ground of all other clarity. Still, the subjective eye can get clearer, and become more fit for this clarity, through deeper explanation of the immediately surrounding terms; therefore I add in this regard another consideration which lies on the system's path anyway. Yesterday, and again today too at the beginning[21] of our meditation, although we constructed being according to its inner essence, if we only remember, we *placed* being *objectively before ourselves*, despite the fact that, though only as a result of following our maxim, we grant no validity to this objectivity:—*factically*,[22] even though surely not *intelligibly* or in reason, being remains separated from itself. But, just as in this reflective process we are grasped by the insight that being itself is an absolute I, or we; thus the first remaining disjunction—between being and the we—is completely annulled, even in facticity, and the first version of the form of existence is also factically negated. Previously [we knew that] at the very least we emerged factically out of ourselves toward being, and [in this process] it could very well happen that being would not come out of itself, especially if we did not wish to be being. We did not accept this being as valid, merely on the basis of a maxim that had its proof via derived terms, and thus might well need a new proof here. As we become being itself in the insight we have produced, we can—as a result of this insight—no longer come out of ourselves toward being, since we are it; and really we absolutely cannot come out of ourselves at all, because being cannot come out of itself. Here the preceding maxim has received its proof, [234–235] its law, and its immediate realization in the insight: because this insight in fact no longer objectifies being. Now to be sure, I say, no other objectifying consciousness arises together with this insight—[23] because in order for that to occur, a self-reflecting would be required to stand in between—however the possibility does arise of an objectifying consciousness: [namely,] our own.[24] Now, as regards the content of this new objectification, it is already clear that it does not bring with itself any disjunction in our subject matter, as does the first—between *real being*[25] and absolute non-being— rather this content brings only the mere repetition and repeated supposition of one and the same I, or We, which is entirely self-enclosed, which encompasses all reality in itself, and which is therefore entirely unalterable; therefore, it does not contradict the original law of not going out of oneself in essence.

But, as the first stage of our descent into phenomenology, we will have to explore whence this empty repetition and doubling may arise; today it is merely a matter of establishing the insight which is expressive of pure reason—that being or the absolute is a self-enclosed I—in its unalterability.

Now on to the second part of the general review. As must arise in any presentation of the science of knowing, we have proceeded factically, inwardly completing something useful for our purpose, and paying attention to how we have done it, compelled always, as is evident, by an unconscious law of reason working in us. On this path, which I will not repeat now, we had elevated ourselves to a pure *"through,"*[26] as the essence of the concept; and had understood {*eingesehen*} that the latter's realization presupposed a self-subsisting being. Having presented this insight as a fact and reflected further about its principle, it turned out either that one could posit the energy of thinking a "through" needing completion as the absolute and thus as the source of intuition and of life in itself within intuition, which was an idealism; or that, considering that life ought to exist in itself, one could take the latter as the principle, with the result that everything else perishes; this latter [was] a realism. Both were supported by maxims. The former on this: the fact of reflection is to be taken as valid, and nothing else; the latter on this: the content of the evident proposition is to be taken as valid, and nothing else; and, for that very reason, both are at bottom factical, since indeed even the contents of what is manifest, which alone should be valid for realism, is only a fact.

Along with the necessity that arose from this to ascend higher and to master the facts genetically, we turned our attention to what promised to be most significant here, [namely] to the in-itself, bound to the realistic principle, [236–237] to life in itself: and this further deliberation was the first step we made this week.[27] It turned out that the in-itself manifests as an absolute negation of the validity of all seeing directed toward itself:[28] that it constructs itself in immediate manifestness, and with its own self-construction even gives off immediate manifestness or light: yielding a higher realism which deduces insight and the light themselves, items that the first realism was content to ignore. A new idealism attempts to establish itself against this new realism. That is, we had to take command of ourselves and struggle energetically to contemplate the in-itself in its significance. So, [we] believed we realized that this in-itself first appeared as a result of this reflection as simultaneously constructing itself with immediate manifestness in the light; and that consequently this energy of ours would be the basic principle and first link in the whole matter.

Realism, or we ourselves, since we are nothing else than this realism, fights very boldly against this as follows: "If you really actually think . . . ," and to what will you appeal for confirmation of this assertion: you can adduce nothing more than that you are aware of yourself, but you cannot derive thinking genetically in its reality and truthfulness, as you should, from your consciousness in which you report it; but, by contrast, we can derive the very consciousness to which you appeal, and which you make your principle, genetically, since this can surely be only a modification of insight and light, but light proceeds directly out of the in-itself, manifestness in unmediated manifestness. The higher maxim presented in this reasoning would just be this: to give no credence to the assertions of simple, immediate consciousness, even if one cannot factically free oneself from them, but rather to abstract from them. What is this consciousness's effect, for the sake of which it[29] is discarded; and therefore what is that which must always be removed from the truth? Answer: the absolute projection of an object whose origin is inexplicable, so that between the projective act and the projected object everything is dark and bare; as I think I can express very accurately, if a little scholastically, a *proiectio per hiatum irrationale* (projection through an irrational gap).

Let me again draw your attention to this point, both for now and for all your future studies and opinions in philosophy: if [238–239] my current presentation of the science of knowing has been clearer than all my previous versions of the same science, and can maintain itself in this clarity, and if clear understanding of the system is to make a new advance by these means, the ground for this must lie simply in the impartial establishment of the maxim that immediate consciousness is in no way sufficient and that hence it does not suffice in its basic law of *projection per hiatum*. Of course the essence of this truth has ruled in every possible presentation of the science of knowing from the very first hint which I gave in a "Review of *Aenesidemus*" in the *Allgemeinen Literatur Zeitung*, because this maxim is identical with the principle of absolute genesis. If nothing that has not been realized genetically is permitted, then projection *per hiatum* will not be permitted, since its essence consists precisely in non-genesis. If one has not made himself explicitly aware that this non-genesis, which is to be restrained in thinking,[30] remains a factical element of the consciousness which is unavoidable on every path of all our investigations and of the science of knowing itself, then one torments and exhausts himself trying to eliminate this illusion, as if that were possible. And the sole remaining way of breaking through to truth is to divide the illusion, and intellectually to destroy each part one at a time, while during this procedure one actually defers the illusion to another piece at which annihilation will arrive later, when the first piece could once again serve as the bearer of the illusion. This was the science of knowing's previous path—and it is clear that it too leads to the goal, although with greater difficulty. However, if one knows the origin of non-genesis in advance, and that it always comes to nothing, although it is unavoidable, then one no longer fights against it, but rather allows it to work peacefully: one simply ignores it and abstains from its results. It is possible

in this way alone to gain access to insight immediately as we have done decisively, and not just by inference from the nonexistence of the two halves.

Let me continue the recapitulation: the realism which presented the
recently analyzed maxim was itself questionable and was brought before the
judgment seat [240–241] of its own maxims. There, on closer consideration,
the *in-itself*[31] (inasmuch as it is assumed to be something original and independent of all living construction and to possess this same guiding meaning)
turned out to be incomprehensible without a not-in-itself. Therefore, in the
understanding it turned out to be no *in-itself*[32] (i.e., something comprehensible by itself alone) at all, and instead it [turned out to be] understandable only
through its correlative term. Therefore, the unity of understanding,[33] which
reason presupposes here, cannot merely be a simple self-determined[34] oneness;
instead it must be a unity-in-relation, meaningless without *two* terms which
arise within it in two different connections: in part as positing one another
and in part as negating one another, thus the well-known "through" and the
five-foldness recognized in it. If one must also now concede that once oneness
has been admitted, the terms incontestably posit themselves genetically, still
oneness itself is not thereby explained genetically; hence it is present simply
by means of a *proiectio per hiatum irrationalem*, which this system, [presenting
itself][35] as realism, has made against its own principles.

With this disclosed, absolutely everything in the in-itself which
pointed to relations was to be abandoned, and so nothing else remained
behind except simple, pure being as absolute, self-enclosed oneness, which
can only arise in itself, and in its own immediate arising or life: which therefore always arises from a place where an arising, a living, simply occurs, and
it does not arise except in such an arising, and therefore occurs as absolute I,
as today's disclosure could be put briefly. Generally, one can think this sim-
plest of all insights in indefinitely many forms, if it has once become clear. Its
spirit is that being exists immediately only in being, or life, and that it exists
only as a whole, undivided oneness.

CHAPTER 16

Sixteenth Lecture

Tuesday, May 15, 1804

Honorable Guests:

The fundamental principle presented now:[1] *"Being is entirely a self-enclosed singularity {Singulum} of immediately living being[2] that can never get outside itself"* is in part immediately clear in itself, and in part it has been shown in the discussion that it is clear to this assembly in particular.[3] Hence, we do not need to linger with it any further.

I said that it contains and completes what one could present as the first part of the science of knowing: the *pure theory of truth or reason*. We proceed now to the second part; in order to deduce from the first part, as necessary and true appearances, everything which up to now we have let go as merely empirical and not intrinsically valid. In advance of this undertaking, I must remind you of only one thing. Resolving this task *in absolute oneness of principle*[4] is not without difficulties; especially since, according to a remark[5] about method I made at the end last time (on the occasion of a general review), this task is *entirely new* and has not even arisen in the earlier presentations of the science of knowing. For that reason, it happens that this resolution cannot remain without some complications.

However, in order to be completely clear with you about this point, I will employ here the method that I have generally used before of giving you an initial factical acquaintance with the terms which come next so as to prepare you adequately for their subsequent combination and connection. This preparation is the next purpose of today's lecture.[6]

1. In the *insight* we[7] had produced into inner being, we began—after fully abstracting from that objectification, about which we already know that it intrinsically lacks validity—from [244–245] this being's construction, to which we expressly challenged ourselves. (You see that I revert to this, partly as it has always been done up to now, and partly because thereby some kind of idealistic outlook enters in again. I refrain from giving an account of this

---

This lecture begins at GA II, 8, pp. 242–243.

here.)[8] Now mark this well, since this point can bring you great clarity, I will not myself reason {*räsonnieren*} here as all previous idealisms have reasoned: "consequently being depends on its being constructed, and this is its principle"; because this claim could have truth and meaning,—but only in relation to being's factical existence in the form of external, objectifying existence, which existence then [is] absolutely presupposed and so—according to our basic maxim—the projection through a gap would not be abstracted from.[9] This factical existence in general is to be put into question in its basic principle and deduced for the first time; but, trusting in the truth of the insight's content and so in our principle, we will thus conclude entirely realistically: if being cannot ever get outside of itself and nothing can be apart from it, then it must be being itself which thus constructs itself, to the extent that this construction is to occur.[10] Or, as is completely synonymous: We certainly are the agents who carry out this construction, but we do it insofar as we are being itself, as has been seen {*eingesehen*}, and we coincide with it; but by no means as a "we" which is *free* and *independent* from being, as could possible seem to be the case, and as it actually appears to be, if we give ourselves over to appearance.[11] In short, if being is constructed, as in fact it seems to us to be, then it is constructed entirely through itself. The basis for this construction, as is immediately apparent and understandable to us, can not be located external to being, but only within itself as *being*, entirely and absolutely; and indeed *absolutely* and *necessarily* apart from all contingency.

At this point notice a)[12] I have said "If being is constructed," expressing myself hypothetically, thereby perhaps reserving a future division of the statement into a true part and a false part. So if someone were to insist that[13] it was actually constructed, you might wonder how on the present standpoint such a one might conduct the proof? I know of no other way than by means of his consciousness.[14] However, we have already given up on [accepting] such a proof as valid by itself; but here for the first time [the question of] to what extent and in what sense consciousness and its statements can be [accepted as] valid is to be decided. In particular, we must decide on the extent to which consciousness suffices in *the highest things* it asserts, of which the fact that being is constructed can serve here as an example.[15] Therefore, we should not reach ahead anticipating the results of the investigation, which we will make possible only by means of the hypothetical assertion.[16]

[246–247] b) To be sure, it has already become immediately clear in our earlier investigation that mere being is of itself, from itself, through itself immediately an *esse*, that it therefore constructs itself, and that it is only in this self-construction. This comprised the whole content of our insight. But the self-construction that we talk about here, which we present only hypothetically as a declaration of pure consciousness, and which we append to being in itself only mediately as an inference, this is—as I ask you to grasp {*einzusehen*} immediately—something entirely different, merely idealistic, imaginal. This is the only way I can describe it in words. In contrast, the first one alone would be *real*, clearly having the predicate "real" only by contrast with the other,[17] and thus negating the absoluteness of the previous insight with this predicate, which is understandable only relationally and through its opposite. Now the task is just to find to what extent—I say not so much being's *ideal* or *real* self-construction—as rather the *analytic/synthetic principle*, which grounds it, is to be [accepted as] valid. This question of validity can only be resolved by deducing the principle genetically.[18] Therefore, we take care not to anticipate, and we grant the entire distinction only hypothetical validity.

2. Let us go back. If being is constructed ideally, as we assume, then this happens directly as a result of its own immanent essence. Be sure not to overlook [the fact] that we have thereby[19] actually won something *new* and *great*.[20] That is, the ideal[21] is posited in this absolute insight organically and absolutely in essential being itself, completely, without any real hiatus in essence, and so without any disjunction in essence. This insight is also genetic, positing an absolute origin as unconditionally necessary on the condition that it be the ground and be assumed.[22] Now this insight brings along an absolute *that*, but by no means a *how*; we cannot see *how* the absolute essence ideally constructs itself, nor can the inner ground of this construction be constructed further. We must not be put off by this, since only thereby does this insight secure itself as the absolute, beyond which there is no other, and this construction as the absolute one, beyond which no other can be placed. To be sure, it must come down to such an absolute insight and construction, and it is clear that, only at this point, with an insight and construction proceeding directly from essence, could we arrive there. The gap *{hiatus}*, which as a result of the absolute insight is in essence nothing at all, exists only in respect of the We;[23] and, indeed, in case [248–249] the essence of consciousness, properly so-called, is to consist just in this, no longer in the absolute and pure genesis but rather in the genesis of the genesis, as it appears here, then, if this *We*[24] (or this re-generation of the absolute genesis) were to be deduced, it would be in *consciousness* that it [the gap] could well remain. [We can then very easily see] that here, quite probably, we have untied in passing the genuine knot at its root; and that the new difficulty, which has not concealed itself, has fallen further down, where it can let itself be easily resolved by closer consideration of the basic point already discovered.[25] In the meantime, since the point has not yet been put as clearly as possible, we will continue our exposition without staying here longer.

3. *We have* now *grasped {eingesehen}*[26] this. Following our consistent method, let us make this insight itself genetic. Under what condition did it arise? Evidently this, that an ideal self-construction of being be assumed, at least hypothetically. "It is assumed," obviously means and can be explained *ipso*

facto like this: it is *projected absolutely* into the form of outer existence, in a provisional way, without any ground or principle for this projection, thus through
an irrational gap.

Now, a major portion of our task is to demonstrate the genetic principle for this irrational gap, which so far we have presented only factically, whose
validity we have denied, but without our being able to dispense with it.[27]

(Observe. A philosophical lecture can frequently count on the unnoticed assistance of the understanding, without always providing the distinguishing grounds for the distinctions that it makes; the fact usually explains
its true meaning through itself and its results. However, in such cases one
always counts on a happy accident that is just as likely not to occur. It is
always more exact not to leave any distinguishing grounds unexplained; and
especially we should not allow ourselves to be led astray by the fact that often,
and on many subjects, the explanation makes more obscure what was clearer
with the unnoticed assistance of the understanding, because it should not be
so, and satisfying ourselves with understanding's unnoticed aide is not the
genuinely philosophical disposition. In the hour before last, we had looked at
the case of a distinction between two ways of thinking about the in-itself,
whose distinguishing ground I specifically stated, although the distinction
might have been clear enough simply as a matter of fact. The present case is
similar. The principle for the irrational gap as such, i.e., for the absolute
absence of principle, [250–251] as such, should be demonstrated. Obviously
not insofar as it is an absence of principle, because then it would negate and
destroy itself, a very different thing from it being provided with a principle.
So, in what respect is it to be and in what respect not?—Let us now make the
meaning clear. Being's ideal self-construction is projected through an
absolute gap, and is thereby made into an absolutely factical and external
existence. Now this existence,[28] as absolute existence, can have no higher
principle at all in the sphere of existence, and in this sense is precisely lacking a principle. Its "principle" in this unprincipledness is just the projection
itself. Hence too it is not claimed, and cannot be claimed, that being in itself
constructs itself ideally, but rather only that it is projected as constructing
itself so; this is important and breaks the doubt aroused by the first remark
at 1. above. Therefore, nothing remains—once this factical being has been
annulled as absolute by the demonstration that the projection is its principle—except the projection itself, and this as an *act*,[29] as everyone is requested
to become aware. To say that a principle must be provided for it means therefore that a principle must be provided for it solely as an act in general, and as
this act that in itself posits something unprincipled.)[30]

What could this principle be? The absolute insight, which forces itself
on us, that the ideal self-construction must itself be grounded in absolute
essence, is conditioned by the presupposition of this ideal self-construction

without any ground, and thus by this projection we ourselves have made to complete the science of knowing. And so, the principle has been found in what is conditioned by it, and the newer, higher insight that is thereby created can be encompassed in the following sentence: If {Soll}[31] the absolute insight is to arise, that, etc., then such an ideal self-construction must be posited entirely factically. The explanation through immediate insight is conditioned by the absolutely factical presupposition of what is to be explained.

4. Now do not forget that everything here remains only hypothetical. If it *should be* seen into, *then must* ___,[32] etc. Should the consequent be posited absolutely and categorically? Undoubtedly, if the antecedent is, and without doubt not, if the antecedent is not; because the latter has no principle except the former. But if the first should {soll} be posited absolutely, then it is not apparent as absolute,[33] because it has been posited as absolute *hypothetically {problematisch}*.[34] As I add now only to arouse attention, [252–253] in this hypothetical *"should"* as our highest point so far, everything comes together whose derivation is now our task: the ideal construction of being as a self-construction, as well as the projection through a gap. Just so, it is clear that this hypothetical quality of the "should" must remain as it has been presented. However, it is equally clear that something categorical must arise too, since otherwise our science would be baseless and without principle through its whole range[35] as well as in its starting point. However, this categorical quality must now just manifest itself hypothetically in the "should" *qua* "should," so that henceforth the chief principle of the process of appearance {Erscheinung} (and, if[36] it were believed, of what appears {des Scheins}) should consist in this: that the absolutely categorical "should" appear as hypothetical in relation to the insight, the true and the certain. That is, [it should appear] as able to be or not to be, as able to be thus or be otherwise.

5. In order to prepare the way for this point, to the extent time allows, I urge you to reflect maturely with me on the essence of the *"should."*[37] Obviously, an inner self-construction is expressed in the *"should":*[38] an inner, absolute, pure, qualitative *self-making*[39] and resting-on-itself. One can assist the intuition of this truth, which in any case also makes itself. It is, I say, an "inner self-construction," completely as such: *nothing else*[40] supports the hypothetical "should," except its inner postulation entirely by itself and without any other ground; because if it had some other ground, it would no longer be a hypothetical "should," but rather a categorical "must." "Inner postulation *entirely by itself"*[41] I have said; hence a creation from nothing, producing itself entirely as such. A "resting-on-itself" I have said, because (letting myself take it up in a sensory form, which harms nothing here) it falls back into nothing without this continuing pursuit of inward, living postulation and creation from nothing. Hence it is the self-creator of its own being and the self-support of its duration.

This, as we have described it, is simply then the "should," and, according to the presupposition, it is grasped intuitively by all of you in this way. Therefore, with all its initially apparent hypothetical character,[42] just for that very reason there is something categorical and absolute here, the absolute determinateness of its essence. Before we now show further what follows from this, let me add today two further comments in conclusion.

a. The "should" bears every criterion of the intrinsic being intuited in the basic principle: [it is] an inner, living from itself, through itself, in itself, creating and bearing itself, pure I, and so forth; and [it is] certainly [254–255] organized and coherent internally, entirely as such. As regards the latter, in case it needs further explanation after the clarity with which it must have already presented itself previously in intuition: we then always objectified the fundamental principle's "inner being" factically, although this objectivity was not valid. We also have previously objectified the *"should."*[43] Finally, however, we have been lost in it factically, in its inner description and insight, and now for the first time we free ourselves from it, and it from us, in reflecting about it, a process which, according to our previous method, can be explained as a projection through a gap taking as its principle the "should" itself. Accordingly, this "should"—purely and simply in its oneness, and without any supplement—can easily be being's immediate ideal self-construction, i.e., that is in no way to be further *reconstructed,*[44] but rather that provides the subject matter *{die Sache}* directly in the construction itself. On the other hand, being's previous, hypothetically posited, construction from the "should" has finally found a principle in this "should," just as inner being finally has too for its projection through a gap, which we had proposed accordingly. [This principle] in itself is *construction and subject matter, ideality and reality,*[45] and it cannot be one without the other. This duality may reside in our objectifying consideration of the science of knowing, which therefore abandons its claim to intrinsic validity.

b. This "should" has constantly, but without notice, played the principal role in all our previous investigations. "Should it come to this or that, to a realization of the through, etc., then must . . ."; our insights have always gone along in this fashion. Therefore, no wonder that after letting go of everything else, what remains for us is only the thing that is truly first in all these cases.

CHAPTER 17

Seventeenth Lecture

Wednesday, May 16, 1804

Honored Guests:

I have stated in the last hour how the part of our science on which we are now working might be different from the part completed first, and what our following lectures intend: namely to introduce for the first time the materials for resolving our second task, and to make you familiar with them. At the same time, I admitted that the next lectures might not be without difficulty and confusion. It is easier to take in and to grasp *{einsehen}* that which rests in reason completely and simply as *oneness*, as did the earlier fundamental principle, since only abstraction is needed for this task.—"Easier," I say, than to trace what in itself and originally is never[1] a oneness back to a[2] oneness in order to produce a completely new and unheard of concept in oneself, for which other arts are undoubtedly required. Now, we first lay out multiplicity in an order in which is most convenient to us for insight. These terms[3] can first be *correctly ordered* and understood *{eingesehen}* on the basis of their *principle*,[4] which itself is first to be discovered from[5] them. At this point in the course of the external lectures, there is an unavoidable circle that can be annulled only by its own completion. It is possible, and indeed expected, however, for one to grasp the process—that, to be sure, has its proper order—and terms, and to give them what clarity they can have under the circumstances.[6] I have said that a new, heretofore entirely unknown, principle must be presented; and also simultaneously I would add this remark: that (thinking of the previous division of the science of knowing into two parts) we are concerned not just with presenting the second part, but also with uniting the latter with the first part.[7]

The course of the previous sessions was this: we *constructed*[8] the pure being, which we had grasped *{eingesehen}*, as an entirely self-enclosed singularity. In this way, I assumed, we could become immediately conscious of ourselves, and, as required, we were actually conscious of ourselves. This therefore was a completely simple, factically objectifying projection of an act that we

---

This lecture begins at GA II, 8, pp. 256–257.

ascribe to ourselves as likewise independently existing entities; and in this manner we could have been tempted to deduce being itself from this act of construction in a one-sidedly idealistic fashion. However, [258–259] we wisely refrained from doing this, well understanding that by this we would return whence we had first arisen and consequently would not have advanced. But we proceeded in this manner, and necessarily had to do so, if we wanted to come to something more than the one being, for example to the latter's way of appearing.—"As concerns the truth in itself of this construction, this can appeal to nothing else besides the bare assertion of consciousness."[9] We cannot now discard this statement unconditionally, as just previously we unconditionally rejected it, thanks to our present, entirely altered, aim; because previously we sought pure being in itself, and it has been shown that consciousness is entirely insufficient for this purpose. Now we no longer seek this pure being in itself, since we already have it and so our search for it is over. Instead, we want to grasp it in its primordial appearance; and so consciousness, and here in particular the construction, could be the first term of this appearance for us to grasp. We cannot allow this term to be unconditionally valid any more than before; since the extent to which and the conditions under which it is valid are exactly the issue. Therefore, we must present this claim hypothetically, without prejudging future inquiry: if, and to the extent that, a construction of this kind *is actual*,[10] that is, takes part in being and not merely seems to be, but has being actually appearing in it, then ____ . *Through* this *then*, we are asked to point out in immediate manifestness the condition for the real and true being of such a construction, in case and to the extent that being could come to it. This condition has now been found and has become evident without any difficulty:—If this construction, which appears to us,[11] *is* actually and in fact connected with *true being*[12] in reason—but in no way connected with factical existence in consciousness, which counts for nothing until it is better grounded (this detail is not to be overlooked)[13]—if the construction which appears to us *is* in this sense, then it is not in any way based in the vain "I" of consciousness that emptily objectifies being; rather it is grounded in being[14] itself. For being is one, and where it is, it is whole; in being *qua* being;[15] therefore entirely and absolutely necessary.

(On the condition that you do not allow yourselves to be distracted, let me add here an additional remark that can spread much illumination. Posit pure immanent being as the absolute, substance, God, as indeed it really is, and posit appearance, that is grasped here in its highest point as the absolute's internal genetic construction, as [260–261] the revelation and manifestation of God, then the latter is understood as absolutely essential and grounded in the essence of the absolute itself. I assert that this insight into absolute inward necessity is a distinguishing mark of the science of knowing as against all other systems. I cannot emphasize it enough, because the absolute absence

{Dunkelheit} of insight strives against it with all its might, since freedom is always the last thing [this darkness] will surrender. If it cannot save [freedom] for itself, then at least it tries to secure it in God.[16] In everyone without exception, an absolute contingency exists next to absolute substance. Here something is seen from the beginning as absolutely necessary in reason and in itself, which afterwards will appear not in reason and not in itself but as contingent in another connection that still is to be worked out. Only on this condition can the science of knowing hope to deduce the phenomenon in a genuine and grounded manner, and not merely as a pretense; because a genuine derivation must have a reliable principle. Otherwise, as has often actually happened, one deduces from the intrinsically contingent something else which is also contingent, and obtains other contingent things from these, which themselves stand firm only on condition of the reliability of the previous thing, whose reliability likewise depends on the first. As if a good, proper, and reliable standpoint could arise when one had two terms, neither of which could stand by itself, each relying reciprocally on the other.)[17]

This remark as well: it is evident that in our present investigation it still seems as if, as I freely admitted at the outset, this investigation is still searching for its principle but has not yet got it, something I have described as erroneous, since its first term—the construction of inward being—still remains hypothetical in connection to that about which alone we are inquiring, true being in reason. So, the thing which can first be ascertained under this condition, being's necessary self-construction, can itself not be otherwise than hypothetical to the same degree. Therefore, from here on [262–263] you should direct your attention to the question whether and when a self-sustaining principle emerges.

If there is a construction of being, then it is grounded absolutely in being itself; we grasped *{sahen . . . ein}* this directly and reflected further on the insight and its inner, law-governed form. Then it was immediately clear that we began with the presupposition of inner being's construction, which we incorrectly attributed to the "I" of consciousness, but we have already learned better than this and let go of the attribution. But this much remains indubitable, that being's construction is projected as an absolute fact.—Have we now brought this implicitly simple, factical projection into connection with other terms by the use we have made of it? Evidently so; we saw *{sahen wir ein}* that if such a construction exists, then it must be grounded in being. Now, we have undertaken this entire speculative venture freely; the resulting insight (which might very well not have been engendered) is conditioned by our procedure (which we might very well have omitted), and therefore it is in no way a firm standpoint. All the same, in order to achieve such a firm standpoint we applied a procedure that, to the extent that it needed to, proved its legitimacy by its bare possibility. We said: assume that the insight, engendered by us, is to arise, then you will see *{einsehen}* that under these conditions the projection of factical being, previously only possible, becomes necessary.

In this way, we would first of all have made good progress beyond everything achieved so far toward a proof that, although to be sure we do not feel firm ground beneath us, we might be on a good path. The absolute projection through a gap, and thereby the form of outer existence, that could not be understood conceptually in all our previous investigations, is explained as necessary under the assumption that a higher term (the insight) should be, an assumption that itself was previously hypothetical. Thus, the hypothetical status departs from the lower term, though only by transferring itself to the higher; but at least with this it is simplified and its proper location is revealed to us, where we can hope to grasp it at the root.

After what I have said about the necessity of a self-supporting principle for this investigation as well, we will next eliminate this hypothetical status completely; and here the most secure means is to look it straight in the eye. It is entirely compressed into the hypothetical "should"; this is sufficient by itself for our next purpose;[18] therefore, we let go of the site where this "should" appears, insight, etc. Quite apart from our current procedure, it could be obvious from the entire previous investigation that one now needs to keep this "should" as one of the deepest foundation points of all appearance, [264–265] as I will observe in passing. All our preceding investigations and engendered insights have started with the hypothetical "should" and have proceeded from it as a *terminus a quo*: "If there is really to be *{soll}* a "through," then there must ____"; " Should the achieved insight arise, then there must ____": *idealism*; "should this life be life in itself, then there must ____": *realism*; all the way up to the highest relation: "Should an *in-itself* be comprehensible, then a not-in-itself must be thought" and so on.[19]

This "should" loses itself entirely only in the insight into pure being and into the way in which we evaporate into it, so that an absolute categorical character enters, without any hypothetical presupposition. As soon as we reflect again on this insight, the process which yielded the historical origin of our second part and our entire present investigation, it[20] reinstates itself with a "should," thus as something contingent, seeking the basic condition for this contingent quality, a necessary *self-construction* of being. Now, so far in the ascent we have clung to the content of the generated insight without reflecting on the hypothetical form in which, as a whole, it appeared. This was entirely correct because we wanted to arrive at the original content of the truth as such. (Here in passing the question that some have asked me concerning the true grounds for our first part's preference for realism and for the maxim that ruled there always to orient ourselves realistically answers itself decisively and fundamentally.)[21] But now as we descend we have to hold on to just this neglected "should," which indeed provides the enduring inner soul of all the idealisms, which consistently excluded themselves during the ascent, and which were struck down by an opposed higher term only in respect to their content; but still persist in their form, as we see. Now this form cannot be disturbed directly by the original content, since everything that the latter can attain has already been achieved in the ascent. Rather, it must be explained and justified inwardly on its own terms. It must refute its own ungrounded claims, to the extent that they are ungrounded; roughly just the way we refuted the content's highest idealism, that at first presented itself as realism, by means of the law that it itself presented, and revealed it as idealism.

In a word, and in order to lead you even deeper into the systematic connection between

a. the term that earlier was the highest in appearance—the distinguishing and the unification of the in-itself and [266–267] not-in-itself in the whole *five-fold*[22] synthesis, and
b. absolute inner being, as the absolutely realistic element, the *"should"*[23] enters here as a new middle term, in which the self-differentiating and likewise synthetic relation of the two indicated relational terms must show itself. To find this is the proper content of our task: to find it as a firm principle is its form.

First, however, the connection to inward being. The form of being is categoricalness. Therefore, something categorical must be found in the *"should"*[24] itself, however hypothetical it might appear. In order to uncover this, I have demanded that the inner essence of a hypothetical "should" be carefully considered (following our consistent method of raising into clarity something that was at first dimly projected).—We have already done this last time; because of the subject's importance, I will repeat the entire operation today.

If you say forcefully and deliberately: "*should* so and so be," then it is clear that thereby an inner assumption is expressed, without any foundation, simply of itself and from itself, thus an inwardly pure creation, and to be sure standing there completely pure entirely as such,[25] because the "should," if it is taken only as purely hypothetical—as is required here and without achieving which the required insight will not arise—expresses complete external groundlessness, simple internal self-grounding, and nothing else. Further, (in this way, I tried to grasp the same thing and make it clear from the other side): the absolute *assumption*[26] is expressed in the *should*, an assumption that is unconditionally allowed to drop, just as it is unconditionally presupposed. Should it (and with it probably the entire "If . . . *should*, then _____ *must*"[27] that depends on it) not drop away, (with which dropping away all knowledge and insight probably drop away as well) then it must hold and sustain itself.—As surely as we have now seen into this, just that surely has the *should*[28] been illuminated for us as an absolute that holds and sustains itself out of itself, of itself, and through itself *as such*, on the condition that it exists. This, I say, is a "should"; and were it not precisely so, then it would not be a "should"; therefore we have a categorical insight into the unchangeable, unalterable[29] nature of the *"should,"*[30] an insight in[31] which we can completely abstract from the outward existence of such a "should." "Can abstract," I say since, with adequate deliberation, I refrain from drawing a conclusion here which easily presents itself, but which is not yet sufficiently ripe, given the context. To the extent that our task simply consisted in discovering something categorical in the "should," it has been fulfilled by what has happened.

In explaining the should, I have not warned you about the illusion that it is we who assume there what is hypothetical and who hold [268–269] and sustain it; since the rule is to leave this "we" of mere consciousness entirely out of action until it is deduced, and being able to do so is the art without which no entry into the domain of the science of knowing is possible. If, in the meantime, this "I" has forced itself on anyone, then let it immediately remove itself at this point. Namely, whether or not you have created and carried the assumption, it is still always completely clear that you have a *"should"*[32] only on this condition of self-creation and carrying forward. Therefore, even if you are the creator, the *"should"*[33] always contains the rule and law of proceeding in that manner, otherwise it is not a "should," and we have not wished to say any more than that here; abstracting completely from the question that you raised and that we will work out in another place.

And now, in conclusion, a very[34] sharp distinction, that will become decisive in what follows, and that cannot be made clear too soon. The strong similarity between inner being as something self-enclosed and self-sufficient in-itself, of-itself, and through-itself, and the should as just the same has already been pointed out earlier. There is nonetheless a distinction between the two that I have named and made dimly[35] recognizable in the stated formula: "the should" is something in-itself, etc., *as such.*[36] I urge you now to clarify this distinction for yourselves along with me. Being was constructed as something absolute in itself, etc. I ask: should there now exist, or is their actually in our insight, if it is of the right kind, another persisting being or substantive, besides this absolute, self-constructing *esse*? Not at all. Instead both merge into each other[37] and into the pure self-enclosed singularity, and the doubled repetition is entirely superfluous, insufficient, and neglected. This is not at all the case with the "should," if you will look into it quite acutely.[38] The latter stands out as a fixed, substantial middle point and bearer of absolute *self-production* and *continuation.*[39] The latter is not just immediate, as was the case with being, but rather only mediate through presupposing and positing a "should"—in brief on the assumption that the "should" itself again should be, and thus should be seen *{eingesehen}* through its own doubling. Here there is

not, as there was before, an immediate rational insight, but rather only a mediate one, conditioned again by a higher projection through a gap, precisely of
the *"should"*;[40] just in the way we have actually proceeded. We have wished to
indicate this relation by the added phrase "as such,"[41] i.e., itself in objective,
factical oneness of essence.

To what further things this new discovery might lead must emerge on
its own. Before [270–271] hand, this much arises in regard to method: that,
just as a projection through a gap (the projection of being's construction) is
deduced as necessary from the fact that a particular insight "should be" *{sein-
sollen}*,[42] another projection, just that of the *"should"* itself, presents itself [on
the one hand] as a condition for this insight and on the other side again as
conditioned by it. We now need to venture further into this; that therefore our
present investigation, just like the previous one, advances upward only in this
precisely delineated circle, because it is still looking for the latter's[43] principle.[44]

CHAPTER 18

Eighteenth Lecture

Thursday, May 17, 1804

Honored Guests:

[Here is] what has been presented so far: we presuppose a construction of being. On the principle that nothing can be except being, the construction is seen *{eingesehen}* as arising necessarily from being—of course, with the same certainly it has generally; supposing therefore "If it *should* be . . . , then ____ *must* be."[1] But the "should" is something in itself, of itself and from itself *as such*." This, and in particular the "as" most recently added, is now firmly fixed for you as another new middle point and bearer for the self-producing and self-sustaining "should."

Today I add another basic observation concerning the true inner spirit of the reasoning processes presented so far, and [we] will then work on our remaining task from another angle.

1. As concerns the first, our higher insight from the standpoint of the hypothetical "should" took the following form: should an insight into this or that occur (in this case in particular the insight that the ideal self-construction is to be grounded in being itself),[2] then ____ must. "Since you now," I would say, "actually provide[3] the content of this insight, which, according to your account hasn't yet occurred but whose condition you are seeking, you already without doubt have it *in sight* and in your concept; you are constructing it really and in fact"; (as is the case here with being's ideal self-construction).[4]

This remark permeates all consciousness and can be illustrated in every case. I cannot reflect *how* and according to what law anything (e.g., a body in space, space, a line, etc.) is conceived or constructed, unless I have already grasped it apart from all reflection and according to a universal law. In the present case, the law is constructed in one of the most general cases, which contains others within itself. "Therefore," I continue, "you seek either that which you already have, or you seek the same vision and the same concept[5] (the same in regard to contents[6]) only in another qualitative form *{Bestimmung}*. That

---

This lecture begins at GA II, 8, pp. 272–273.

the latter is the case becomes clear through a more exact consideration of the proposition laid down.[7] The content of your vision, which, as the content of *mere seeing*, is separated and existing for itself,[8] should be brought into connection[9] with something else in seeing, both as its condition and as conditioned by it, initially through what *you* call *insight*.[10] Thus, in order to state the true result of your desire definitely and exactly: just to arrive at your demand, a seeing that is already completely determinate in and of itself (and that you must presuppose as determinate) should [274–275] be further qualitatively determined in this persistent, objective determinateness *as* seeing, since the objective determinateness remains. Therefore, to put it briefly, you demand a new genesis in the seeing that has already been presupposed as existing and as remaining the same objectively.

A new inner genesis of seeing, as formal seeing itself, without any *alteration in the* [seen] *content*;[11] (what we have already called objectivity[12]). Now, the material of this formal genesis, its result, is itself again a genesis: the constant content should be brought into a genetic relation with another term, that creates, and is again created by, it; thus the entire familiar "through," or the relation in its synthetic five-foldness, should come in. As things stand, it can well be that this external material genesis with and out of the content, which is nonetheless not changed in its inner nature, is itself grounded in mere seeing's formal genesis, and resides not so much in the subject matter as in the altered eye, through which the entire present multiplicity is traced back to the oneness of the same principle, of the formal *further*[13] determination. This formal further determination, or new genesis, is called for through a *"should,"* which has itself been recognized as a genesis in its inner nature unconditionally as such. And so this genesis could have its ground in the *"should"*[14] itself as the relation and five-fold synthesis within the formal genesis, so that the "should" is the basic principle for everything, as we have previously already taken it to be. In brief, the spirit of our whole reasoning process, conducted since the beginning of the second part, is the demand for an *inner genesis*[15] in the seeing presupposed for genesis[16] itself. This process adds nothing to the seeing in its true meaning, and so it must be inoperative in relation to this meaning, just as we have always wished. Likewise, this very inner formal genesis, as wholly concerning only the *way* of *viewing*,[17] may be the principle of absolute idealism = of appearance; and we ourselves have entered into a new and higher idealism through the principle presupposed in our entire reasoning process: that being is constructed ideally, i.e., separately from its real self-construction.

That just this insight, now characteristically distinguished from the presupposed *original seeing*, presents itself alone as certain, compared to which the original seeing is to be only hypothetical in relation to its content (it is clear on immediate reflection that the matter stands so, and our certainty appears finished and closed)—this circumstance probably lies in the partiality of idealism itself, which here gives testimony for itself, knowing nothing else. Now we have to investigate this claim for the first time.

[276–277] 2. A recognized basic rule: nothing can be accomplished in any way against an idealism except from the standpoint of realism. Therefore, as soon as our reasoning has been traced back to its spiritual oneness and understood to be idealism, we cannot stand by it any longer without being driven around in circles. We must turn instead to the corresponding realism and consider this more deeply in its origins.

a. As we remember, we entered this realism after the last consideration of the *in-itself*, and of the insight that, in our knowing, this in-itself is relation and multiplicity; therefore, that it is not absolute oneness, thinkable without any composition or division, but is rather, as we said: a *oneness of understanding {Verstandes-Einheit}*.[18] We discarded this knowing entirely, and yet knowing still remained, which thus was absolute inner oneness, without any combination or separation: oneness *in itself*. We also refrain from saying for example that *we* have produced it in this oneness; since we truly would not have wished that something should remain behind after abstracting from everything, or [have wished] to encompass what remains with our will, had we willed or been able to will this, so that it would indeed have been left over for us: instead it was just unconditionally left over: oneness *of* itself. Everything depends on this last point; it is what has been overlooked in every system and what becomes clear only to the deepest deliberation. What we are naming the *We*, that is our freedom, which is derived here for the first time from the previously mentioned, new formal genesis of the absolutely presupposed seeing= re-construction, can only abstract from its own creation of the act of reconstruction, but it cannot creatively construct primordial reason; although after complete abstraction primordial reason enters without delay. So then anyone who—in inseparable[19] awareness of the simultaneity of his completed abstraction and the arrival of primordial reason, and in the equally inseparable[20] awareness that he is the one freely abstracting—immediately transfers his own freedom to reason's emergence, such a person deceives himself and remains trapped in an idealism. This final illusion is negated here in immediate manifestness by means of deep reflection. After abstraction from the highest oneness of understanding, *a knowing*[21] remains, just because it remains, without any possible assistance from us, pure light or pure *reason in itself*.[22]

b. This pure reason is equally immediately inner *being*[23] and completely one with it. Previously[24] we called what remained after all abstraction "inner being"; here we have called it "pure light," or "reason." [278–279] But whatever we may wish to name it, it is what remains unconditionally by itself after all abstraction, an entirely indivisible singularity; and I would very much like to know whether any disjunction can be made in the presented concept, and whether the insight that it is a completely self-contained singularity does not clearly show that, whatever variation in the words used to name it, one and the same nature could be meant.

c. Previously as well as now, we have named it a real self-construction *in itself, of itself, and through itself*, and we could not describe it differently. Now, abstracting completely from the facticity of this description, which to be sure can only be a reconstruction, and through which we happen into the first named idealism, [let us] reflect [instead] on its inner truth, and—with this I ask for your complete attention—on the surprising result that I intend to bring out. I ask: does it not now depend entirely on the pure thing itself remaining after all abstraction that it exists *entirely from itself*—whether you call it *being* or *reason*?[25] For example, is it arbitrarily posited as existing on its own? How could it be? For this would be a genuine contradiction, since in that case it would not be from itself but would exist through an arbitrary act of positing. If it is posited as something left over after abstracting from everything outside itself, then it is necessarily posited as *of itself*. For if it were not *of itself*, then it would be *of another*,[26] so that in its absolute positing—i.e., in the original creation of its being—it would not be possible to abstract from this other. (That because of babble and thoughtlessness this other might not be considered could be factically true and still should be *explained*;[27] it is not true in the one absolute, self-consuming oneness.) Once again, it is *posited absolutely*, creatively, as something *of itself*[28]—it is evident that this of itself is actually manifested and is not just thought up;—so it is posited as existing absolutely and remaining behind after abstraction from everything.—Hence it is clear that light, or reason, or absolute being, which are all the same, cannot posit itself as such without constructing itself, and vice versa: that both coincide in their essence and are entirely one.[29]—Notice here: 1. the insight that being must construct itself unconditionally has arisen here through the mere consideration of its inner nature entirely immediately and without any factical presupposition, an insight that, according to idealism's pretensions, should only be producible mediately from the factical presupposition that a constructive act is present. By this means idealism is first of all fully refuted, insofar as it grounds itself in the necessity of a presupposition for a [280–281] particular insight, although merely a possible one, since the insight has actually been produced without the presupposition. Idealism must therefore look around for higher support, if we are still to come to it. Further, the proposition alluded to in passing has therefore come up, that this same insight is possible in two different ways: mediately, from presuppositions, and completely immediately. How would it be, if the entire distinction that we have sought between philosophical and common knowledge, between the standpoint of the science of knowing and that of ordinary knowing (and in case within the latter there should be degrees of mediatedness, the distinction between the various standpoints of this common knowing) were to lie in just this distinction between these differing ways. Philosophical systems are always closest for us:—the presupposition that idealism wants as the principle of mediate[30] insight, is factical. How would it be if, for example, the proof of absolute being from the factical existence of finite entities, which is conducted in nearly every system, and according to them in ordinary consciousness as well, were just this idealistic path of mediate insight, with which one remains satisfied, for the lack of the immediate path. In itself this is correct and is applicable in its place within the gradual process of cultivation, i.e., in rising up to the highest; but it generally fails the test against criticisms that strive ahead to the highest! 2. The distinction between being's *real* and *ideal*[31] self-construction that we made earlier, and on which idealism built, is now completely annulled. Being, or reason, and light are one; and this one cannot posit itself, or be, without *constructing*[32] itself; this is therefore *grounded*[33] in its *nature*, and is entirely unitary, as is its nature. Therefore, if we are to return later to such a distinction,[34] then it must first be derived.[35]

3. We saw {*einsahen*} that, in reason per se, its self-positing and its self-construction[36] as "from itself," etc., coalesce entirely into one.[37] And as certainly as we saw into this, *in this insight*[38] we were the oneness of reason itself. Now a *duality* still remains here, not however as in the oneness of understanding, whose parts are to be integrated—since parts within the oneness are rather completely denied and negated here; and the oneness does not understand itself through parts but rather posits itself unconditionally and absolutely—but rather as a means for achieving oneness. Therefore, it may perhaps turn out that a re-construction is already present here, one that would be posited backwards toward the idealistic side by an absolute "should," and which we could not avoid merely factically, even though its intrinsic validity is not admitted; therefore that we stand at the precise place from which our task could be completed. How things may stand with this I reserve for further investigation.

[282–283] Now I add a supplementary remark, with which I did not previously wish to interrupt the course of the inquiry. As the opportunity has arisen, I have tested those recent philosophical systems, which have made the greatest impression in regards to their principles, in order thereby to bring greater clarity to the science of knowing; thus Reinhold's system and thus Schelling's system. Next to these, and perhaps even more than they, Jacobi's system recommends itself, because with great philosophical talent it tries to jettison philosophy itself, and thus it flatters the prevailing spiritual indolence and denial toward philosophy. The scene for testing this system's principles was just above. It proceeds from the following principles: a. We can only re-construct what originally exists.—We ourselves have precisely presented and precisely defined this claim, which for Jacobi is almost a postulate: the seeing, determined primordially in its content, is formally genetic[39] in relation to an unaltered content, and therefore it is the insight into a connection; and we ascribe this genesis to ourselves, a genesis that is only re-construction in relation to the truly original content and that is truly original construction and creation from nothing in relation to the terms added factically.—Regarding the last point, the absolute creation of everything factical from the I, he very clearly took this over from us; and it is very plausible that he granted being to the factical, i.e., to what is sensible outside the one rational being, and thereby left us only reconstruction. b. Philosophy should reveal and discover *being in and of itself.*—Correct, and exactly our purpose.—Through the persistent assertion of these two principles this author has earned the age's great thanks, and has favorably distinguished himself from all of the philosophers who just reconstruct impartially, [284–285] or even just fool around with nature and reason. c. Therefore, we cannot philosophize, and there can *be no philosophy.*[40] This latter claim, just as I have stated it, is his true opinion, and must be his true opinion, if he is to have any opinion at all. For he contributes nothing by his usual addition: philosophy *as a whole.*[41] Because, if there is no philosophy as a whole, then there is no philosophy at all, but rather only edifying remarks for every day of the year. I grant him everything as it is presented, only taking it more seriously than its original proponent does. *We*, the we who can only reconstruct, cannot do philosophy: equally there is no philosophy individually and personally;[42] instead philosophy must just be, but this is possible only to the extent that we perish, along with all reconstruction, and pure reason emerges pure and alone; since this latter in its purity is philosophy itself. From the perspective of "we" or "I" there is no philosophy; there is one only [once one has gone] beyond the I. Therefore, the question about the possibility of philosophy depends on whether the I can perish and reason can come purely to manifestation. This author could demonstrate that this must indeed be possible from his own words. Because when he *says*: we can only reconstruct, he achieves ipso facto in that very moment something more than re-construction, and has at least drawn himself happily out of the "We" of which we have spoken. For if he could [do] this, then for his whole lifetime he would enact {*thun*}, but without speaking about it, just as by his previous statement he enacted elevating himself to reconstructing the reconstruction. Of, if we will free him from this, he [can] tell us how he came to the universal statement by which he prescribed an absolute law for his "We," and thereby pre-constructed the "We's" essence for them, and did not merely re-construct it. In which case he would have to resign himself to express himself like this: "I and everyone I know, as many as I can remember to the present could only re-construct; whether perhaps tomorrow [286–287] something else will happen, we will have to see." Finally he will have to tell us whether he understands this concept of "reconstruction" without presupposing something original, independent prior to all construction. As surely as he understands himself, he must become aware of such a thing beyond all reconstruction. Grasping this original something and reconstruction as following from it as an absolutely essential law of the "We," just as we have articulated it here *is* the task of a philosophical system, which we have presented entirely according to its sense, but have only partially solved.

CHAPTER 19

Nineteenth Lecture

Friday, May 18, 1804

Honored Guests:

Since today we finish the week, I do not wish to let you go without having equipped you with some definite result. This resolution compels me for now to pass by certain middle terms that still remain for deeper consideration between that with which I ended yesterday and that which I will attach to it today, in order to reserve them for the descent.

1. As an introduction to our essential business for today, [here is] a clarifying remark that should direct your subsequent attention and that at the same time also briefly and concisely repeats the first major part of yesterday's lecture! I say: in all derivative knowing, or in appearance, a pure absolute contradiction exists between enactment *{Thun}* and saying *{Sagen}: propositio facto contraria*. (Let me add here by the way, as I thought previously on an appropriate occasion, a thoroughgoing skepticism must base itself on just this and give voice to this ineradicable contradiction in mere consciousness. The very simple refutation of all systems that do not elevate themselves to pure reason, i.e., their dismissal and the presentation of their insufficiency even though their originator is not thereby improved, is based on just the fact that one points out[1] the contradiction between what they assert in their principles and what they actually do [in asserting them]: as has been done with every system that we have tested so far, and yesterday with Jacobi's as well.) In the first half of yesterday's talk, this contradiction showed up in what we had identified so far as the highest principle of appearance, that is in the *"should,"*[2] immediately after we had conceived it in its firm and completely determinate nature as something from itself, etc., *as* such; namely, a particular insight (which in our case was this: that being constructs itself) is posited through the "should" as not present but rather merely as possible, and as possible only under a certain condition that is still sought. If we are even to arrive at the consideration of its conditioned possibility, this [condition] finally must be presupposed as a

---

This lecture begins at GA II, 8, pp. 288–289.

seeing that is fixed in its content and to that extent unchangeable,. Hence, [two things] stand in complete contradiction in this "should," its *enactment {Thun}*—its true inner effect, to presuppose a seeing that is unalterable in its contents—and its *saying*—a different action *{Thun}* on its part, according to which the insight is supposed to be not actual but only possible under a condition yet to be added. I add only for the sake of recapitulation that the true external nature of this "should" is found as the [290–291] demand for a further inner and merely formal determination of a presupposed seeing that is unalterable in its content, through which further determination this presupposed seeing comes into a genetic connection with another term that is created purely by this further determination. And I immediately formulate the following conclusion: absolute reason is distinguished from this relative knowing by the fact that, in the case of absolute reason, what exists, or what it does, is expressly said in it; and that it does what is expressed in it in absolute qualitative sameness.

2. In the second part of yesterday's investigation, we tried to represent pure reason in ourselves. I noted at the end of this presentation that, because of the *duality*[3] that to be sure was annulled intellectually but that remained factically inextinguishable in you, it became evident that pure reason could not display itself immediately in you and could rather only be reconstructed.—The same qualitative determination of a presupposed seeing that is unalterable in its contents, a determination pointed out within the "should," we also called reconstruction; therefore, the contradiction between saying and doing just discovered in all derivative knowing is contained within reconstruction itself, a fact that can itself be made clear immediately. To be sure, reconstruction explicitly puts itself forward as reconstruction and therefore in its own concept quite properly posits the point of origin *{das Ursprüngliche}*, and in that there is no contradiction. But since it leaves the content unchanged and can actually create nothing new without completely negating the relation between itself and the absolute—its construction is therefore groundless and the fact itself contradicts the postulate of the *absolute necessity* in the pure, *positive in-itself*.[4]

I should now immediately climb past this contradiction [we have] discovered and relieve it (that is, past the groundlessness of the concept of a reconstruction). However, in accordance with my initially stated resolve, I am retaining it [in order] to annul it mediately in the descent; and so [let's turn] directly to yesterday's reasoning to indicate the location of absolute reconstruction,[5] and to remove this circumstance.[6]

We brought the already established absolute insight to life in this way:

a. it arose for us after we abstracted completely from all relations, and it remained behind as a oneness, not just because we wished it, but[7] simply by itself. Pure light, or reason.

b. Previously we named it inner being, here light or reason; but it is clear that no distinction whatsoever occurs in the one singularity that remains behind by itself as one, and that consequently both designations are only two different names for the one that is grasped *{eingesehene}* as completely indivisible and inseparable.[8] [292–293]

c. We saw into this "one," and still see into it now as something from-itself, etc. = [as] self constructing.[9]

I asked: should not then this *from-itself*[10] reside completely in its nature as absolute truth?[11] And I discussed it even further in the following consideration: out of its self-positing as *this*,[12] self-construction follows, and vice versa; because if it is posited as *this*,[13] as remaining after abstraction from everything else, then it is posited as remaining and persisting because of itself; since if it were not because-of-itself, it would be because-of-another, from which it would not then be possible to abstract in its true original creation, or which could not be absent for this creation. Conversely, if it is a true, *actual*, energetic *from-itself*, then it is not from another;[14] since then it would not be truly from itself. Therefore, it is necessary to posit it, as it has been posited.—But let us take a keener look at this reasoning itself and the procedure within it.—(And I remind you that this is the most difficult and significant thing that has so far come before us.—)[15] First of all, without exception in our whole argument process and in the entire conduct of our lectures up to now, the absolute has been treated as what is left over after abstraction from everything manifold; and if equally we have expressed specifically enough the absolute from-itself and pure oneness in-itself, then with these words which we have added as clarifications, we have surely again made use of this same relation; as more certain[16] proof that even we ourselves, the scientists of knowing and what we actually did and pursued, found ourselves in the previously uncovered contradiction between *saying* (of the from-itself) and *doing* (explaining by means of the *not* from-itself).[17] Thus the first premise of our proof here reads: "If it is posited as *this*, i.e., as left over after abstraction from everything else . . .";[18] which is a sure demonstration of reconstruction. Second, in the center of our entire proof we have absolutely presupposed both genesis and the absolute validity of the Law of Principles.[19] The center of the proof was, "If it is not from another, then it is from itself; and if it is not from itself, then it is from another." If someone now were to say to us: "Quite right: one of the two— from itself or from another—and in case one, then not the other, if of course I grant you the use of your "from" at all. But if I say instead: in brief it *is*, and that's all, who will then ask about a "from" *(Von)*?" To be sure we can answer such a one as follows: "You are reflecting; so in addition to this "is" you also have consciousness; you therefore have not one but two, that you can never make into one [294–295] and an irrational gap lies between them; you are in the familiar death of reason";—so the loophole always remains open to him that is taken by every non-philosopher:[20] "I must just stay in this 'from' and it is impossible to escape it"; so everything finally comes down to this that we justify ourselves in the use of the "from."[21] Therefore this would be our next task, to justify the "from" in general as *such*, entirely abstracting from its application. So far, as I ask that you recall, it has not arisen in any other way than in factical necessity.

This justification will disclose itself if only we rigorously pursue the analysis of the preceding argument. In the first half are to be found the remarkable words that without doubt became immediately evident and clear to you: "if it were not because-of-itself, it would be because-of-*another* from which it would not then be possible to abstract in the true *primordial* act of creating *{Creiiren}*, or which could not be absent for *this creation* {Creation}";[22] and yesterday I also added: "even for truly primordial creation," since through thoughtlessness and foolishness one could easily forget the other through[23] which alone the first can be. What then is understood by this primordial creation which likewise in total tranquility provides the center of the proof? Evidently that our thinking, or the light, if it should be of the right kind, must accompany the genuine real creation of things and originate along with it: hence if the one were to be through another, it would have to take the "through another" up into itself and express it; contrariwise, a thinking that omitted this "through" would be mere thinking and not absolute, and would set down a true creation only factically as bare, dead existence. This was the first point.[24]

Now it seems here as if the real creation, as real, could exist on its own and go its own way; and some assert it. The basis for this illusion has in fact been grasped here. That is, it rests in the possibility of viewing primordial creation too in a pale and factical way, as a result of which it seems to be capable of existing independent of, and separated from, its appearing *{vom Blicke}*. But we have already seen earlier that light and inward being (by no means the external existence created by faded thought) are entirely one and the same; or, in case we had not yet realized this, then this is the place to prove it immediately; because if absolutely unchanging and unchangeable self identical light must accompany creation, then there is no light without creation and creation is likewise inseparable from light: since it is only because of the *light and in the light*.[25] Creation = "from," "through," etc., so absolute light is itself an absolute "from." This was the second point.[26]

[296–297] Now we, the scientists of knowing, have tacitly presupposed this as the inner principle of the possibility for the entire subordinate proof procedure, which we are now dropping, and indeed—this is the important thing—we have done it without any design or plan before the deed and immediately through the deed itself. But I claim that the bare possibility of this presupposition shows its truth and correctness. Let me prove this first indirectly. We ourselves in our doing and pursuing are knowing, thinking, light, or whatever we wish to call it. If knowing were now absolutely limited, i.e., to the faded thought of an existence separated from thinking, then we could never have been able to get out of it to this presupposition of an absolute creation. Since we have really posited it, and the light as absolutely one with it, since we ourselves are immediate light, we have quite certainly validated the truth of our claim in immediate being, in action, since we enacted in that place the very thing we said, and said what we enacted; and the one could not be without the other. Results: 1. The contradiction we have noted up to now in what we ourselves are and pursue, between doing and saying = the real and the ideal, is now annulled, as it alone can be, ipso facto in us ourselves, and since this is the criterion of pure reason, we are ipso facto pure reason. 2. Light has a primordial conception of its own nature that ipso facto preserves itself in immediate visible completion of itself. (Note well: here we are holding simply to the immediately evident content of our sentences. It is obvious that questions can still be raised about their form. These questions will raise themselves, and the basic principles for deriving relation from the absolute may well lie just in answering them.) 3. On the very grounds given, let us leave our factical conception of the nature of the light, which may well give rise to the entire *we*[27] whose origin we are seeking, and let us hold simply to the content. In light, *absolute genesis*.[28] Obviously, the *light*, as light, is *qualitative oneness* (which in fact enters as just plain seeing that cannot further be seen), which *permeates* the entire *inner genesis*[29] as bare *pure genesis* (I am relying here on your [powers of] penetration; since language can in no way bring us to our goal[30]—). I can now construct this for you further as follows: this oneness[31] permeates the duality in the *"from a–b"*; which duality exists only in the absolute "from"—but not at all outside it in some independence and [in an] independent differentiation of terms—so that [the duality's terms] may be reversed with complete indifference.—These all are [298–299] constructions in sensory terms, through which I anticipate myself. The ground of their possibility must lie in and be derived from me myself, insofar as I am the factical concept. In the strictest sense, nothing matters more than this: light is the qualitative oneness that penetrates the "from." This was the first point.[32]

Now likewise, following our concept, this "from" and (just for that reason and consequently) the light's permeation of it, and also therefore the entire qualitative oneness of the light, that indeed can only be thought in relation to a "from" and its duality in order to annul it,—all this, I say, has its ground in the light itself,[33] no longer as qualitative but rather as an inscrutable oneness. Therefore, there exists between the light in itself and the entire preceding relationship a new, only entirely one-sided "from"; and this latter denotes the absolute effect of the light; to the contrary, the entire first relationship simply shows the appearance of this effect, of the qualitative immediately self-effecting light. This was the second point.[34]

As a genesis, every "from" posits light;—just as previously light posited genesis: and indeed, since the absolute "from" of the pure, inaccessible principle rests here, it posits absolute light, without the genesis *ever* becoming visible, and [posits] itself *only in this*[35] absolutely factical light and from this factical light.—If you have seen into this, then reflect now on yourself. *We* have seen into the "from" in just this way, and by means of it have seen into the 0 whose inaccessibility we have previously admitted, and have seen into it as unconditionally *existing, objective*[36] and so as having to exist, if appearance is to arise. This is the fact. How have we *explained*[37] it? Thus: there is an *absolute, immediate* "from," which as *such* must appear in a seeing, itself moreover invisible.[38] Hence we ourselves, with the whole content of our immediate seeing, are the *primordial appearance*[39] of the inaccessible light in its primordial effect, and a–b is mere appearance of appearance. And so the *primordial facticity*, the original objectification of reason, as existing and genetic, is thereby clarified from the original law of light, and our task has been completed in its highest principle.

I have no reservations in letting you go for the week with these provisions.—Monday [21 May]—a discussion.

CHAPTER 20

Twentieth Lecture

Wednesday, May 23, 1804

Honored Guests:

Being is an unconditionally self-enclosed, living oneness. Being and light are one. Since in the light's *existence*[1] (= in ordinary consciousness) a manifold is encountered—we have initially expressed our problem empirically[2] and we must continue to speak this way until it has been solved—a ground for this manifold must let itself appear in the light itself as absolute oneness and in its manifestation, a ground that will explain this entire manifold as it occurs empirically. "In the light and its *manifestation*"[3] I have said: therefore we must first of all derive the appearance of the light *from the light*, [and] the manifold will arise in the former.[4] This is roughly the main content of what has been achieved so far and of what remains to be done. This is to be noted especially:—[the task is][5] to present appearance in general and as such. (Obviously, as soon as appearance has been explained and the principle of the manifold has been explained from it a priori and in principle, all appeal to empirical experience falls away, and what was previously held factically will be conceived genetically.)

At present we have already pushed ourselves quite near our highest principle. If transcendental insight has been opened for us, then having in mind the most recent link in the chain is sufficient for understanding the lectures; if the earlier links by means of which we ascended to the later ones are not equally present, nothing is lost; we will rediscover everything anew on the descent. I must bring you back to this last link by repeating the previous lecture, at the same time {*bei welcher*} I will also expand and add. It has already been proven earlier that the *absolute*, simply *as absolute*,[6] must be *from itself*, whatever else it may be (earlier it was "being," "light," and "reason," none of which mattered to this argument and did not belong to it); and this proof further coheres with the postulate that inner being could not be constructed from outside but must rather construct itself, with which postulate we opened the

---

This lecture begins at GA II, 8, pp. 300–301.

entire so-called "second half" of our investigation. (In this fashion, everything achieved so far toward bringing out the second part, and with it the whole, could also again be reproduced.) In the last hour, this completed proof was itself investigated in its central nerve and points of manifestness, and what turned out to be its foundation was the simple presupposition that genuine true seeing, or light, must have accompanied the actual *Creation*;[7] and since being and seeing had already been grasped *{eingesehen}* earlier as being the same, that genuine true light must itself be an immanent creation, or an absolute *"from" {Von}*. This, I say, [302–303] turned up as a mere *presupposition*,[8] grounding the process of our proof regarding the essence of the absolute, but itself based on nothing. Still, a little reflection[9] shows us that this presupposition proves its *correctness*[10] simply by its mere possibility and facticity; because we ourselves were the knowing, insofar as we conducted the proof and made the fundamental assumption concerning the essence of knowing: that it is a *"from"*;[11] and, note well, we certainly could be, and indeed are satisfied, that knowing cannot be both something in and for itself apart from any view *{Ansicht}* into itself and also a "from," but rather that it can be both only within [such a] view. By the actuality of this view within ourselves, we have proven directly and factically that in this respect it is so. It is, and it is this; because it quite certainly is, and quite certainly is this, and we ourselves, the scientists of knowing, are it as such. This is an immediate demonstration of the essence of knowing, conducted through the fact itself and its possibility. At this point let yourself take in even more fully what was established last time, although only in passing: we did not make this presupposition because we wished to, or with any sort of freedom; and if only this free element, which is to be summoned in response to some particular reflection, is to be called *We*,[12] then *we*[13] actually did not make it; rather it made itself directly through itself. All our preceding investigations have started from the fact that we were requested to think energetically about something we were aware of internally and also were able to ignore; so both took place only in consciousness; this provided our premises, and, to be sure, this energetically considered object was always accompanied by the explicit supplement of a "should"—"If this should be so, then ____." From our thinking this premise energetically, manifestness grips us without any assistance on our part, and carries us away, attaching to the controversial premise that conditions it and is conditioned by it. Therefore, the knowing, which we pursued in this way, instantiated the basic characteristic mentioned before of being merely reconstructive and was, in this reconstruction, a secondary and merely apparent knowing, transferring knowing's implicitly unconditional content into a conditioned relationship. All systems without exception remain fixed in this knowing; their premises therefore are hypothetical *for them* only (but not absolutely in reason, by which even they themselves are driven, although to be sure without their knowing it) and the relationship alone is *evident*, which however gives no final or fixed manifest-ness, since the relationship itself depends on the reality of its terms. They sup-plement the lack of this strength only by an arbitrary [304–305] reliance on the premises and by averting their eyes from their difficulties; without this reliance they could release themselves to absolute skepticism at any moment.

Up to this point [it has been] this way. Now, absolute manifestness has extended itself to the premise, to the absolute presupposition itself; and thereby it has annulled both all freedom and every "We" that was presup-posed[14] as a premise in relation to the secondary manifestness of the context. Hence, we are transposed into a completely different region of knowing, not simply *as* something purely self-grounding {*Vonsich*}, but rather immediately, and ipso facto from itself {*von sich*}. But as for what relates to the premise *as a premise*,[15] undoubtedly in this quality a consequence is posited through it, and these two in turn posit a relation; therefore, in this quality, it serves admirably to explain secondary knowing; and, since it is absolute, to explain the latter from the absolute, which is exactly our task. As a premise, it is undoubtedly the principle of appearance we have been seeking. But since appearance is not itself the purely self-contained absolute—as becomes evident in the premise: the simple fact that it requires a consequence and a context shows it to be insufficient by itself—there must therefore be a higher notion of knowing. This remark can cast a great deal of light over what we still have left to achieve, so I want to analyze it further.

Now we let go of the point that we presuppose it, or more accurately, that it posits itself as a presupposition, and thus let go of the proposition's form for reasons having to do with method, and simply hold on to the con-tent of the proposition: "the light is an absolute "from""—analyzing what we actually mean by this.

1. All along, and obviously in this proposition, light[16] is posited first and foremost as an essential, qualitative, and material oneness, not further conceiv-able, but instead only to be carried out at once, just the way we carry it out in all of our knowing, from which we cannot escape. I want to be understood on this point that is easy in itself, that requires simple, strong attention. Question: what then is *knowing*? If you know, then you just know.[17] [306–307] You can-not know knowing again in its qualitative absoluteness; since if you did know it, and even now were knowing it, then for you the absolute would not stay in the knowing that you knew about, but rather in the knowing by which you knew it; and it would go on this way for you even if you repeated the procedure a thousand times. It remains forever the same, that in absolute knowing you recapitulate knowing as essential qualitative oneness. Initially this insight needs only to be *carried out*; reflecting on the law of its completion still remains before us. This light is now absolutely presupposed as a "from" without prejudice to its qualitative oneness; since [if it did not preserve this oneness][18] the *light* would

not be "from," and so [it is presupposed] as permeating this *"from."* Notice first what is new and important here: it is *presupposed*[19] to be like this, unconditionally. Thus it has presupposed itself in a particular act; and this presupposition is now proven[20] by its facticity and possibility, and further by the possibility of a deeper determination of knowing, which opposes the simple existential form in its attachment to the mere dead "is."[21]

In our insight, it in no way *follows*[22] from our insight[23] into the essential light as such (which we once again should have been grasping energetically and freely), by means of which manifestness descended into the connection between light as such and the "from." And we again lapsed into secondary and merely apparent knowing with which there must, to be sure, eventually be an end, an end we have sought so avidly from the beginning. "It does not follow," I said, since, as we have seen, there is generally no such insight into the light in itself, hence, I said: the light posits itself as a "from" in a particular and absolute act or genesis; an act that cannot be mastered immediately in this genesis, as the genesis of genesis, because otherwise the genesis would not be an *absolute genesis*. (What this latter means, and does not mean, since here as well is yet another disjunction, will show itself it what follows.) I say: according to the preceding observation, it thus *posits*[24] itself absolutely; the act is a self-contained, self-sufficient act; it is posited by us merely in our inferential chain, which we now entirely let go of, as the mere means by which we have ascended to our present insight, until we find it again on the descent. This is the first, and significant, point.

That the light in its changeless qualitative oneness is a "from" therefore means: it is a qualitatively changeless permeation of the "from."[25] In the previous hour, we made the following application of this point: disjunction is found everywhere in the "from"; absolutely out of, and from, the "from";[26] by no means [308–309] presupposing terms that were primordially different independently of the "from," instead [they were] produced absolutely as terms, absolutely distinguished as such only through the "from" and otherwise through nothing at all. The one, eternally qualitatively self-identical light, by virtue of its identity with the *"from,"* must, in this qualitative oneness, spread itself over these terms, whatever their distinction from each other.

Let me now apply and animate this insight right away, and thereby make it unforgettable for you. A "from" is posited immediately through the light:

$$L$$
$$a - b$$

Hence, if light exists, then necessarily there is also a *"from."*[27] Now if the light is identical with the "from," then, as surely as it itself exists, it spreads itself in unchanged qualitative oneness across every "from," and comprehends every "from." And if one again posits within the first "from" another one that is deducible and conceivable on the basis of the original synthesis of light and the "from"[28]

$$a \longrightarrow b$$
$$\vert \quad \vert$$
$$a\text{–}b \quad a.b$$

it is completely clear that the same original light, qualitatively unchanged, by means of its identity with the original "from," must at the same stroke accompany all subordinate divisions of the original "from"[29] into further "from's." And it is also clear that whatever possesses the principle of this secondary splitting of the original "from" accompanies this progression of the light as entirely necessary and at one stroke, and can reconstruct it purely a priori and without any empirical presuppositions; which indeed is the second and subordinate task of the science of knowing, since we now are pursuing the much higher task of presenting the principle of this principle. This "from," in pure, absolute, immediate oneness[30] and without any disjunction, as the pure self-positing of the original light, is the light's first and absolute creation; the ground and original source even of the *is*, and of *everything* that exists; and the disjunction within this "from," in which true living perishes and is reduced to the mere intuition of a dead being, is the second re-creation in intuition, that is, in the already divided original light. And thus the science of knowing justifiably presents itself as the complete resolution of the puzzle of the world and of consciousness.

This, I asserted, was the next application that I made last hour of the proposition, "The light is a 'from,'" attending to the disjunction in the "from." But it is even more important to look at the essential and qualitative oneness of this "from" and at the words that were said previously about the original creation. Recall them. In its pure qualitative oneness, *"from"* is genesis: that the light is identical with it and permeates it in this its essence, means: in this its second power (namely its appearance), it is itself genesis; [310–311] genesis and seeing converge together completely and unconditionally.—The words are easy to understand; it is not so easy to give them the deep meaning intended here in living insight; and it is nearly true that the only way I am able to guide you forward is with an example. The subject matter that I wish to present to your intuition appears in every transition from lassitude to energy, and for our purposes, the example cited just above will serve best: the one in which we had tacitly presupposed absolute knowing to be a "from"; when interrogated about the justification of this presupposition, we *recalled* that indeed we knew ouselves in this presupposition and were the knowing. I ask: does not this new awareness, that was not yet there prior to our presupposing, seem as if it were a popping up, a new production? Now at this point you are certainly able to abstract purely, as is my present demand: that this *is* consciousness, is a consciousness of knowing, and what is more of knowing as a "from." What remains for you after this [act of] abstraction? Evidently just a knowing/seeing/light, exactly absolute, qualitative, as it has already been described, and [it *was*] this therefore because you abstracted completely from all content, which you could do according to the presupposition; consequently, [it], as itself light, conducted the proof of legitimacy empirically; further, [it is] a consciousness of *absolute genesis*. Now—note this addition, the proof becomes more rigorous and the insight purer through it—you can more suitably posit this genesis or freedom in the act of abstraction from all content of the presented consciousness, which is thus required of you. As things stand, it is immediately clear to you that this *pure* light, as it has been described, could not arise without abstracting from all content,[31] nor can the latter appear without arriving at pure light; that therefore the appearances of both terms are indivisible, and permeate one another; and that hence pure light appears as permeating genesis, or as producing itself. By means of this proof more is nearly proved than should be proved, and future research is anticipated, as I note in preparation; the light's positing of the "from," and the fact that it posits itself as a "from," has already become immediately visible. What we have to be concerned with next here can be shown with a little preparation in two examples. Because you were instructed to reflect energetically and a new consciousness emerged for you, this new consciousness is not to exist *{soll . . . nicht sein}* as something new without the energy; this consciousness [312–313] and the energy should open up together indivisibly. Now you certainly posit genesis here partly in yourself, in the energy of your reflection, and partly in the essence of reason itself, since the manifestness is to emerge without any further action on your part; but this entire distinction ought to have no validity in itself, and it should be abstracted out, and so—leaving undecided whether genesis's true principle lies in me or in reason itself—there always remains an absolute, self-producing knowing that does not possibly occur without the genesis.

Now this means, as was said before, that light permeates the "from" in the qualitative oneness of its (the "from's") essence: the presented intuitions of this penetration were only explanatory means. But, independent of all facticity, we have seen a priori that if light is to be, such a permeation is necessary.

This is the one side of the previous proof for the content of the sentence: the light = "from," that we have repeated and enriched today. There is still another, and of this more tomorrow, equipped with today's new discoveries!

In conclusion another comment about the whole of the science of knowing, one that I share with you not so much for your own guidance, since I hope you do not need it, but rather as a weapon of defense against the ignorant. Already earlier, and again today in passing, the proof of knowing's essential criteria is conducted on the basis of our capacity to see it thus. The nerve of the proof is clear: we ourselves are knowing; since we can know only in this way, and presently actually know thus, then knowing is constituted so. It is equally clear that the failure to discover this principle of proof, or not paying attention to it once it has been found, grounds itself on the truly foolish maxim of searching for knowing outside of knowing. Concerning this, nothing more needs to be said. I would only bring this to your attention: the proof simply does not succeed for anyone who is really not able to make clear and intuitable what can only be made so by his own capacities; through his incompetence he is barred from the subject itself and from any judgment about this world that is entirely concealed from him. It is the same for those who could but will not, that is, who will not submit themselves to preliminary conditions of sharp thinking and strong attention; because everyone who can, will do the thing itself; and everyone who will, can do it. This is true when the science of knowing does not yet stand at the apex.[32] One should not therefore wonder how that which has in itself the highest clarity and manifestness, cannot in any way be made clear and true for very many people {Subjekten}; one can rather himself lay out the grounds for this impossibility, if they will just come to understand the premise that there might be something they do not now know; and that they are not able to know directly and without much preparation and strong discipline, as things are with them now.

CHAPTER 21

Twenty-first Lecture

Thursday, May 24, 1804

Honored Guests:

(We will make use at once of what we have already understood, and take a shortcut without further repetition and closer definition of subordinate terms.[1] You know that such a thing is possible in the science of knowing, and why. That is, [it is possible] because the subordinate terms will recur in their full developmental clarity during the descent; and the ascent is undertaken not for the subject matter itself, but for clearing our vision and opening it to the absolute by abstracting from all relations.[2])

I connect this with what has gone before: the light has been *presupposed* as an absolute "from." Then we immediately proved the legitimacy of this presupposition by means of its bare possibility and facticity, because we ourselves were light and knowing. Based on this last key step in the proof,[3] the presupposition is true and legitimate in the "*We*"; not, of course, in the previous "We" that freely posited premises, (since in this case knowing posits itself, as was clearly explained yesterday). Instead, [it is true and legitimate] in the We that merges into the light, and is identical with it. Moreover, it truly is just as it factically occurs, but it occurs as a presupposition. Hence, taken strictly (as we have not so far taken it, and for good reasons)[4] it has been truly and factically proven that the light can presuppose itself as a "from," and that in us it actually does so. In us, to the extent that we have merged, and disappear identically, into the light itself = [we] are the science of knowing. Unnoticed, this presupposition has made itself, and we will build on that. But [the We][5] on the occasion of which it made itself, has in that sense not even made itself, instead we, who are freely abstracting and reflecting, have made it. Consequently, by this "We" one may well mean that light makes itself into a "from" only in the science of knowing, as a higher, absolute knowing; and so we provisionally indicate a distinguishing ground (for which we have been searching) between lower, ordinary, empirical knowing and higher, scientific, genetic knowing.[6]

This lecture begins at GA II, 8, pp. 316–317.

We said, "It is *presupposed*."[7] However, all presuppositions bring along a hypothetical "should"; and let themselves be expressed through it. In fact, we have not argued differently than this in the two previous sessions when analyzing the contents of this "from": "Is there light" = "if light is to be"—and "Is there an absolute 'from'" = "If there should be an absolute 'from,' then must ____ ," etc. However, we have not only presupposed the absolute oneness of the light hypothetically; [318–319] instead we have also realized it unconditionally. To be sure, we have done so only in its qualitative character[8]—which as you will remember, was itself a result of the "from"—as was the case with the absolute origin in knowing as permeating the "from" in its qualitative oneness, as we discovered yesterday. Hence, both are a result of the hypotheticalness, so that only pure, bare oneness, henceforth presented as inconceivable and understood as categorical, remains left over. I wished to undertake the delineation of this very boundary in passing, and it is commended to you.— Now back. Our reasoning has proceeded in the hypothetical form of a "should"; and this to be sure unconditionally as itself knowing, and as primordial knowing, since knowing itself has posited this "from," then transcended this *posited* and objectified "from," which we analyze from below[9] and derive from it.

(This as well about method. Obviously we are once again reflecting about what we were and did in the previous presupposition and analysis, in the same way we have proceeded in our entire ascent; and I could have proclaimed our activities in just this form. Purely because we have left the realm of arbitrary freedom behind and have arrived with our own effort in the realm of organic law, I preferred to compel you to the present reflection through the reminder that indeed everything grounds itself simply on the presupposition, rather than appealing to your freedom.)

2.[10] In its *innermost essence*,[11] a "should" is itself genesis and demands a genesis. This is easily understood; you ask, If such and such *should* be, then is it or isn't it?[12] The "should" tells you nothing about this. What then does it say? It sees[13] a principle; therefore, it explains categorically that being can be admitted only on the condition of the principle. Thus, only genetic being, or being's genesis, can be admitted. Thus, it is the absolute postulation of genesis; and since everyone whose transcendental sense has been awakened will allow no genesis to be valid in and for itself without such a postulation, even[14] immediately absolute genesis, and the genesis of objective genesis only mediately, according to a law that we have yet to exhibit. Or this as reinforcement: I have said [the "should"] is the postulation of genesis. Now it is immediately clear that the "should" is a postulation, and that a postulation is a genesis, at least an ideal one; otherwise, it is, as such, completely incomprehensible and accordingly the addition "of genesis" would not be worth while in any way. So it is evident that, in our hypothetical "should," being's[15] genesis is demanded, which, as a genesis of being, the hypothetical "should" is content not to be able to provide. Instead, it waits for it from a principle outside itself. The demand, as itself a genesis (*ideal* [320–321], as we have called it, in order to name it only provisionally with this partially clear term), however, lies in the "should," and the "should" is it. Thus, there can be a disjunction within the absolute genesis itself, through which it would be *real* and *ideal*. This entire disjunction, discovering the basis of which may well be our most important task, can now[16] follow from genesis, or the "should." Through resolving this disjunction, those words, which we have used so far only provisionally and according to a dim instinct in the hope of an eventual clarification, will themselves become clear.[17] This is merely a hint at a part of our system that necessarily must remain obscure here.

However, the following is completely clear in what has been said: in virtue of yesterday's demonstration, genesis = the "from" in its qualitative oneness. We ourselves, or knowing and light as such, which are entirely the same as us on the level of our present speculations, are this "from" immediately, in that which we pursue and live. So there is no further need for the "from" that is posited and presupposed through some specific act of ours or of the light, nor for anything that we have derived from it in our analysis. Therefore, we let it all go as just a means of ascent, until it shows up again on our descent. I said, "in that which we pursue and live"; and this very pursuing and living, as pursuing and living, follow directly from [our] dissolution into genesis.

3. By virtue of the hypothetical "should," the we, or knowing, is absolutely genetic *in relation to itself*. Because we ourselves were knowing, we pursued it in the following way: "should knowing be (that is, should we ourselves be, since we ourselves are knowing), then ____ must" and so forth. Thus, [it is the] genesis of nothing else, but rather of itself, of the simultaneously productive [one]. Thus, with this it is absolute genesis, which carries in itself the already sufficiently seen {*eingesehen*} character of being or light: that it is completely self-enclosed and can never go outside itself.

4. This absolute self-enclosure of genesis in its fundamental point (in which it should be a genesis of genesis) does not prevent two points of origin {*Genesen*} or two knowings from appearing impermanently. We ourselves conduct one when we say, "If knowing (or we ourselves) should be ____"; and the other one should be, if its principle is fulfilled.[18]

I regard insight into this distinction of two aspects of knowing, a distinction that is still only factical, as simple. Yet, it is so important that I cannot very well leave it to mere luck, and so a bit more by way of elucidation. We ourselves are the absolute light, the absolute light is us, and this is genesis itself. Nothing can depart from this; therefore, a distinction [322–323] cannot be admitted within the subject matter itself, without contradicting our first fundamental insight. Hence, the disjunction that remains is not a disjunction between two fundamentally distinct terms, instead it is a disjunction within one, which remains one throughout all disjunctions. Something of this sort has already presented itself to us earlier. Stated popularly: it is not a disjunction of two things, but rather just different aspects of one and the same thing.

5. Letting this disjunction stand provisionally, just as it has appeared to us factically, with the intention of working further on the basis of it, the question arises, which of the two aspects is to be considered provisionally as absolute in order to explain the other from it? [It is] obviously the first term, in what we ourselves live and pursue, given the insight aroused in us yesterday, that seeing and light reside always only in immediate seeing itself and never in the seeing that is seen. By no means could it be in the objectified *is*, that waits [to receive] its being from a principle and is therefore truly dead within. This choice can be shown to be completely necessary through another circumstance as well. For if we wish to work further, then we wish to pursue and live knowing further as well. Therefore, in fact and absolutely, we must remain in life and cannot *abstract* from it, as is evident. To do so would exactly be not to live and search further, but instead to remain here, which would contradict our intention not to stand still and instead to go further.[19]

(In passing, this aspect is the one that we have always called idealistic. Thus, our science, standing between idealistic and realistic principles, would at last become idealistic, and indeed, as we have seen, be forced to do so by necessity, and contrary to its persistent preference for realism. We will not promise that the matter will come to rest with this principle, as it now stands and as it will at once be explained more clearly. We can promise more confidently that we will never again use objectivity as a principle. From this it will follow that, if the idealistic principle too should prove inadequate, we will need to find a *third*, higher principle that unites the two.)[20]

6. Just as is demanded in this principle *{Satze}* of absolute idealism, the inner *self-genesis*[21] is presupposed as a living inward oneness—what this is, on that point you understand me—as oneness, thus as light, qualitatively absolute, only as something to be enacted and by no means as something to be understood. This latter [oneness is to be presupposed] as *genesis* (i.e., as was made obvious yesterday in each transition from dull to energetic thinking), as disappearing into the arising of an absolute "from"[22] that in turn merges into it, so that seeing and this [324–325][23] arising are entirely inseparable—that is, as genesis of self, or I, so that accordingly what emerges in immediate light may be an "I"—as a result of which, light and this very We, or I, would merge purely into one another. The principle demands this: inner self-genesis is to be presupposed as intrinsically living oneness, then also knowing's objective aspect is allowed to stand and to be united with the previous [aspect], as it can be united in knowing alone. From the genetic principle, it would then follow

that a principle must be assumed for the absolute, inner, and living self-gene-sis, and that this latter [event must occur] in a higher knowing that united both, as is obvious. This latter knowing is then the highest, and the two sub-ordinate terms {*Seitenglieder*} are merely what is mediated through it.

That in the higher knowing a principle is presupposed for absolute self-genesis means that inwardly and materially this higher knowing is *non-self-genesis*.[24] Yet it does not *not* exist, rather it exists actually and in fact; thus [it is] positive non-self-genesis; and yet it is *immanent*[25] and is *itself* an *I*, because this is its imperishable character, as absolute. What else is negated besides genesis? Nothing, and to be sure this is negated positively; but the positive negation of genesis is an enduring[26] *being*. Thus, knowing's absolute, objective, and presupposed *being* becomes evident in this higher knowing, hence directly genetic, as it has previously appeared merely factically.—Once again, in order to review the terms of the proof: as a result of positing a principle for self-gen-esis within knowing itself, [we derive] the explanation of genesis as not absolute; consequently, [we infer] its positive negation within knowing; and consequently [we also infer] the positing within knowing of knowing's absolute being.

If you have just grasped this rigorously, then I can add something else in clarification.[27] This knowing, that only ought to exist, is of course a self-genesis of knowing, its self-projection beyond itself, as we, who are standing over it reconstructing the process and its laws, very well understand {*einsehen*}. However, the question still always remains as to just how we arrive at this insight and so apparently get outside of knowing. Yet, in contrast to an absolute self-genesis, which is itself annulled as absolute by the addition of a principle, the immanent knowing that never can get outside itself for just that reason can never appear as self-genesis but only as the negation of all genesis. Here, therefore, there is a necessary gap in continuity of genesis, and a pro-jection *per hiatum*—but here presumably not [326–327] an irrational one. Rather, it is [a projection] which separates reason in its pure oneness from all appearance, and annuls the reality of appearance in comparison with it.

"Reason," I say, in order to clarify this for us; in this case we were only concerned with deriving the form of pure being and persistence. In our case, this persistence is now, and certainly always and eternally, *genesis*. This exist-ing knowing—which to that extent, is not genetic as regards its external form—is enclosed in itself in unchangeable oneness, and so indeed [is] also genesis, just as it seems to be above. Thereby the absolute, inward awareness declares itself, without any external perceiving, knowing, or intuiting, all of which fall out in self-genesis—[an awareness] of an original principle and an original principled thing {*Urprincipiat*} in a one-sided, and certainly not reci-procal, order; or pure reason, a priori, independent of all genesis, and negating it[28] as something absolute.

Let us go further: in what we most recently lived and pursued, we ourselves have not become pure reason itself, nor dissolved into it, instead we have merely deduced it from[29] an insight into it. However, this was possible only to the extent that we presupposed self-construction as absolute, as we did; because what should follow, follows only on the condition that it [that is, self-construction] is annulled as absolute in itself, from itself, and through itself; and this was the center {Nerv} of our proof. Since it was mentioned previously that the higher knowing, which projects reason, is also at bottom self-genesis and consequently does not just appear to be, we can very appropriately call this self-genesis the reconstruction of the non-appearing original genesis, thus the clarification of the terms of the original genesis, hence [we can call it] *the understanding.*—Accordingly, it follows for us that there is no insight into the essence of reason without presupposing understanding as absolute; conversely, [there is] no insight into the essence of understanding except by means of its absolute negation through reason. However, the highest, in which we [328–329] remain, is the insight into both, and this necessarily posits both, although [it posits] the one in order to negate it. From this standpoint, we are the understanding of reason, and the reason of understanding, and thus both in oneness. Now the disjunction stands forth in its clearest definition. Just one more principle and the matter will be completely explained. [We will talk] about this, next Monday.

This besides; I regard what I have just presented to you as not at all easy. However, that lies in the subject matter, and we have to go through it sometime, if we want to see solid ground. I can promise you a bit more illumination on this from an insight into the principle we are still seeking, but then the difficulty will lie in the principle itself.

One cannot speak properly in front of others about speculation in these heights freely and without preparation, since one has enough work speaking of it in formal, prepared lectures. For this reason, and in order to escape our mutual impulse nevertheless to handle this matter freely, [we will now have] a special discussion period.

CHAPTER 22

Twenty-second Lecture

Monday, May 28, 1804

Honored Guests:

Although I can justifiably report that our speculations now already hover at a height not reached previously, and have introduced insights that fundamentally change the view of all being and knowing (and I hope that all of you who have historical knowledge of philosophy's condition up to now will agree), nevertheless, all of this is still only *preparation* for really resolving speculation's task. We intend to complete this resolution during the current week. Hence, your entire attention is claimed again anew. Whoever has completely understood everything so far, and seen into [it] to the level of eternally ineradicable, forever immovable conviction, but who has not yet seen into, and achieved conviction about what is to be presented now, such a person has achieved at least this protection from all false philosophy: he can set each of them straight fundamentally. He also possesses some significant truths, disconnected and separated from one another; but he has not yet become able to construct within himself the system of truths as a whole and out of a single piece. I now intend to impart this capacity to you, and after that the main purpose of these lectures on the pure science of knowing will have been achieved.

Whether one names the absolute *"being"* or *"light,"* it has already been completely familiar for several weeks. Since attaining this familiarity, we are working on deriving not, as is obvious, the thing itself, but rather its appearance. The request for this derivation can mean nothing else than that something still undiscovered remains in the absolute itself, through which it coheres with its appearance.

We know from the foregoing (which, to be sure has been discovered only factically, but which nonetheless would have its application in a purely genetic derivation) that the principle of appearance is a principle of disjunction within the aforementioned undivided oneness and at the same time, obviously, within appearance. However, as regards the absolute disjunction, I urge

---

This lecture begins at GA II, 8, pp. 330–331.

you to recall an analysis conducted right at the beginning of this lecture series, in which the following became evident. If disjunction were to be found directly within absolute oneness, as is unavoidably required by the final form of the science of knowing, and is what we intend here, it must not be grasped as a simple disjunction, but rather as the disjunction of two different disjunctive foundations. [It must be] not just a division, but rather the self-intersecting division of a presupposed division that again presupposes itself. Or [332–333], using the expression with which we have designated it in our most recent mention of it, [it is] no simple "from," but rather a "from" in a "from," or a "from" of a "from." The most difficult part of the philosophical art is avoiding confusion about this intersection, and distinguishing that which is endlessly similar and is distinguishable only through the subtlest[1] mental distinguishing. I remind you of this so that you will not become mistrustful if, in what follows, we enter regions in which you no longer understand the method and [in which] it should even seem miraculous. Afterwards we will give an account of it; but beforehand we actually cannot.

This much as a general introduction for the week:—Now back to the point at which we stood at the end of the last hour.—Absolute self–genesis posited and given a principle, obviously within knowing, which is thus a "principle-providing"[occurrence].[2] Thus within this knowing there follows the absolute, positive negation of genesis = completed and enduring being; and indeed, because this entire investigation concerns light's pure immanence, our investigation has long ago brought in {über die Seite} a presumed being external to knowing, knowing's [own] completed and enduring being.

Now *We* saw into this connection during the last hour and see into it again here; as is evident, we see one of the two terms in and through the insight into *this* connection, determined as such. Thus, this latter is itself mediated, and just we (= the insight we have now achieved) are therefore the unconditionally immediate [term].

Two remarks about this. 1. I have just recalled again, that here the inner being and persevering is knowing's being, the very thing already recognized as absolute genesis and [the thing] we have also already validated in the last hour as a priori rational knowledge of an absolute principle. At this point, we must hold on to the fact that it is knowing's being, even in case we should let go of the addition as a shortcut in speaking; because otherwise we will fall back into where we were before, far removed from further progress. Therefore, our entire chain of reasoning must always be present to us, now more than ever.[3] 2. It is said that every philosophical system remains stuck somewhere in dead being and enduring. If now a system derived this being itself in its inner essence, as ours has done, by positing a higher principle for absolute genesis, whereby it then necessarily becomes the positive negation of genesis, and therefore [becomes] being; if too this being is not the being of an object and so doubly dead, but rather the being of *knowing*,[4] and so of inner life; then such a system seems [334–335] to have already accomplished something unheard-of. However, we are required to see *{einzusehen}* clearly here that by this we have not yet achieved anything, since even this saturated being of living is again something mediate and is derived from that which alone now remains for us, the insight into the connection. Now let us apply this directly for our true purpose, which we have long recognized. Knowing's derived being will now yield ordinary, non-transcendental, knowing. Through our present insight into the genesis of the former's principle (that is, the principle of the recently derived knowing), and through reflecting on this insight we elevate ourselves to genuine transcendental knowing or the science of knowing; and [we have done so] not merely factically, with[5] our factical selves, so that we are the factical root. We have already been *this* since the time when we dissolved into pure light; instead [we have done so] *objectively* and *intelligibly*, so that we, achieving insight factically, at the same time penetrate the law of this insight. Henceforth we have to work in the higher region that has now been opened. Only here will the principle of appearance and disjunction that we seek show itself to us; which then should only be applied to existing (= ordinary) actual knowing. Now also this addition: since the beginning of what we have provisionally called the second half, a hypothetical *"should"* has been evident as simply creating a connection, and as linking a conditioning and conditioned term (which are both produced absolutely from it) to a knowing, which must be originally present independently of the "should" and its entire operation, if one just understands it correctly. This could be called the first sub-section[6] of the second part. Since we concerned ourselves with an absolute presupposition about the essence of knowing as an absolute "from," we wished to know nothing more about this entire hypothetical "should" and its power of uniting and joining, as a merely apparent knowing. We said at this point that so far *we* (the we that still has not been grasped so far) have concurred about the premise's arbitrary positing, pointed out by energetic reflection, and only the *connection*[7] has made itself manifest without our assistance. Now the premise too presents itself without our assistance; therefore in the premise too we coincide with the absolutely self-active light. Let's hold on to this. We have been doing this for a long time in our discussions about the "from," until I thought you were sufficiently prepared for the higher flight that we began in the last hour. You may take this as the second sub-section of the second part.—In the last hour, the bare connection[8] presented itself again, and (as we might suspect, but will more exactly show and demonstrate) [336–337] with it the hypothetical "should," from which we had already hoped to be free. This should surprise us. If this "should" has reappeared with the same significance in which it was previously struck down, then we have not advanced and are just sailing on in the seas of speculation without a compass. Through the hint given recently as to the difference between ordinary knowing (based on the principle of knowing's being) and transcendental [knowing] (based in the genetic insight into this same principle), it is probable that [the "should"] does not arise in the same way. Instead, the "should" that we have dropped operates in ordinary knowing with tacitly assumed premises; in contrast, the "should" arising now operates in *transcendental*[9] knowing, which grounds its premises genetically—as emanating from a "should." Therefore, in the preceding lecture, we have begun a third sub-section of the second part, and the two extreme sections come together in the *middle* (with the premise) once again distinguished by a duality in the premise. By this means, the two outermost parts (= transcendental and actually existent knowing) would be the two different distinguishing grounds, proceeding from the middle ground of the premise, which both unites and separates them. This is the compass that I would share with you for the journey we have already begun.

2.[10] I said that a hypothetical "should" appears again in our completed insight. To begin with, this is obvious. "Given [that there is] a principle for self-genesis, then it follows that ____ ."[11] Previously, we have found the two terms factically, and to that extent separately; but in the last hour, we have united them genetically, according to our basic rules and maxims. Because we comprehend them mediately in the insight into their connection, then, given this insight, we no longer need to assume them factically. They reside a priori in the insight, and we can drop the empirical construction, until perhaps it arises again in some deduction.

3. Now let us grasp this hypothetical character at its core. According to the maxims and rules that we arbitrarily adopted at the beginning of our entire science, and hence arbitrarily, we appear to ourselves—so it has been, and so it now is openly admitted—as genetically uniting both terms. Here is the inner root of hypotheticalness (now fully abstracted from the hypothetical character of the subordinate terms), precisely the "should's" admitted inner production, containment, and support of itself as identical with the [338–339] free We, i.e., the science of knowing. This very inward hypotheticalness could be what first shows itself and breaks through in the subordinate terms' hypothetical character. Hence, it is only a matter of negating this inner hypotheticalness, so that thereby the quality of being categorical will be manifest in it, and thereby we will justify our insight in its truth, necessity, and absolute priority. In that case, the inference, made[12] here only provisionally, first achieves categorical validity; namely, the inference that both terms (i.e., knowing's self-genesis and its being) occur only mediately in a genetic insight into the oneness of both, and in no wise immediately.

(A remark[13] belonging to method: One must not allow oneself to be distracted [as to] how I legitimately assume this. This is more necessary than ever, since here the method itself becomes absolutely creative; further, nothing besides a remark like this can be adduced in explanation of what happens here. Our insight has come about through the application of the basic maxims of our science, to apply the principle of genesis thoroughly and without exception. This has been required, and it should prove itself. Likewise, the maxims of the science of knowing itself, and with it all of science, have been required, and they should prove themselves. Science itself should justify and prove itself before it truly begins. Thereby, the science of knowing would be liberated from freedom, arbitrariness, and accident; as it must be, or else one could never come to it.)

4. Without digression, we conduct the required proof, according to a law that has already been applied, thus. We could produce this insight, and we actually did so; we *are* knowing;[14] thus this insight is possible in knowing and is actual in our current knowing.—Just a few remarks about this proof. a. The genesis first accomplished by us is an absolute, self-enclosed, genesis; by no means is it a *genesis of a genesis*,[15] because it negates itself inwardly within knowing, as we have shown in the last hour. To us, however, who are contemplating further and constructing the process in its laws, it manifested as genesis. In immediate knowing, however, it was merely a persisting intuition, as external in its result: which explicitly was *non-genesis*[16] = being. b. The proof of absolute genesis was conducted purely through its possibility and facticity, and thus [is] itself only immediately factical. In this case, therefore, facticity and genesis entirely coincide. Knowing's immediate facticity is absolute genesis; and the absolute genesis is—exists as a mere fact—without any possible further ground. [340–341] To be sure, it must happen so, if we are ever actually to arrive at the ground. c. This is a cogent example of how much in the science of knowing depends on one always having the whole context present, since the distinctions can be drawn provisionally only through this context. Knowing, as genesis, is proved factically in this way. What then happened several sessions ago when we proved knowing as a "from" factically in the same way? Is the "from" something other than genesis, and have we not conducted the identical proof? Yet the present, factically demonstrated, genesis is something entirely different from the one proved earlier. You could grasp this distinction *{Character}* only by noticing that in this case it is a question of the genesis of absolute knowing in its fundamental construction, whereas previously [it was a question of] the genesis of its absolute self-genesis. In that lecture, to be sure, I had to let this criterion go and abstract from it, looking simply at the core element of the new proof (since otherwise we would never arrive at this new proof) and relying on the solid insight already engendered in you. However, you can add this criterion now, and can use it to rebuilt and reinforce the insight, in case it begins to waver. Later of course I will add inner distinguishing criteria, e.g., for both these points of origin *{Genesen}*, by which they can be distinguished in themselves, independent of their relation. However, they are not even possible, or

comprehensible, before the distinction in the thread of relatedness has been completed factically, because these inner distinctions are nothing but the genetic law of the factical difference, which arises only in the fact. For just this reason, the science of knowing is not a lesson to be learned by heart, but rather an art. Presenting it, too, is not without art.[17]

d. I also want to make you aware of the following. Even in the recently conducted proof, within whose content facticity and genesis should merge purely into each other, there still remains in the minor premise of the syllogism the same term that arose above factically and still has not been genetically mastered.[18] "We know, or are knowing." [This is] of course immediately clear and intelligible, but its principle is by no means clear. Investigations remain to be made here, and herein lies perhaps the most important part of our remaining solution.

Let me announce the process that will follow. For good reasons lying in my art, I will not proceed at once with this point, but instead I will wait until it arises of itself. On the contrary, I will add this also: in the insight we have completed, an insight has now indeed arisen for us that is objective, immediately compelling for us, as well as intrinsically determinate and clear. It is this, if [342–343] we abstract from the subordinate terms as hypothetical and as themselves just the externalization of the inner hypotheticalness of our performance (of course, we need to abstract from this hypotheticalness as well), then we intend to turn from the form of our insight to its content, in order to explain the form from it, as we have frequently done and as is actually a realistic move {Wendung}.

To repeat briefly: the content of the insight we have recently achieved must be clearly present to you. Providing absolute self-genesis with a principle yields absolute non-genesis = being. As we just recently undertook to do, today we have abstracted completely from the two subordinate terms. And, looking only at our insight itself and the manner of its production, we have justified, as was possible only in a factical manner, the absolute application of both the maxim of self-genesis and this procedure. This is the essential content of the little, easily remembered, bit that we have achieved for our topic.

Further, at many turning points {Wendungen} we have made extremely penetrating remarks about method, which I urge you to keep in mind, because only with them will you find your way through the maze which we confront.

CHAPTER 23

Twenty-third Lecture

Wednesday, May 30, 1804

Honored Guests:

Providing a principle for absolute self-genesis, as we have described the light, creates non-genesis, or *being* (of knowing, it goes without saying). We have seen *{eingesehen}* this, have reflected about the method for producing the insight, and have justified it factically. It is possible and actual within knowing, because it is possible and actual within us, and we are knowing. However, no genetic derivation of this last point has occurred just yet.

We can justify this procedure even more deeply and from another point of view. An objective, and absolutely compelling insight has actually arisen for us; this process hereby has also shown itself to be coherent with the absolute, self-producing light. Consequently, the task which we reported at the end of the last hour as coming next *(to investigate this objective insight in respect to its true content)*[1] will simultaneously be our first attempt at justifying more deeply what has up to now been presented only factically, and perhaps even to make the point genetic.

—And so to the content of the self-presenting *objective insight!*[2]

1. Evidently, the absolute relation of both subordinate terms. However, these are still hypothetical; but without them, there is no connection; it itself is the result of hypothetical terms, and so itself is hypothetical; a fact from which we should abstract. What is still left? Plainly nothing other than the insight's inner certainty; and because even the insight as such depends on the terms, [it is] nothing more than a purely inner certainty.

The first claim on you is to grasp this certainty sharply and altogether purely. It is not certainty about anything in particular, as the relation of the subordinate terms was in our case, because we have abstracted from that. Rather, it is certainty pure and as such, with complete abstraction from everything.

At first, accordingly, it is immediately clear that certainty would have to be thought completely purely. Moreover, the ground of its material what-ness

---

This lecture begins at GA II, 8, pp. 344–345.

{*Washeit*} lies in the *"what"*[3] (that it is, that it is *what* it is, that it is *certain*[4]); but the ground for certainty cannot in any way be located there, because this does not belong to the *"what."* Therefore, certainty lies simply in itself, unconditionally and purely as such; and it is unconditionally of and through itself. It must be thought in this way, or else certainty is not conceived as certainty.

(In passing, being is not a reality that is derived from the sum of all possible realities [346–347] (i.e., from the possible determinations of a "what"); rather, it is completely closed into itself, and outwardly, in its properties, is first the condition and support of every "what." Kant was the first to validate this proposition—misunderstood almost entirely by the old philosophy. As regards the first half of the sentence: being is something living from itself, out of itself, and through itself, absolutely self-enclosed and never coming out of itself, as we grasped {*eingesehen*} clearly at the end of what we called the first part. Kant merely added the second part of the sentence, "condition and support of the 'what'"[5] factically, without ever deriving it. We will append it genetically. In brief, the task of deducing[6] *appearance* (as we have so far labeled our second part)[7] is entirely the same as completely proving the stated sentence from being {*esse*}.[8] Now so far we have inferred, and proved to this extent {*in tantum*}, that light[9] and being are completely identical, because we are, and are light, all of which is surrounded by facticity. Further, in our view the light carries another qualitative character, the *"from,"* and lastly absolute genesis as well. At the highest point of our speculation, we said that the light is absolute, qualitative oneness, which cannot be penetrated further—briefly, thus, an occult quality. Now for the first time we have arrived at a property of light through which it shows itself immediately as one with the being previously seen into: *certainty* {*Gewissheit*}, pure and for itself, as such.)[10]

2. How would you proceed, if I asked you to describe this certainty more closely, to make it clear? Not otherwise, I believe, than by conceiving it as an unshakable continuance and resting *in the same*[11] unchangeable oneness; in the same, I said, and therefore in the very same *"what,"* or quality. Accordingly, you could not describe pure certainty otherwise than as pure unchangeability; and [you could not describe] unchangeability otherwise than as the persisting oneness of the "what," or of quality.

3. I inquire further, is the main thing for you in describing pure, bare certainty that the "what" be something particular, or does your description not rather explicitly contain absolute indifference toward all more exact [348–349] determination of the "what"? Only the latter, you will say, and without doubt you will admit *that*[12] the "what" remains one; but by no means *what* else it may be. Therefore, in this case merely the pure form of the "what," or quality in general, is employed in the description, and it is the required description of pure certainty only on condition of this formal purity.

4. With this, the concept of the "what," or quality, is completely explained and derived for the first time. This is a concept that has so far always remained in the dark, as much in its content as in its factical genesis. Quality is the absolute negation of changeability and multiplicity, purely as such; i.e., the concept is thereby closed without any possibility of further supplements. I add here as a supplement that through this negation, the negated term (changeability) is posited at once, purely as such, and without further determination. (Quantifiability through quality, and vice versa.)[13] "Genetically derived," I have said. As such, certainty cannot be described otherwise than through absolute quality. "If it should be described, then ____ must" and so on. Therefore, we have taken a very important step for our primordial derivation of the "what" = appearance. Now everything depends on how the description (i.e., reconstruction) of certainty arises.

5. We argue thus: In this way we have seen into and described certainty. However, is our description of certainty itself then certain, true, and legitimate?

As we have always done with similar questions, let us pay attention to our manner of proceeding. We have constructed *a general "what"*[14] and posited it as unchangeable. The essence of certainty appeared therein. I ask, if we repeat this procedure infinitely many times, as we seem able to do, could we ever do it any differently? The "what's" construction is entirely unchangeable, and in all these infinitely many repetitions, it is possible in only the one way we have described: through negating changeability. Therefore, we view ourselves in the very same way we have described certainty, as persisting unchangeably in the construction's single same "what"; we are what we say,[15] and we say what we are.

6. Certainty is grounded completely and absolutely in itself. However, according to its description, certainty is persistence in the same "what." Thus, in the description, the ground of the "what's" oneness is to be posited completely inwardly within certainty itself. The oneness of the "what" lies in this, that certainty is, and in no other external ground.

[350–351] 7. "Certainty is grounded in itself" also means that it is absolute, immanent, self-enclosed, and can never go outside itself; in itself it is *I*; in just the very same way that the proof of being's *form* was previously conducted. Therefore, it is clear that the externalized and objectivized certainty we presented previously is not the absolute one, according to its form, although in its content and essence it may very well be. Hence, it is clear that in searching for the absolute we must abstract from the latter, and search simply in what manifests itself as immanence, as I (or We).

In this We, we have now surely found certainty, as the necessity of resting in the procedure's qualitative oneness;[16] and there the matter now rests (this enumeration demands all our attention). First and foremost, *absolute certainty*[17] is, in and from itself, the same as "I" or "We," us or its own self (all of which mean the same thing), completely inaccessible, purely self-enclosed, and hidden. For if it (or "We," which means the same thing) were accessible,[18] then it would have to be outside itself, which is contradictory. As a result of the preceding insight, we must abstract from just this: that we are actually speaking about it now, and thus are manifesting it; and this is the appearance (which is mere appearance, because it contradicts the truth) whose possibility we must deduce from the system of appearance.

In a way that arises from a ground that will show itself very soon but that is not yet clear, certainty now *expresses* itself immanently in itself (that is, in us) and thus in every expression, as *perception {Anschauung}* of a particular, completely unchanging process. This manifestation shows up here, but only as an absolute fact, and so an obscurity still remains. (Process is living as living; the process's unchanging qualitative oneness is life's immanence and self-groundedness, expressed immediately in life itself.) Let us press ahead toward clarity, to the extent that we can do so here. Immediately living and immanent being-a-principle is light, and is intuition with an inner necessity.—I say, "being-a-principle," therefore just projecting and intuiting. I say the projected term *{das Projectum}* is "immediately living and immanent"[19] simply in intuiting, from intuiting, and out of intuiting; and the projecting is just light's life as "principle-providing" *{Principiieren}*.[20] I say "with an inner necessity," and thus that this necessity must completely express itself, because it is just *"principle-providing"*[21] as being principle-providing.[22]

It is absolute, immanent *projection*, and so it is a projection of nothing else than itself, wholly and completely as it inwardly is.—Note, as it is, it is projecting, first of itself inwardly and qualitatively, but not [352–353] at all understood objectively. Thus—*making itself into an inward intuiting*, immediately by way of inner, living "being-a-principle," as thinking and intuiting unconditionally at a single stroke; but, in fact and truthfully, it is the latter as a result of the former. Thus in this inner qualitative self-projecting, it necessarily projects itself, objectively *(et in virtute eius, minime per actum specialem)*;[23] not yet to be sure as an objectively present I, but rather as it inwardly is: first of all as living, one, and grounded in itself formally; but this is process in pure *qualitative* oneness.[24] This is the intuition of inner certainty and oneness of process that concerned us previously. This oneness expresses itself with necessity,[25] because it is the result of the absolute, living principle-providing. We called this process "describing certainty" and sought a ground for it. It has been found. I ask to wit, does such a description of certainty happen in itself and actually? But how could it; it is nothing else than the necessary expression and result of certainty's life as pure "providing-itself-a-principle" *{Sichprincipiierens}* completely derived and explained by us. Yet this life is unconditionally necessary in being or certainty.[26] Further—it projects itself as it inwardly is; but it is not merely living, instead it is its own life, and, as such, it is *self*-projection. The life derived in this way as a constructive process is therefore the construction of itself in the projection (and therefore likewise in the certainty taken objectively), which we found as a first term at the beginning of our investigation, when we were unfamiliar with the higher terms. In the living description, certainty is more primordial in us than it is objectively in itself without any description. It is the latter only as a result of the construction, which is also projective.—[27]

Now let us more clearly and definitely grasp the three primary modifications of the primordial light, which we have disclosed today.

Certainty, or light, is an immediately living principle, and thus the *pure absolute oneness*[28] of just the light, which cannot be described further in any way, but rather can only be carried out. If we wished to describe it, then we would have to describe it as a qualitative oneness, which in this case does not serve us. It is always and eternally[29] *immediate* I. Therefore, since we said the foregoing, we already contradicted ourselves in what we say.[30] When we said, "it is a *living principle*"[31] we began to describe it, but [to do so] primordially. "Principle-providing" *{Principiiren}*[32] is already its effect, but its primordial effect[33] in us, since we are it. It (or we, which is the same thing) describes itself in this way. Principle-providing, if only you [354–355] think it precisely, is *projecting*,[34] immanent self-projecting. To be sure, since it lies immediately and directly in living[35] itself, it [consists in] making oneself into projection and intuition,[36] not through a gap and objectively, but inwardly and essentially[37] through transubstantiation. Notice, because this is situated in *light's* very *life*, all light whatsoever is immediately[38] self-creating, and so it *is* like this:—thus, it is absolutely intuiting. Even the science of knowing, in all its living activity, cannot avoid this fate. We have not avoided it either, despite the fact that, according to a law that we have not yet explained, it invades the principle and becomes a *self-making*[39] in it, because otherwise [the principle] remains just a being. This entire insight into the primordially real principle-providing is a matter for the science of knowing—which is the first factor.

Living knowing intuits itself unconditionally as it is inwardly just because it really projects itself. However, above all it is unconditionally[40] from itself; it must therefore intuit itself as being thus, and here specifically as not existing outside intuition. Here, therefore, the absolute gap arises, and the projection through a gap, as a pure, rational expression of the true relationship of things: the notion of intuition, or the concept, in its separation from essence, not as the essence itself, but rather merely as its image, and the negation of the latter beforehand.

Hence, it is a "principle-providing," and it must intuit *{anschauen}* itself objectively and through a gap. At this point it is clear that this "principle-providing," its process, must appear within the intrinsically immanent view as from itself, out of itself, and through itself; as by no means grounded in it, but rather as happening because it projects through a gap.—However, the scientist of knowing, who understands {*einsieht*} the view itself in its arising, knows very well all the same that this entire independence is not intrinsically true as self-producing, but instead is only the appearance of a higher, absolutely unintuitable, principle-providing. Therefore [he understands] that all the flexibility {*Agilität*} lying in the procedure's appearance is not grounded in truth, so that it can only be grasped with difficulty, just as the qualitative oneness of intuition by no means comes to an end with it.

So then, it is an *absolutely immanent*[41] providing-itself-a-principle {*Principiiren seiner selbst*} and indeed, as will now be explained more exactly, in absolute fact, without any other intervening light, or seeing: as *intuition*. This very intuition must itself be intuited, or projected through a gap: through which arises the intuition of a primordially complete and persisting knowing, what we previously called the being of knowing. The first described [356–357] principle-providing in intuition relates itself to this "being of knowing" as reconstruction. So, from certainty we have derived both subordinate terms (which previously just stood there hypothetically) out of a deeper insight into the essence of their relation.

We have not sought to conceal[42] where the difficulty now still remains. That is, [we need] to ground the possibility, and justify the truth and validity of the science of knowing's presupposition that living certainty is genuinely "principle-providing."—I say carefully "principle-providing," not "providing-itself-a-principle." If we prove the first, then the second follows from absolute immanence and self-enclosure, as is completely obvious from itself. More about this tomorrow.

CHAPTER 24

Twenty-fourth Lecture

Thursday, May 31, 1804

Honored Guests:

We have posited the primordial light as "principle-providing" living immediately in itself, and from this, we have derived three necessarily arising fundamental determinations of the light. At first, it was enough for us to understand this proposition and the inferences following from it, which demanded energetic thinking and inwardly living imagination above all. However, I believe that I have succeeded in being comprehensible. Finished with this business, we raised the question, what authorized us, as scientists of knowing, to make this assumption? We held ourselves back from answering this, until today. a. To begin with, consider the sense in which we then asked the question. We know that the science of knowing is I, that light is completely I. Further, someone could attempt to conduct a proof here in the same way we did it previously; the science of knowing as I, and therefore light, can and does; hence the light can and does. Nevertheless, this mode of proof must fall away and receive its higher premises. When this occurs, the place is revealed where, at the very same time, the I that can act *{könnendes Ich}* and the light that can act fall away, along with all arbitrariness, the appearance of which our presupposition certainly still carries.

So much generally. Now I request that you undertake the following reflection with me:

1.[1] If arbitrariness is to vanish, an *immediate, factical necessity* of immediate self-projection must show up in the science of knowing. "Immediate[2] necessity," I say; the science of knowing must really do this, or better the necessity must take place itself, without the science's help. I say "necessity" and "factical":[3] it must be immediately intuited as necessary, *but without additional higher grounds*. The remark, which we make from time to time and made yesterday, that we cannot escape from knowing's projecting and objectifying, does not suffice for our purpose. It has not been shown *under what conditions and*

This lecture begins at GA II, 8, pp. 358–359.

in which context we cannot escape. Thus, if we could not escape only in attentive thinking, we nevertheless seem to escape in weak thinking. We should explain just how it stands with these two contradictory appearances.

However, as I will show you briefly and without further derivation, the following suffices and leads to our goal. I cannot predicate anything of the light,[4] unless I just project and objectify it [i.e., the light] as the subject of the[5] predicate. *"Non nisi formaliter obiecti sunt predicata."*[6] [360–361] If one merely ponders this proposition attentively, it is immediately clear, without any further possible *{anführbaren}* grounds; and if it is to belong here, then it must be just so, according to our previous remark.[7] It is more important for us to understand its contents properly. "I predicate of the light" (or, what is synonymous, the light predicates of itself) means that it projects itself through a gap, by means of the enduring intuition sufficiently characterized yesterday. "I cannot do so without projecting it" generally means: without projecting it in the primordial, real, inner, and essential projection, which first makes it intuition, as again was sufficiently described yesterday.

Let us look back at our task. We put forward the very claim about which we admitted that it was not made in any factical knowing whatsoever (which is always limited to already completed intuitions) but rather is made only by the science of knowing—light's absolutely primordial act of making itself an intuition. This claim should be demonstrated in an immediately self-producing insight and manifestness. This is the case with the insight produced by us. Therefore, absolute necessity, etc., is comprehended *{eingesehen}*.

But how is it comprehended? Not unconditionally, but under conditions. Our insight brings it into connection with something else. If [something] should be predicated (that is, be intuition), then _____ must. However, should the antecedent *{erste}* be?[8]

In that case neither is the consequent *{andere}*: the first *can be seen into* only under a condition—thus it is conditioned intellectually; if the consequent happens to occur—that [would be] real conditionedness. So everything is just about what we wished; but not the unconditionedness and oneness for which we strove.

(a. A logical clarification: Predicate = minor premise; absolute objectification of the logical subject = major premise. Both posit themselves unconditionally reciprocally; and so something else underlies the inference much more deeply than the major premise, with discovery of which we began. Ignoring this, all philosophical systems without exception fail to arrive at an absolute major premise. Therefore, if they do not wish their thinking to stand still somewhere arbitrarily, they must sink into a rootless skepticism.

b. With the repeated appearance of the *"should,"* of hypotheticalness, and of relatedness, no one now[9] fears that we would be driven back again to the old point that we have already abandoned. Because obviously the currently related terms are higher than were the previous ones. Previously, [we understood] self-construction to be the procedure that arose yesterday in the already established {*stehende*} intuition, and, [we] took the being of knowing to be the highest, the established [362–363] intuition. Now, though, the established intuition itself is not displaced by a higher one in relation to pure and real *self-projection*, rather it is simply discovered in it.)

2. Since I, a scientist of knowing, see into this connection as absolutely necessary and unchangeable, I myself project and objectify knowing as just this relation, as a "oneness through itself," determined without any possible assistance from some external factor; [a oneness] which I simultaneously permeate and construct in its inner essence and content. What then is the content?—Above all, something arbitrary and dependent simply on freedom and the fact, therefore something unconditionally necessary, which, facticity, if it happens to be called into life, grasps and determines without further ado. Both in relation to one another, so that the one is indeed the completely proper principle of its being, but cannot be this without in the same undivided stroke having its principle in the other. Likewise, the other is not actually a principle unless the one posits itself. We can best name the former *"law,"* i.e., a principle that, in order to provide a principle factically {*welche zu seinem facktischen Principiiren*}, presupposes yet another absolutely self-producing principle. [We can name] the latter a pure, primordial "fact," which is only possible according to a law.

3. This is what knowing is, absolutely and unalterably, without any exception, and it is understood {*eingesehen*} as such. Now, in the insight just produced and completed, I myself, the scientist of knowing, am a knowing. Indeed, as it seems to me, I am a free and factical knowing, since I could well have omitted the preceding reflection, and moreover [I am a knowing] predicated of knowing, describing its entire essence.—According to my own statement, facticity always and everywhere takes up the law of primordial projection, therefore in actual fact it must have taken me up, albeit invisibly. Formal projection in general rests in the law, and this is evident enough factically; I add here only that it exists as a result of the law. The fact also rests in the law that it [facticity] is projected just as it *inwardly is*, or, (as we could say more accurately in order to be safe from all misunderstanding) *nota bene*, as it must be projected[10] according to the law. However, at the heights of our speculation, we know no other law at all except the law of lawfulness itself, *that*[11] it is projected according to law. This is just how it expressed itself to us earlier in factical terms; therefore, we have nothing else to do regarding this material point than to add that this projection occurs according to the absolute law. In that way, [364–365] by applying its own material assertion to its own form, we have genetically derived the very insight from which we began today, and which previously was produced factically. This is the first important result.

a.[12] No doubt, we will get to say more about such an application of what a proposition asserts to the proposition itself. *It is remarkable.*[13] It seems to be just the determination of the major premise by the minor premise that we mentioned previously; and therefore truth seems to begin running back into itself, which in all other systems would have neither beginning nor end, if they were consistent. b. On every occasion, we have posited as the absolute of its kind that which posits itself; and so, in the investigation just completed, we have [posited] a law of law, or lawfulness itself. That this is the absolute law cannot be doubted; nor that the act we carry out in accord with it is the highest, immediately law-conformable act of the science of knowing. (What the stated limitations mean will become evident at the appropriate time.)

4. Now we proceed to another investigation that is of the highest importance, interesting (if I can succeed in making myself understandable to you), and even agreeable.

Without doubt the absolute law—according to which we projected knowing in its essence in the insight that we completed today and then analyzed—has absolute real causality on the *inwardness* of the act (I do not speak of its outward form, which appears free). So that the law and the act permeate one another inwardly (and indeed the act with the oneness of all its distinguishable determinations) without any gap between them. The projection is in part formal (objectifying), and in part material[14] (expressing the essence[15] of knowing). It is by no means the latter without the former, but instead is both at a single stroke, because it is both through an absolutely effective law. Hence, the material expression must simultaneously express the projection's form. Or, to say it exactly: disregarding the prior proof of the opposite, knowing in projection, at least formally, cannot simply be just what it is in itself or according to the law, without any projection. What could it be that projection alters in it? Of course, you do not forget that we are speaking here only about projection's inner material form, abstracting from its outer form, on the basis of which we merely argued and which we now drop. The inner essence of projection is living principle-providing; this [latter] must remain in [the former] completely and absolutely as such, and can never be destroyed. What is this? Answer: only absolute [366–367] description, as description, which stepped between the two terms in a wonderful way. Among other things, [it is] quite evident in the relation as such. For what is the relation except describing one on the basis of the other? The latter must remain immanently[16] in the former and can never be destroyed, precisely as intrinsically living "principle-providing." Thus, it must allow itself to be perpetually renewed as such, although the content, determined by the absolute law, remains the same. On this basis, one can now explain the appearance of energetic reflection, and the infinite repetition of the content that qualitatively remains absolutely one, content which, to our great astonishment, has not yet wished to leave us. I said that the law should determine the inner content. While we examine it, if we now think of description as an absolutely living "principle-providing" in itself, then it is clear at once that it must appear just through the law as the reconstruction of an original pre-construction, and so, in a word, as an *image*. Or, [it must appear] as the oft-mentioned mere *statement*,[17] only the enunciation and expression, of that which to be sure should in itself be just thus. In a word, [description is] the whole simply ideal[18] element, as which we must consider our seeing to be, if we transfer ourselves into the standpoint of reflection, i.e., of "principle-providing."

Therefore, to apply this at once, this is how it stands with knowing. The entire form of objectivity, or the form of existence, has in itself no relation to truth. Knowing itself, however, and everything which should arise in it, splits itself absolutely into a duality, whose one term is to be the primordial, and whose other term is to be the reconstruction of the primordial, completely without any diversity of content, and so again absolutely one; differing only in the given form, which obviously indicates a reciprocal relation to one another. (It is really like this in every possible consciousness, if you wish to test the proposition there. Object, representation.)

However, let us carry this reasoning further. At the beginning of our investigation, because the looked-for absolute oneness created us, we stood (as we later discovered) under the law without knowing either it or our[19] act as such. Only when we reflected on this act were we able to apply the content of our discovered insight to it as the middle term of our inference, and arrive at an insight into the previously concealed law. Without doubt, we constructed or described the law itself in this insight, and could catch ourselves in the act.[20]

Therefore, we truly stand under the law just in case no law [368–369] arises in knowing; and we are beyond the law, constructing it itself, if it does arise in consciousness. Thus, our entire inference grounds itself on a mere fact, without law, which therefore cannot be justified; and the inference itself only *speaks* of a law without being or having one. Hence, this reasoning too, however much luster it shows, unravels into nothing.[21]

Applying this to the preceding: the ostensible primordial construction, which is supposed to justify the reconstruction (that admittedly presents itself as such), is itself really just a reconstruction, but one that does not present itself as such. However, the entire appearance disappears on closer inspection.

We must be glad that it now drops away as well, and that this standpoint was not the highest. Because yet another *disjunction* lies in it, whose genetic principle is not yet fundamentally clear, and at which we cannot remain. Of course, it is not the outward disjunction into subject and object, which fell away by means of the full annulment of the persistent form of projection and objectivity; rather [it is] the inner living difference between both: two forms of life.[22]

Just how this difficulty is resolved and where our path will go on from there can be gathered very easily. We described and constructed the absolute law; that is the difficulty. It must be evident that we cannot construct it; rather it constructs itself on us and in us. In short, it is the law itself, which posits us, and itself in us. On this subject, tomorrow.

CHAPTER 25

Twenty-fifth Lecture

Friday, June 1, 1804

Honored Guests:

We understood {*sahen wir ein*} that, as a condition, if knowing is to predicate something of itself, then it must in general simply project itself. Looking simply at the form of this insight, it contains a free, arbitrary fact and an absolute law, of which this fact, becoming actual, should immediately avail itself. This is the first point.[1]

Now in this "understanding" {*Einsehen*}, we—as scientists of knowing—are also knowing, indeed a free factical knowing, and so in the same circumstance of which we have spoken. Therefore, we ourselves, along with this fact of ours, come under the law to project knowing in general, and to project it as it is inwardly, or according to law. Thus, knowing has disclosed itself in our insight as objective and unchangeable oneness, and with the absolute manifestness that it behaves in just the way we have said. We add only the new[2] point that this too exists in this way because of the invisible law.

This point was argued further as follows. This projection occurs (at least according to the material, or to the content of knowing stated in it) according to an absolute law, which cannot not be a law and cannot not have causality. Hence, it is an absolutely immanent projection and can never escape being so; and, as we very illuminatingly add, the light in the projection can not be just the same as it is inwardly or (according to the law) apart from all projection. What does this mean? It must permanently bear the mark of the intrinsic living *principle-providing*;[3] and [it must] appear in its form as the product of that sort of "principle-providing." Therefore, [it must appear] repeatedly to infinity as a *re-construction*[4] related to the primordial projection through the law. This establishes the fundamental disjunction in knowing. At this point, we raised this objection: is not the law itself reconstructed by us? Obviously; therefore, we never really arrive at a primordial construction and law, instead, viewing the matter aright, [we] merely have two reconstructions, one of which

---

This lecture begins at GA II, 8, pp. 370–371.

presents itself as what it is, and one of which lies. However, [we] can uncover this illusion. Thus, we still find ourselves in the realm of arbitrariness, not yet having entered the necessary. Now to solve this.

1. In the first place, why is it, really, that we will not trust this reconstruction of the law? Because it seems arbitrary. If it showed itself as necessary, then it would show itself also as something conforming to law and as itself the immediate inner expression and causality of the law. We received an [372–373] immediately factical law, pervading the facts: posit the law. Now, merely because it is projected, the projected law can always be the result of a reconstruction; but at least the *inner construction*[5] of this objective law is not a reconstruction, but rather the primordial construction itself.

2. Can this proof of a law's reconstruction be carried out? I say: as it seems to me, it can be done easily in the following way. The first, primordially permanent projection intrinsically bears the *character of an image*,[6] of a reconstruction, etc. However, the image as such refers to a content; and *re*construction[7] as such refers to an original. Hence, the task of understanding this concept of intuition completely and lawfully contains another [task], to posit this prior one.—Now I ask, how then is the image an image, the reconstruction a reconstruction? Because they presuppose a higher law, and exist because of this law, we have said; and therefore [they] point in the image, as an *image*, to the law, which is already contained there, at least virtually and in its results.[8] We, scientists of knowing, stand presently just in the image as an image; thus, it is the law implicitly and virtually present in us ourselves that constructs, or posits, itself ideally. So, what we undertook to prove yesterday is completely proven,[9] "The law itself posits itself in us ourselves." Image as image is the crucial premise *{nervus probandi}*.[10]

Notice also: 1. In order to conduct the proof we have just completed, we first had really and intrinsically to presuppose the law as the image's primordial ground, without giving any account of how we arrive at[11] the concept or its projection. Now we have completely explained how we arrived at it; but the variation of this concept's form has not yet been explained. I content myself here with merely pointing out this as yet obscure section historically, and adding that its clarification lies in the reply to the question of the science of knowing's possibility as a science of knowing, which will now be addressed continually, but achieved only at the end.[12]

2. We have now changed the following in yesterday's sketch of knowing. Knowing stands neither in the reconstruction as such (representation), nor in the original (the thing-in-itself), but rather wholly in a standpoint between the two. It stands in the image of the reconstruction, as an image, in which image the *positing of a law* arises immediately through an *inner law*.[13] This permeation of the image's essence is the primordial, absolute, unchangeable oneness. As wholly internal, in projection, it just divides itself projectively into a permanent objective image and a permanent objective law.

[374–375] I wish to be completely understood on this. The light lives what it is in its very self, it inhabits its living. Now it is image—*as* image, I have added, that is living, self-enclosed imaging. You have to attend very closely to the latter; because otherwise, it is not yet clear how you could have come to the former, to the image as a closed oneness that you have undoubtedly objectified. It is an imaging, formally immanent;[14] it images, or projects itself as just what it inwardly is, as an image. It is intelligibly immanent and self-enclosed.[15] Yet, the image posits a law, therefore it projects a law; and it projects both as standing completely in the one-sided, determinate relation in which we have thought them.

Note further here: according to yesterday's disjunction, both primordial image and copy should be qualitatively one, because otherwise they could not cohere. Now, both cohere inwardly and essentially as image, positing a law, etc., and qualitative oneness can not come into it in any way. Qualitative oneness is the absolute negation of variation; therefore, it can come into play only where *variability*[16] can be posited. However, image, as image, is intrinsically invariant. It is essential oneness, the *law* of the image is likewise oneness, and they posit one another entirely only through their inner essence, without any further supplement. This total removal of the material, qualitative oneness, which so far has not left us, is a new guarantee that we have climbed higher.

Since we end the week today, I will not begin any new investigation; instead, I will estimate what we have left to do in the coming week, during which I intend to complete this entire presentation, should that prove possible.

Initially, it is readily clear that, if we only establish ourselves correctly in what has just been presented, no possibility can be foreseen as to how we should escape it and go further. Here we are immediately absolute knowing. This is an "image-making process" *{ein Bilden}* positing itself as an image, and positing a law of the image-making process as an explanation of the image. With this everything has been unfolded, and is completely explained and comprehensible in itself. The terms come together to form *{bilden}* a synthetic cycle, into which nothing else can enter.

The particular point at which we have closed off further progress is very clearly evident above. [We did so] through the total negation of the concept of qualitative oneness. By negating this concept, quantifiability was established at the same time that we opened a more comfortable way to descend into [376–377] life and its multiplicity, as we know from the preceding. Now, this qualitative oneness has been negated through positing a *oneness* of image and its law that repels all variability, a oneness essential in itself but still merely hypothetical. Since this oneness has become manifest absolutely, it must be applicable here, so that we cannot possibly prevent ourselves blending this quality in, without further ado.[17]—As to this, I wished particularly that you had noticed for yourselves, that we had to descend again to this quality only through a term of the necessary relation, one which is produced lawfully. (The occult quality is entirely cut off.)

Noteworthy too is the fact that the concept of the science of knowing as a particular knowing has now disappeared completely. What we have derived is the one pure knowing in its absolute disjunction, which is explained from its essence as oneness. We now are this one pure knowing; we are now the science of knowing as well and [we] hope to become it again, so the science of knowing is absolute knowing itself, and we are the latter too only to the extent that the science of knowing is it.

The last consideration leads us to the path on which we can go further; the science of knowing must emerge again as a particular knowing. Of course, we know very well that we have not always been the one insight that we now are and live, but that we have ascended to it by means of all our previous considerations. We must retrace this, our *transformation {Werden}* into absolute knowing—not empirically and artificially, as we have before; instead, we must explain it. In short, we must once more see *{einsehen}* in its genesis what we *are* at the conclusion of today's lecture. This insight into the genesis—not of *absolute*[18] knowing in itself, because this knows no origin; but rather of absolute knowing's actual *existence* and *appearance* in us[19]—this would be the science of knowing *in specie*, in so far as it is a particular knowing whose nonexistence is as possible as its existence.[20]

Now, it may happen that ordinary knowing is the primordial condition for the genetic possibility of absolute knowing's existence, or of the science of knowing. Hence, [it may happen] that its determinations can be explained simply from the presupposition that the science of knowing ought to arise,[21] and the sum of our entire system resolves itself into the following rational inference. "If absolute knowing is to appear, then ____ must, etc." Now, knowing is determined like this, so consequently this should clearly happen.

I have said that all determinations must be explicable and understandable simply on the basis of the presupposition: "It should unconditionally ____, etc."; and I ask you to take this in its full strength. By way of explanation, I add the following: we have seen *{eingesehen}* that knowing in itself is unconditionally one, without any material [378–379] quality or quantity. How then does this knowing descend in itself to qualitative multiplicity and difference,[22] and to the entire infinity of quantity and its forms (time, space, etc.) in which we encounter it? We have to prove the following: simply because absolute knowing's being can be produced only genetically, and because it can be so only under just the types of conditions that we find originally in living, therefore life coheres indivisibly with the science of knowing, and with that which it produces. Everyone must confess that, apart from the extent to which he elevates himself to absolute knowing, his entire life would be nothing, would lack worth and meaning, and would truly not even exist.

In brief: absolute affirmation[23] of the genesis of the existence of absolute knowing (according to the preceding, no term in this description is superfluous) unites both ends of knowing, the ordinary and also the absolute and transcendental, and clarifies them reciprocally. We must put ourselves into this point, as the genuine standpoint of the science of knowing *in specie*. With this, I believe that I have shared with you a very important conception of our entire procedure up to now and into the future.

Hence, the entire outcome of our doctrine is this. Simple existence, whatever name it may have, from the very lowest up to the highest (the existence of absolute knowing), does not have its ground in itself, but instead in an absolute purpose. And this purpose is that absolute knowing should be. Everything is posited and determined through this purpose; and it achieves and exhibits its true destination only in the attainment of this purpose. Value exists only in knowing, indeed in absolute knowing; all else is without value. I have deliberately said "in absolute knowing," and by no means "in the science of knowing *in specie*," because the latter is only a means *{Weg}*, and has only instrumental value, by no means intrinsic value. Whoever has arrived no longer worries about the ladder.

This result, that only true knowing or wisdom has value, is very shocking in our age, which counts only on external workings, and undoubtedly it appears to us as a great innovation. It is remarkable that this doctrine, which is an innovation to our age, is really the primordial one, as is almost always the case with all our characteristic works and ways. I will prove this, not to support by age and authority what can prove itself, but rather to give you a parenthetical opportunity for comparison. In Christianity, (which may in its essence be much older than we assume, and concerning which I have frequently [380–381] said that, in its roots and especially in its charter [i.e., the Gospels], which I hold to be its purest expression, it [Christianity] completely agrees with realized philosophy) the final purpose, especially in the record of it, which I hold as the purest,[24] is that people come to *eternal life*,[25] to having this life and its joy and blessedness in themselves and out of themselves.[26]

In what then does eternal life consist? "This is eternal life," it says, "that they *know [recognize]*[27] you . . . and [him] whom you have sent"[28] (for us, this means the primordial law and its eternal image); merely *know [recognize]*. Yet, indeed, this recognition not only leads to life, instead it *is* life. Thus, from that time on, through all the centuries and in all forms of Christianity, and consistently with this principle, *faith* in the teaching that true knowledge of the supersensible is the main and essential thing, has been insisted upon. Only in the last half a century, after the almost total decline of true scholarship and deep thinking, have people changed Christianity into a doctrine and ethics of prudence.

This doctrine has not forgotten to teach that in genuine, truly living knowledge right conduct[29] arises on its own, and that, even if he wishes to do

so, the one in whom the light has inwardly dawned cannot fail to shine outwardly. Our philosophy forgets it just as little. Yet, there is a great difference
in doing right from such different sources. Doing right from self-interested
cleverness, or from self-regard arising as a result of a categorical imperative,
yields cold, dead fruit, lacking blessing for both agent and the recipient. Now,
as ever, the former hates the law, and would much prefer that it not exist.
Therefore, happiness with himself and his act never arises. The latter cannot
animate and bring to life that which fundamentally has no life. Only when
right action arises from clear insight does it occur with love and pleasure. Only
then does the act, self-sufficient and requiring nothing else, reward itself.

Discussion.[30]

CHAPTER 26

Twenty-sixth Lecture

Monday, June 4, 1804

Honored Guests:

Absolute knowing has been presented objectively and in its content, and if that were the only issue, our work would be completed. However, the question still remains how *we* have become this knowing, since we have become it; and, if this has further conditions, what are they? The first [is] the transcendental, in all its determinations, the second [is] ordinary. Our proper standpoint [is] the reciprocal determination of both.[1]

Based on our previous experience, I assume that we are sufficiently constrained by the shortness of time from easily comprehending the difficulties. Therefore, today we will pass immediately into the indicated central point. In the subsequent sessions, this will make it easier to fill out the remaining gaps between the center and the designated end-points. I tell you in advance that this investigation is important and raises entirely new topics.[2]

1. How, I say, have we arrived here? It is quite clear that we do not want to see the steps that we have taken historically retold, and that this entire "how" contains the *de jure* question rather than any historical one. Without further ado, it is clear that, in the knowing just presented, *we* have, and are the same as, absolute knowing only on the condition that we are *certain* of this, or that we are formally certain in general and that we express this formal certainty within ourselves in fulfilling this knowing. Otherwise, it could always[3] be certain for someone else without being so for us, and *we* would in no way have elevated ourselves to the absolute, although we are able to repeat[4] the word quite properly. This is the first point.[5]

The content presented should itself be the expression of absolute knowing, or certainty. Therefore, thought in relation to what has gone before, the following two modes of inference are possible. *We* are certain, and so what we say in this situation of certainty is *certain*, i.e., it is an expression of inward certainty; or, this is certain, we see into it; therefore we are certain, or expressing

---

This lecture begins at GA II, 8, pp. 382–383.

certainty. Whichever of the premises one chooses, one presupposes that the nature of certainty is *known*. Without doubt, we will carry out one of the two inferences. Hence, we must presuppose that the essence of knowing is known.

2. If it is known. Previously we designated it as resting in itself, thus a oneness of qualities. We cannot assume it here as this, since this [384–385] oneness has been completely lost to us in the foregoing. Indeed, it has been lost in relation to an inner essential quality, as in an image, or in the law of an imaging, which excluded, in the second power, all variability and hence all qualitative similarity. Here we must characterize certainty with this higher concept. Thus, it is essential, immanent self-enclosure (as absolute being was previously seen to be).

3. Now, for the judgment that we wish to pass, that "we are certain," we presuppose a primordial concept, or description, of this immanent self-enclosure. How is this concept or description primordially possible? That means, the law for such a description should be presented, i.e., be understood {*einge-sehen*} by us simply as a primordial description.—[6]

Since in fact I rise here to a higher term than all those presented so far, I cannot connect what is to be presented to these, nor can I explain it from them. Rather, I can rely only on your creative intuition, which I merely hope to guide. Everything will become completely clear in context, if only one can make a beginning toward clarity based on the parts.[7]

I say that, *description*, as such, is inward, *immanent projection*[8] of the described. Above all, this in no way means an objective projection through a gap. Instead, [it means] a projection that recognizes itself as a[9] projection (i.e., as something superficial) immediately in itself and negates itself as such; and so posits something described only through this self-negation, an inwardness. In a word, it is just pure ideal *seeing*, or *intuition*,[10] permeating itself simply as such. I do not say that this permeation exists in itself. Instead, I commend it to you, as the "We" of the science of knowing, as that through which alone you become this "We." You permeate it, if you grasp it as self-negating, yet positing in this negation something described, positing itself and us as the external, and so negated. "*Seeing* X" means not regarding the seeing as X; thus negating it.[11] In this negation, seeing becomes a seeing,[12] and something seen arises simply if it abstracts from X. This, which must now be grasped in intuition much more deeply than I can express it in words, is what I want to point out. It is the inner essence of *pure seeing*, as such, which we have actually realized here in its essence, as surely as you have followed my intuition. This is the first point.[13]

Here now should be a description of certainty, as absolute enclosure within itself. If we just stay with the elicited intuition of pure seeing, or the purely formal description, [386–387] then we can derive from it alone this content: that it is a description of an enclosure within itself. *Being* is what it intuitively projects in this negation of itself in which it still *exists* {*ist*}. Because it projects this within, and by means of, its own ineradicable essence, this essence is an *expression*, an intrinsically self-expressive being, i.e., an intrinsically living and powerful being.

(Because I think that I can cast the highest clarity over the whole, I make the following remarks:

1. Seeing (which reveals itself intrinsically as material and qualitative external-ity and emanance, as anyone can discover for himself, if he notices what *see-ing* means), thereby annuls itself in the face of absolute immanent being. I do not say, and have not proven, that it does this on any particular grounds, but, according to the presupposition, it has done so in our own person.
2. Yet in this self-disclosure in essence and self-negation, it *is*, because we continue to know; and it exists with its unchangeable *basic property*, as expression. Hence, the being in front of which it negates itself is none other than its own higher being, in the presence of which the lower, which is to be objectified as seeing, vanishes. This, its being, therefore carries its pri-mordial feature, expression, which, since it has now become absolute, expresses itself.
3. Therefore, when it negates itself *as seeing*,[14] seeing becomes actual seeing, inwardly and truly effective, or, as is better here, pure light. Thus, pure light does not *come to be* as absolutely inward self-expression, power, and life, instead it just is. It emerges only in insight; and in that case it comes to be through seeing's absolute self-negation in the presence of being.
4. To what extent then, and on what grounds, is seeing negated? Answer: because it is the *expression*[15] of another and is set over against another as what it sees (which other, as a result of its own self-negation, lies within see-ing itself), therefore, what is negated is simply absolute intuition as such.
5. This intuition is likewise present in our recently generated insight into absolute light as a living self-expression, and it is to be negated in relation to inner essence and truth, despite the fact that it may always factically per-sist. We could point out its origin, and we have done so in the third remark. It lies in this insight's genesis from the negation of another.
6. Now, to make a review of the foregoing. The insight that was so significant at the end of our first part—that being was an absolutely self-enclosed, liv-ing, and powerful *esse*—was nothing other than merely the factically fulfilled absolute insight whose genesis we have realized here. [388–389] Indeed, it had come about factically in just the way we have understood {*eingesehen*} here that it had to come about, by abstracting from everything, or factically negating all intuition. Thus, our requirement at that time to abstract, as regards validity, from the objectivity that did not factically weaken as a result of intuition, was completely correct and has now been proved.)

We continue, and on good grounds we stay with the standpoint originally held: what seeing intuitively projects in this self-negation, and has been seen into by us as intuitively projecting, is *being*; and a powerful being at that. However, being as such, or objectivity, is self-enclosure. Moreover, a living self-enclosure *{in sich Geschlossenheit}* (= living self-enclosing *{in sich Schliessen}*) posits a principle of coming out of oneself, which is annulled by the former. Therefore, this principle is better named a "drive."

And so we would have realized what we sought, a *description* (i.e., liveliness and construction of certainty) as a self-enclosure based simply on the closer and deeper description of *seeing*, of ideality, and of intuition as such.[16]

In this description, four interrelated terms *{eine Vierfachheit der Glieder}* disclose themselves, and this enumeration can clarify for you what has been presented. First, [there is] seeing in *its essence*, as absolute *externality in relation*[17] to another, thereby as self-negating, and, in this negation, regarding this other as inwardly[18] self-enclosed being. This yields two terms.[19] Things would have rested with this pair of terms, if we had not added that, despite this partially valid self-negation, seeing continues in the insight into being's necessary arising, and remains what it ineradicably is, an inward externality.[20] Therefore, being must intrinsically carry its characteristics of life and externality. Pursue this a bit deeper. Strictly speaking, here there is a two-fold view of seeing, from which there follows a two-fold view of being; or perhaps the other way around. Thus, [there is] seeing, as intuition, which therefore intuits itself, from which mere dead being follows; and [there is] seeing in its inward essence as absolute externality, whence follow the potency and life of being.[21] It is clear that, in being, both should exist together completely in one, a living self-enclosure, or an intrinsic self-occlusion, and therefore being must likewise merge into knowing, from which it has been deduced. A self-negation resulting from the construction of its essence as ____ , and a projection [390–391] of this essence into being as a result of its negation of itself. Finally, the fourth term, the principle of coming out of oneself through the self-enclosure's liveliness and energy, which is simultaneously posited in its being and negated in its effect—this principle is immediately clear and needs no further proof.

It is not difficult to add the fifth term, which should belong here according to historically well-known rules so that a complete synthesis can arise. That is to say, the arising and persistence of these four terms in our insight depend on the fact that one understands seeing in its essence as externality, as we have understood it, and that one negates it as absolute immanence (that is, as intrinsically valid) in the face of the recognized being. Still, [one must] observe it as itself factically enduring above and within being. This seemed to us a possible insight, and, if it is brought about, an absolutely evident one, which in general we freely produced and to which we were summoned. Further, the continuance of these four interconnected terms as a whole (I say "as a whole" because if one is posited, the others follow as well) depends on this, that within the insight that we have described (and which is properly a description of certainty) one preserves what appears there too as dependent on our freedom.

Enough about this. I commend it to your memory for future use.

1. Prevented by time from introducing new syntheses, I will merely prepare you for them. If being's living self-enclosing {*in sich Schliessen*}, which we mentioned, really is literally a living *enclosing*, as we express the matter, then it posits an *act*, and indeed an absolute act *qua* act, an effect of the drive to come out of itself. Now it should annul this latter without resistance. Both can very well be united if we consider that this entire "livingness" is only a result of seeing's inner expression and projection, as such and as intuition. This latter has been overthrown as valid in itself, although factically it cannot be eradicated. Therefore, the former can always exist and remain in factical appearance, while in truth the second does not occur in any way. In this way, the unification of truth in itself and its appearance first provides again a true ground for the oneness of quality. Previously, we assumed this only factically, then lost it in the face of a higher truth, and now have been working to reinstate it. The drive for coming out of oneself [392–393] always emerges in appearance and is struck down; undoubtedly, it can form {*bilden*} the appearance of freedom and genesis themselves, but it does not enter into truth. Just so this drive provides the true real ground for quantities.[22] Through the unification of these quantities with the principle of quality, we hope to arrive at a deduction of the phenomenon of ordinary knowing's primordial form.

2. This being, then, resides simply in absolute seeing itself and it is to be sought only there. As much as in *appearance*, it does so in the *truth*, which can of course remain inconceivable and indescribable in its oneness. [It remains so] not simply because it lies outside of knowing, which is the old fundamental error; [it does so] rather because absolute knowing itself is inconceivable, and absolute conceiving is by no means the same as absolute knowing. According to the standpoint we have adopted, then, where should we look for it? This clearly confirmed itself in the insight we completed previously.—For no reason, we saw very directly on the basis of the matter itself that seeing is an externality. We perceived equally immediately that this was clear to us, or that we ourselves saw in the very seeing of seeing, and in the insight into the latter; it was certain for us. Yet, certainty remains to be described, and it is described as an inner self-enclosing {*Sich-schliessen*} against the principle of coming out of oneself. It has come out of there, seeing sees itself, coming out as coming out. It sees itself just as externality; it was enclosure {*Geschlossenheit*}. Everything was one in the same oneness; simply seeing into self, which cannot be described further, but can only be lived. Hence, it was actually not just a re-description, like the first one presented, rather it is the primordial

description, i.e., authentic completion of the one *certainty*, or of knowing. For the reasons given, we could later also add to it being arising from negation, which of course lies within knowing itself as a part of its original description, along with that which flows further from that in the preceding synthesis. But the last thing which flows from it was the necessity that knowing hold and sustain itself within its one unchangeable standpoint, which now for the first time fully points out knowing's independence, which does not surprise us. The one knowing would be completely enclosed by means of this complete synthesis in its formal oneness, and by means of the multiplicity which proceeds from its essence, if this entire reflection did not appear to be freely created and (if we wish to pay attention to ourselves) appear as objectified by us ourselves—as was just mentioned and as it consistently seems to us. *Objectivity* and *genesis*[23] are entirely one, as we have seen previously. However, genesis is this inner externalization and principle of this oneness. Hence, if our appearance is correct (and it must [394–395] of course hold good and be explained as an appearance), there must be yet another specific manifesting principle, to which everything just recapitulated is related as to a oneness that contains it all. It can only be derived from this as the enclosing oneness, and this, as enclosing oneness, can only be derived from it.

CHAPTER 27

Twenty-seventh Lecture

Wednesday, June 6, 1804

Honored Guests:

Our continuing task is to show that, if transcendental knowing (= the existence of absolute knowing) is to arise, then another, ordinary knowing must be presupposed.

The permanent result of the last hour is this: seeing permeating itself as *seeing*[1] necessarily surrenders itself as something *independent*,[2] and posits an absolute *being*. The latter enters into a further synthesis, which yields a description of certainty as an enclosure into itself.

I presented this as the center, and did not fail to recall that continuity of connection had not been achieved from there out to the endpoints, but rather that gaps remained. Today's project is to fill these gaps from the midpoint outward, according to absolute knowing in its oneness. Clearly, this requires new terms that are not to be developed from the foregoing. Meanwhile, this new investigation can thus be tied to the previous one. Undoubtedly, it was we, scientists of knowing, who created this insight into the essence of seeing, and therefore the other as well, that seeing is necessarily a form of intuition, etc. I also add that another entirely different insight, which we have overlooked, is contained in this mastering of seeing's essence, and we will present it now.

1. Namely, I say: if *seeing* is *posited as seeing*, then it follows that seeing actually takes place; or, seeing *necessarily* sees. So that you do not overlook this sentence's importance because of its simplicity, I can justifiably make it more difficult, by therefore adding the following preliminary remarks. Evidently, this sentence is the completion of what is required, but never achieved, in the scholastic proof of God's existence as the most real being—a proof with which you are all familiar—to infer the existence of a thing from the bare thought of it. Seeing posited as seeing means that it is thought, i.e., formed and constructed in its inner essence, just as we have done in the last hour; and this is done hypothetically, as follows immediately from this construction, without

---

This lecture begins at GA II, 8, pp. 396–397.

further ado. Because, from positing what something is, nothing at all is established regarding its existence or non-existence, and instead, it remains hypothetical. As surely as this latter alone is posited, and if "seeing-into" and certainty are enclosed in that, nothing can be said about it definitively.[3] However, we reasoned as follows: "*Seeing*[4] *necessarily* occurs, and so its existence is positively established and expressed." This is the first point.[5]

[398–399] Thus, we genetically derive *being there {Dasein}*, the true inner essence of existence *{Existenz}*. Providing this derivation has been our task, and indeed, the sole immediately derivable existence is that of seeing. This is the second point.[6]

2. For either the proof in its full significance or the insight intended here to arise requires strenuous attention. For instance, one could well say life lives, which is of course correct; but whether life is situated in *seeing*, completely as such, as we have most intimately intuited it in ourselves, that is the question.—I handle it like this: seeing's self-permeation is an absolute negation of itself as independent, and a [matter of] relating itself to something external. It exists only in this self-negation and relating, and otherwise not. Yet this negating and relating is an act that exists *{ist}* just in itself and in its immediate completion. Hence, it is necessary, immediate, and actual; and if the whole is to be, then it must be and exist. Seeing cannot be posited, except as immediately living, powerful, and active.

3. The insight that we have just completed is now the absolute insight of reason, that is, absolute reason itself. In this insight, we have immediately become absolute reason, and have dissolved into it. Let us analyze this insight more closely, and with it reason as well. First, reflect purely on the last thing, the insight itself, abstracting from the way we came to it: it itself is a *seeing*, insight, thus something external. It is a seeing *of seeing*,[7] thus seeing itself as existent, absolute and substantial, a seeing grounded in itself and as such self-expressive, [a matter of] certainty and self-enclosure by virtue of inner necessity. Thus, as a result of its absolute inner essence, it is a light that determines and declares itself, that simply by itself absolutely cannot not be, and absolutely cannot not be what it is, just *self-positing*. Self-positing, I say, but not *as itself.* We have added the last in a way that must now be explained. Reason's absolute insight *sees*, just the seeing under discussion, but not immediately again its first-named seeing, because this is an absolute insight. Proposition: the absolute insight of reason brings absolute existence *{Dasein}* (of seeing, in fact) with itself. It does so immediately [in the course of] performing this action, and as the expression of doing so. Said differently, absolute reason permeates itself as reason, in exactly the way we have indicated, as absolute effect. The proposition is important: I think [it] is immediately clear, and if for this one or that one it is not, I can help in the following way. In the previous hour, formal seeing permeated itself as something [400–401]

absolutely outward, negated itself therein, and thereby posited being; not immediately, but rather by means of _____ , etc. It is otherwise here in absolute reason; this happens without any mediation. Thereby, reason shows itself in us, as reason's reason, thus as absolute reason in this self-permeation and being permeated by itself.—A *doctrine of reason {Vernunftlehre}*, through itself, from itself, and in itself, as this duality *{Duplicität}* can be expressed. A doctrine of reason, as the first and highest part of the science of knowing, which does not *become*, but rather *is* unconditionally in itself, and is that which it is.

Let's go to the other side of this insight, that is to the genetic aspect. On the condition that seeing has been permeated in its inner essence, reason posits absolute existence, and permeates itself as positing. I ask: were we intended to assume a seeing and a permeated-ness of this seeing, apart from what we have here in reason itself and on its basis? I hope not, because then we would have two absolutes, which certainly could not be brought together. Thus, this itself is the expression of reason, grounded in reason itself, occurring in order to arrive at its result of positing being and permeating itself in this positing. Therefore, reason is intrinsically genetic; and it is intrinsically completely consolidated, necessary, and lawful in unchanging oneness. However, it is genetic insofar as it *is* actually and truly living, and expresses itself actively. Now, however, it *exists* necessarily and cannot not be, because it is absolutely self-directing existence and authentic existence. Therefore, it is inwardly and secretly what it asserts outwardly about external seeing, and its inwardly grounded existence and life consists in just this [act of] speaking about seeing. But further:

4. [To say] that reason itself is the ground of its own proper existence, here inward, living, and active, would mean that it posits its life and existence unconditionally and inseparably from itself. No living and existence is possible apart from this one, and it is impossible to escape it. Now, however, although we say that it cannot be escaped, we ourselves have obviously done so. Consequently, reason's genetic life, which we have described in positing seeing's absolute existence in case this latter is merely thought, is still not reason's primordial and absolute existence. That it is not this, also follows for another reason. We appear to ourselves as having completed the very insight just completed, with *freedom*. We indeed are reason, because reason is simply the I, and cannot be anything else than I, according to the proof conducted long since. Thus "we seem," or "reason seems," are completely synonymous. Now we appeared here [402–403] actually as the ground of the insight's existence, but not as absolute ground of its actuality, but rather as the ground of its possibility, or its free ground. Thus, we are only a mediate, factical appearance and insight, and hence not absolute reason.—This mere possibility is also evident in another way. Evidently, this entire insight appears as the *reconstruction* of an original construction in reason, and we objectify this primor-

dial reason, along with its construction. We appear to ourselves as yielding ourselves to the original law of reason by a free act, and now, gripped by it, as made into manifestness = certainty. This surrender and this manifestness appear to us as able to be repeated indefinitely. Further, the following in particular should be noted and made more precise. The premise for the absolutely completed, rational insight into seeing's inner essence as something absolutely external (despite the fact that we do not let it serve as an absolute premise, but have instead derived it from pure reason itself), is still an intrinsic genetic power for the rational insight into existence, which has been brought about. It conditions the latter just as the latter has conditioned it. Hence once again the circle between reciprocal conditionings remains, and thus the old hypothetical character. The absolute condition has by no means been disclosed. That hypotheticalness remains can also be shown in another way, and it is interesting and instructive to give this demonstration.—"If seeing is, then thus and so are as well, and from this follows _____, etc." Precisely, therefore, what lies in the conclusion is presupposed hypothetically in the premise, and so it holds only on condition that the first is given. Now, to be sure, we say that *absolute reason*[8] posits it; but it is only *we* who say it, that is, arbitrariness and freedom. Of course, reason speaks in the connection; but we have provided it with speech in the first place, and should not trust it. Reason itself must start talking directly.

5. In what we have achieved so far, we have at least learned where this might be discovered. "Reason itself is immediately and unconditionally the ground of an *existence*, indeed of *its own* existence, since it cannot be of any other." This means: this existence *{Dasein}* has no further ground. It is not possible, as before, to provide a genetic premise, on the basis of which it can be explained further, since otherwise it would not be grounded in absolute reason, but in a reason that would have to be interrogated in its turn. Instead, we must simply say, it is grounded in reason. [It is] a pure absolute fact.

Now just what is this fact? It has accompanied us all along, and thus in this last investigation as well. It is expressed in the formula: "Reason is the absolute ground of its own existence." If anyone does [404–405] not yet see it, this is because it is too close to him. We ourselves have continually objectified reason, and therefore posited its existence, as existence, in the "form of outer existence." Now we are reason. Therefore, in us ourselves, that is in itself, absolute reason is the absolute ground of its existence *{Daseins}*, that is, of its existence *{Existenz}* as such. This is a fact from which we cannot ever escape, and that cannot be explained or understood from any further genetic premise, as must be the case if it[9] is to be an expression of absolute reason. (Someone has encountered the enduring objectification of the absolute, and has opined that therefore there is no absolute. How could that be, if, as is the case here, true absoluteness is not found in what is objectified, nor in the objectifying [agent], but rather in the immediate event of *objectifying* itself? From time to time, one sufficiently remembers and makes clear the fact that the absolute must not be sought outside the absolute, and especially that we would certainly never *grasp* the absolute, if we did not even live and conduct it.)

6. Now in this case we are not just the bare fact, but instead we are simultaneously the insight that this fact is reason's pure original expression and life; that the fact is origin and the origin, fact. The characteristic mark of the science of knowing consists purely in this synthesis. The bare fact, as fact, yields ordinary knowing. So initially, this self-presentation of reason itself occurs *through reason*,[10] we say: for us, then, how is the latter reason? I think, if we view it properly, [it is] objectified in the same way as the former, and undoubtedly the same one reason as the former. Thus—our life, or the life of reason, does not escape from its own self-objectification.[11] And that which is one implicitly (and probably for ordinary knowing as well) divides itself within the science of knowing's insight into a twofold appearance. Indeed, this division arises only from the *insight*,[12] or the genesis of that which in itself is an absolute fact. This is the first point.[13] Further, and most significantly—we have not just found this insight (that reason alone is the absolute ground of its existence) immediately in our proposition. We could not have done so. This insight alone is what has turned us into scientists of knowing. If we had, the highest fact would have required another genetic premise above itself; and this in turn another, and so on to infinity. Then our system would have met the fate of other systems and found no beginning. Instead of that, we have found it in the more profound insight carried out at the beginning of today's lecture. Now it is merely applied as a universal and absolutely valid proposition. [406–407] Hence, the absolute insight, on which everything depends here, our science as well, is possible only through a deeper one, which likewise is possible only through another, etc. In this way, the genuine ground for the connection between knowing's various basic determinations is opened up and made accessible. The deduction can start from the principle: if the insight obtained in this way—i.e., the science of knowing—is possible in its principles, then must ____, etc. This was the second point.[14] Finally, reason is the ground of its own existence *as*[15] reason. For, note well, this and nothing else was the absolute fact with which we are concerned. However, it is so only in the insight we have created, because it is duplicated (i.e., is reason as reason) only within this insight. Therefore, this very insight, or the science of knowing, is reason's immediate expression and life: the single life of reason unfolded immediately in itself and permeated by itself. Precisely because, just as one lives in it there is seeing, or it appears, thus reason itself lives and appears. In its existence, the insight appears to be possible only by means of freedom; it is also thus actually and in fact. That is, in this way reason shows[16] itself as freely self-expressing. That freedom should appear is simply its law and inward

essence. If it appears as conditioned, then it actually is so; that is, it must appear thus, as it is conditioned, etc. This is all unconditionally *true* and *certain*, but [it is] true and certain to the exact extent that it lies within reason as its necessary appearance and expression. By no means is it as certain as reason *in itself*, to which it in no way comes, except in its expression. The task on which the truthfulness and certainty of our insight depends is simply this: to see everything in its context, and to articulate it in this context. *Appearing*[17] truly exists when it is conceived as the absolute appearing and self-expression of absolute reason, and without the latter qualification, it is not true. It is true that reason appears[18] thus and so, e.g., as inwardly free, only insofar as it also appears as inwardly necessary and actually existing. Without this qualification, it is not true, etc.

Absolute appearance, or genesis, has been presented. The law for deriving it, and for deducing inferences from it, has also been presented, and the deduction can proceed. With this, I stop at the border of a *philosophia prima* (I would have wished to regard these lectures as being this), [408–409] presenting only appearance's first basic distinction, which in its oneness constitutes the concept of pure appearing as such, without any further determination of the latter. In this work, I can either go to work on the details (in which case I will not end this week), or I can present the main point briefly and forcefully in a single lecture. To do the latter, I will need more time for the preparation of this lecture. I prefer the latter, and ask you to permit me to defer tomorrow's lecture, so that I can end on Friday.

CHAPTER 28

Twenty-eighth Lecture

Friday, June 8, 1804

Honored Guests:

Here is where we stood: reason is the unconditional ground of its own existence and its own objectivity for itself, and its primordial life consists just in this. I assume that this intrinsically dull sentence has become familiar to you in all its importance in the preceding lectures, especially the last.

Without doubt, we see {*sehen ein*}[1] this, ourselves intuiting and objectifying[1] reason—as the logical subject of the sentence, which according to us should now further objectify itself—as its predicate. Numerically reason occurs here *twice*, once *in us* and once outside *of us*. I ask, which one is the sole absolute? That is, does *our* projection perchance result from the primordial projection of the external reason, about which we have been speaking, so that we ourselves *said* what it is that *we were*? Or is the reason projected outwardly the result of its own immediate self-projection in us? In a word, reason exists in duality, as subject and object, both as absolute. This ambiguity must be removed.

1. We can *ground*[2] this entire existence most effectively with the formula already previously used and proven: reason *makes itself*[3] unconditionally intuiting. I say "it *makes itself*,"[4] and not "it *is intuiting*."[5] It positively does not arise with intuition's being, and to the extent that it appears to arise there, we must abstract from it. I say, "it makes itself *unconditionally*";[6] i.e., as we express ourselves meanwhile: this making is in no way accidental for it. Instead, it is entirely and completely necessary. If its being is posited, the latter [intuiting] is posited as well, and being unfolds in it. This is its proper, immediate, and inseparable effect. (All these propositions are easy, if one just takes them up in the strength of energetic thinking. Taken weakly and inconsistently, they are confusing and lead to nothing.)

NB: pure, intrinsically clear and transparent *intellectual activity*[7] consists in this "*making* itself unconditionally *intuitive*"[8] in genuine vivacity and exis-

---

This lecture begins at GA II, 8, pp. 410–411.

tence. It is raised above all objectifying intuition as itself the latter's ground, and it completely fills the gap between subject and object, thereby negating both.[9]

Further: This *self-making*[10] is just *effectiveness {Effectivität}*, inner life and activity; indeed, the *activity of self-making*,[11] [is] thus a making oneself into *activity*.[12] Here arise at one and the same time an absolute primordial activity and movement, and also a making (or copying) of this primordial activity as its *image*. (The [412–413] former fundamentally explains the self-making and presenting manifestness that has grasped us in every investigation; the latter explains our reconstruction of this [manifestness] as it has also consistently appeared to us.) Now, though, we have to stand neither in one nor the other, but rather in the midpoint between both, that is in the absolutely inwardly effective self-making, real through itself, without any other making or intuition. We must abstract from the fact that we go on to objectify this midpoint as well, and should in no way admit the validity of that intuition. Because otherwise we have in no way explained the subjective and the objective, but only added it factically. This was the first point.[13]

Reason is this, as certainly as it *is*: but it *is* unconditionally. Now, reason is an absolute, immediate, *self-making*; thus, it sets itself down as *existing*, objectively, and as *making itself*, objectively. The permanent object and the permanent subject, which initially come into question; *neither one [exists] by way of the other*, as we initially thought, but instead both [exist] by means of the same original essential effect in the midpoint. This was the second point.[14]

Now, the effect through which it [i.e., reason] throws down *{hinwirft}* a permanent object is the same one through which it threw down *{hinwarf}* objective living, and therefore the primordial construction, *objective* reason, devolves onto this objective life. In addition, the effect through which it threw down the persisting subject is the same one through which it threw down imaging as imaging, and so this imaging devolves onto the *subject*. This was the third point.[15]

Result: reason, as an immediate, internal, self-intuiting *making*, and to that extent an absolute oneness of its effects—breaks down within the *living* of this making into being and making; into the *making of being* as made and not made; and into the *[making of] making* as likewise primordial, existing, and not primordial, i.e., copied. This disjunction, expressed just as we have expressed it, is what is absolutely original.

2. Now, in the business we have just concluded, *we* indeed have objectified and intuited the one reason as the inwardly self-intuiting making; but we realize that we must abstract from this, if we want to recognize reason as *the one*. We are also aware that we can indeed abstract from it. That is, although we are not able to exempt ourselves from it factically, we can indeed think of it as not valid in itself. In this way, reason is *actually seen into*. That is, as the primordial *self*-making, it fully merges into our imitative image *{nachmachenden Bilde}*.[16]

Therefore, it is the very *same relation*[17] immediately in us that we have just presented objectively. We, or reason, no longer stand either in that objective reason nor in subjective reason; since [414–415] we must just abstract from both— instead [we, or reason, stand] purely in the *midpoint* of the absolutely effective *self-making*.[18] In the science of knowing, reason is completely, immediately alive, opened in itself, and has become an inward "I," [both] periphery and center,— since this is the site of the science of knowing—as it had to come; and all this has happened completely through abstraction. Absolute reason is *absolute*[19] (accomplished) thinking *{Intelligieren}* of oneself.[20] Thinking oneself *{Selbstintelligieren}* as such, is reason.

I can then objectify this very *absoluteness*[21] of reason (or the science of knowing), produced in this way, or I can not objectify it, because I abstract from the objectivity, which factically ceases without my help. If I do the latter, then everything ends here, and reason is enclosed in itself. If I abandon myself to the former, then I give myself up to a *mere fact* that is completely cut off and *without any principle*.[22] It does not arise out of reason, since only those things derived here arise from it; just as little does it arise from something else, since it is simply absolutely factically given.[23] Therefore, it is completely inconceivable, i.e., without a principle; and, once surrendered to it, nothing remains for me except just to abandon myself to it. It is pure, simple appearance.

3. I *want* to surrender to it. Now if I objectify this absoluteness, then it appears to me as an *objective*[24] situation, to which *I* raise *myself*[25] through *free abstraction* from my initially objectifying reason. "*I* want to surrender,"[26] I say;[27] hence, within appearance I find an objectively complete "I" as the original ground and original condition for this situation. (Consciousness, and *self*-consciousness, as the original fact underlying all other facticity. The thing whose validity has so far been completely denied [is] once more derived and justified.) From the preceding knowledge of reason, I know very well what the "I" is in itself. I need not to learn it from appearance, which would not give me any information about its essence. It is the *result*[28] of reason's self-making. Consequently—a very important conclusion, and the only possible one if appearance itself is to be traced back to reason—appearance itself is inaccessible only to me, to the "I" projected absolutely through appearance; it itself is a self-making of reason, of reason's primordial effect, and indeed as an *I*. (The imprint of reason's effect rests solely in the I, as such).[29]

However, a. that I must simply abstract, if this consciousness is to arise, and b. that I could either do this or not, are found purely in *appearance*, that is, in reason's effect, which is inaccessible to me only in its principle. Thus, that I am *free*.

4. What arises through abstraction for me, as a result of the assertion of appearance? Reason as *absolute*[30] oneness: this arises, and appears *as* arising. However, [416–417] all arising appears as such only with its opposite. The

opposite of absolute oneness, which in this oppositional relationship in turn becomes qualitative oneness, is absolute *multiplicity* and *variability*. Therefore, if this oneness is to appear genetically, then consciousness, from which one must abstract as the beginning point, must itself appear as absolutely changeable and multiform. This is the first fundamental principle. It is also the first application of our basic principle: if the science of knowing is to arise (i.e., if the science of knowing is to be precisely an *arising*,[31] an origin) then such and such a consciousness must be posited.

5. The I of consciousness in appearance is an inconceivable effect of reason, above all materially. This inconceivability as such enters immediately into the primordial consciousness, which genesis presupposes, which is unconditionally changeable, and which exhausts itself in infinite multiplicity. It does so explicitly as inconceivable, i.e., as *real*. Reality in appearance is the same as the primordial effect of reason—the one eternally selfsame.[32]

6. The I of consciousness is reason's effect in the conceptual form of this effect, which we conceived earlier in the four presented terms. So far, we have presented these four terms collectively only insofar as we have penetrated reason as an inner oneness. As a genetic abstraction, [this oneness] presupposes external oneness just as before, and as a primordial effect of reason within experience, [it] presupposes inner multiplicity.[33]—However, the inner multiplicity and separateness must necessarily consist in the lack of correlation in realizing these four terms, thus in their apprehension as separate principles. Then, in an absolutely necessary differentiation of principles, we would have four fundamental principles:

1. In the enduring[34] *object*, and indeed in what is absolutely transient: the principle of *sensibility*,[35] belief in *nature*,[36] materialism. 2. In the enduring *subject*: belief in personality, and, given the variety of personalities, the identity and equality of personality, the principle of *legality*.[37] 3. Holding to the absolutely real forming[38] of the subject, which, since this forming is connected to the enduring subject, conceptually makes the latter into a oneness, leaving multiplicity just to the former.[39] [This is] the standpoint of *morality*, as an activity that proceeds purely from the enduring I of consciousness, continuing through infinite time. 4. Holding to the absolute imaging and living of the absolute *object*,[40] which [418–419] becomes a oneness for the same reason introduced in 3. above. The standpoint of religion, as belief in a God, who alone is true for all lifetimes, and alone is inwardly living.[41]

Now all of these standpoints are effects of reason, although not realized as such in their principle, and reason is completely as it is, wherever it is. Therefore, it is evident that, simply as effects of reason, the three other standpoints insert themselves immediately into each of the four, without any apparent free act of abstraction. Yet they do so colored by, and in the spirit of, the dominant principle. Thus, among religious people morality exists as well, but not, as with those having the latter as their principle, as their proper work. Instead, it is a divine work in them, which brings about in them will and fulfillment, as well as the resulting desire and pleasure. Other people also exist besides themselves, and a sensible world. Yet, they do so always only as an emanation of one divine life. Likewise, too, God exists in morality as a principle, but not for his own sake; instead, so that he maintains the moral law. If they had no moral law, they would not need a God. Further, other people exist apart from themselves, but only just so that they can be, or become, moral, and they have a sensible world simply as a sphere for moral action. Likewise, God is present for the legal standpoint, but he exists only in order to manage the higher police work that lies beyond the reach of human policing. Legality also has a morality; however, it coincides with outward integrity in relation to others, and ends there. Finally [there is] a sensible world, for the purpose of civic industry. Fourth, God surely has a place within the principle of sensibility, if it is left to itself and does not become unnaturally depraved through perverse speculation. That is, God exists so that he can give us food in due season.[42] With this comes a certain morality, namely to spread one's pleasures wisely, so that one always has something more to enjoy, especially not to ruin things with this God who provides. Finally, there is also something analogous to reason and spirituality and that is also to enjoy these pleasures in the right order and with prudence. Hence, there are four basic factors in each standpoint (five if you also add the unifying principle). Together these yield twenty main factors and primordial fundamental determinations of knowing; and, if you add the science of knowing's indicated fivefold synthesis, which we have just completed, this becomes twenty-five.

It has already been proved that this division into twenty-five forms coincides with the absolute breakdown of the real, [420–421] or [with the breakdown] into absolute multiplicity of that effect of reason, which is immediately inaccessible in its oneness. This follows because multiplicity in general arises out of the genetic nature of reflection on oneness. However, this reflection on oneness immediately breaks down into five-foldness. Therefore, the manifold from which it is necessary to abstract breaks down in the form of fivefoldness, by the same rule of reason.

Above, we have made it immediately clear factically that this entire consciousness is posited and determined solely by the genesis of the science of knowing. If we abstracted from our rational insight, as a condition objectifying itself immediately in us, then things would rest there, and we would not attain anything further. The insight into the law of all consciousness arose for us only insofar as we reflected on it, and thus posited the science of knowing as genesis, as something that ought to arise, because of our absolute decree.[43]

The task we had assumed is therefore completely finished, and our science has closed. The principles have been presented with the greatest possible clarity and determinateness. Anyone who has truly understood and penetrated the principles can carry out the schematism on his own. Making many words does not contribute to clarity; it can even obscure things for the best minds. Perhaps there will be time and opportunity this coming winter for applying these principles to particular standpoints, for example to religion, which always should remain the highest, not only in the partiality and sensible form in which it was grasped previously, but in our science's inherent spirit, and from there to the doctrine of virtue, and of rights. Until then, I ask for your benevolent remembrance for myself and for science, and I give you my thanks for the new courage and the new happy prospects for science, which you have given me so amply in the course of these lectures.

Appendix

Fichte's Letter to Appia:
Together with Aphorisms on the Essence of Philosophy as a Science

[*GA* III, 5, pp. 244–248]

June 23, 1804
Berlin

Fichte to (Paul Joseph?) Appia[1] (in Frankfurt am Main?)

Enclosed, my highly esteemed sir and friend, you will find a concept of transcendental philosophy, and of the labors of Kant and myself on its behalf, as sharply delineated as one can make it, without entering the subject itself.

In order not to leave this concept completely empty and uncomprehended, the following as well:

1. in relation with §2, that one puts oneself into consciousness in a truly living way through an extraordinary effort of attention. In ordinary reflection, which I call "faded," consciousness is immediately objectified and set over against us. In that way, arises the illusion reproached in §1, of our spirit, soul, or whatever other name this ghost might have. And in this way one never arrives at even the presentiment[2] of the transcendental organ in us. One must become vividly aware that in consciousness one is oneself immediately this very consciousness, not more and not less.

2. in relation with §4, and the empirical domain *{Empirie}* which is reproached there, even in Kant—One must accept the possibility, at least in a provisional way, that the "wisdom" in which we have all be raised (namely, that experience, observation, and the empirical domain are the highest and final thing, and that no one can go beyond them) is rather correct, true, and pure foolishness; because this is the very thing that *Kant* (although he has not remained true to himself all the way to the end) and

203

I (in addition to all the old ones, i.e., Plato, Jesus, and Christianity as a whole) presuppose. We can *prove* to someone that one can know completely a priori, and that order and manifestness *{Evidenz}* come into our knowing only through the a priori, only by means of the act itself, by actually leading that very person beyond all experience into this a priori knowing. For this purpose, however, the individual must first of all accept our presuppositions.

In Germany things run quite contrary to these two compulsory conditions; and among us there are many fewer people than foreigners think, who could know, or who are capable of conceiving, even what I have written in the attached document *{Beilage}*. If, as one can well assume without being blinded by patriotism, the other European nations as a rule and on average are even more faded, distracted, and superficial, are even more deeply sunk into the empirical domain in their mental activities, than are the Germans, then one can hope for even less good fortune from them on behalf of a system like the one we have described. Therefore, dear sir and friend, you will have to make a clear choice of those to whom you will confide about this subject, and be prepared for the strangest opinions.

—Fichte

ह‌ॐ

Aphorisms on the Essence of Philosophy as a Science

1. All philosophy up to Kant takes *being {objectum, ens}* as its object. (For instance, in dualism consciousness itself becomes being as a known object (spirit, soul, etc.). The purpose of these philosophies [is] to grasp the connection of being's manifold determinations.

2. Purely through a lack of attention, they have all overlooked the fact that *no being arises except within some consciousness, and* conversely, *no consciousness arises unless it is of some being.* Therefore [they have all overlooked] that the true in-itself as the object of philosophy can be neither in *being*, where all pre-Kantian philosophy looked for it, nor in *consciousness*, which admittedly has not even been attempted. Instead it must be found only in being [combined with] consciousness, or consciousness [combined with] being; that is, in the absolute oneness of both, beyond separateness. Kant made this great discovery, and thereby he *became* the discoverer of *transcendental philosophy*.

Corollary: With this discovery the miraculous question of how being arises in consciousness or how consciousness comes to being (which until now has been solved by *influxus physicus*, occasionalism, or pre-established harmony) completely dissolves. Being and consciousness have never been separated, and so they do not need to be united, but instead they are intrinsically one and the same.

3. *Addition:* Of course, even after this total alteration of its proper object, philosophy still retains the same task: to make the connection of the fundamental object's manifold determinations understandable.

4. In this, derivation's final task, one can,
Either, proceed by assuming that certain basic distinctions, which can be found only in factical self-observation, cannot be further unified. Then one will trace the [terms] which can be derived from these [distinctions] back to them as *particular* basic unities. This yields a philosophy that partly is incomplete and never itself comes to an end, i.e. to absolute oneness, and that partly is based on *factical data*, and so is not strictly scientific, even though (because of §2) it remains a transcendental philosophy. Kant's philosophy is of this type.

5. *Or,* one can proceed by penetrating and presenting this primordial oneness of being and consciousness (§2) as what it is in itself prior to its division into being and consciousness. (I *name* this oneness "reason," ὁ λόγος as in John's Gospel, or "knowing," so one will not confuse it with "consciousness," which is a lower disjunctive term that is found only in opposition to being. Therefore, [I name] the system *"Wissenschaftslehre"* or "λογολογια." In order to present this really inwardly to someone, and to make it understandable, requires a long preparation by means of the most abstract speculation.)

If one wants to have presented this oneness properly, one will simultaneously grasp {*einsehen*} the reason {*Grund*} why it divides itself into being and consciousness. Further [one will] grasp why, *within this dividedness*, it divides *itself further* in a particular way. One will conceive all this completely a priori, without the assistance of any factical perception, out of this insight into oneness. Thus, [one will] truly conceive the all in the one and the one in the all, as has always been philosophy's task from the beginning. The philosophy just described is *the*

"Wissenschaftslehre."

ج

Explanatory Addition

Berlin, June 23, 1804

As regards the last further split in being and consciousness, already grasped as one, in the science of knowing *{Wissenschaftslehre}* it turns out that this happens because of consciousness and according to its immanent laws. Consequently, being in and for itself, and conceived as separate from consciousness, is completely one, like reason itself. It divides itself only when united with consciousness, because this latter necessarily divides itself, as a result of its proper essence. Consequently, a manifold being exists only in consciousness. So, for example (as it turns out in the *WL*), it first splits into a *sensible* and a *supersensible* consciousness, which, when applied to being, must yield *sensible* and *supersensible* being. Then, according to a law not to be given here, supersensible [consciousness] then divides further into religious and moral consciousness, which, when applied to being, yield a *God* and a *moral law*. Sensible consciousness divides again into *social* and *natural* consciousness, which, when applied to being, yield *juridical law* and *nature*. Finally, and as a result of the *absolute* (i.e., infinite, never to be fulfilled) split in consciousness, absolutely divided being is expanded, as nature through infinite space and as consciousness through infinite time. However, this time and space no more exist *in themselves* as a part of pure being, or of pure reason, than does the disjunction mentioned previously. They occur only in consciousness. Nevertheless, consciousness, with these its laws and results, is by no means an illusion; because no being and reason exist, except in consciousness. For the same reason, so long as we live we cannot give up consciousness and its necessary results, even though we can and ought to know that these results are not valid in themselves. With this latter knowing we can protect ourselves from the monstrous confusions and contradictions that have been brought about through this false presupposition.

—Fichte

Notes

Acknowledgments

1. See, *Johann Gottlieb Fichte; Die Wissenschaftslehre, Zweiter Vortrag im Jahre 1804*, ed. Reinhard Lauth, Joachim Widmann, and Peter Schneider, *Philosophische Bibliothek*, vol. 284 (Hamburg: Felix Meiner Verlag, 1975), as well as Lauth and Gliwitzky, *J. G. Fichte Gesamtausgabe, Der Bayerischen Akademie der Wissenschaften*, II, 8 (Frommann Verlag: Stuttgart-Bad Cannstatt, 1985).

Introduction

1. Dan Breazeale has translated these wonderfully in two volumes: *Early Philosophical Writings*, ed. and trans. by Daniel Breazeale (Ithaca: Cornell University Press, 1988); and *Introductions to the Wissenschaftslehre and Other Writings*, ed. and trans. Daniel Breazeale (Indianapolis: Hackett, 1994)

2. *Foundations of Transcendental Philosophy*, ed. and trans. by Daniel Breazeale (Ithaca: Cornell University Press, 1992).

3. Reinhard Lauth, "Introduction" to Johann Gottlieb Fichte, *Die Wissenschaftslehre, zweiter Vortrag im Jahre 1804* (Hamburg: Felix Meiner Verlag, 1975), p. xviii.

4. "Some Lectures Concerning the Scholar's Vocation," in Breazeale, *Fichte: Early Philosophical Writings* (Ithaca: Cornell University Press, 1988), p. 174.

5. A thorough discussion of the probable invitees and attendees can be found in Lauth and Gliwitzky, *J. G. Fichte Gesamtausgabe, Der Bayerischen Akademie der Wissenschaften*, II, 8 (Frommann Verlag: Stuttgart-Bad Cannstatt, 1985).

6. For instance, Ludwig Siep, *Hegel's Fichtekritik und die Wissenschaftslehre von 1804* (Freiburg: Verlag Karl Albert, 1970), Wolfgang Janke *Fichte, Sein und Reflexion* (Berlin: DeGruyter, 1990), Peter Baumanns, *J. G. Fichte. Kritische Gesamtdarstellung seiner Philosophie* (Freiburg/München: Alber, 1990), and Joachim Widmann *Grundstruktur des transcendentalen Wissens* (Hamburg, 1977).

7. Günther Zöller, "German realism: the self-limitation of idealist thinking in Fichte, Schelling, and Schopenhauer," in *The Cambridge Companion to German Idealism* (Cambridge: Cambridge University Press, 2000), p. 217.

8. See R. Kroner, *Von Kant bis Hegel* (Tubingen: Mohr, 1921). This influential book drew on Hegel's own, somewhat self-serving views. Establishing what has been the standard interpretation of German Idealism, Kroner presents the period as a continuous movement begun by Kant, culminating in Hegel, with all others playing subordinate roles along the way.

9. See my essay "The Shadow of Spinoza in Fichte's WL 1804^2," *Idealistic Studies*, Volume 33, Issues 2–3, 2003, pp. 163–176.

10. *Johann Gottlieb Fichte's Nachgelassene Werke*, ed. I. H. Fichte, 3 vols. (Berlin: Veit and Comp, 1834–35). Reprinted as volumes ix–xi of *Fichtes Werke*, ed. I. H. Fichte, 11 volumes (Berlin: Walter de Gruyter, 1971).

11. *Johann Gottlieb Fichte; Die Wissenschaftslehre, Zweiter Vortrag im Jahre 1804*, ed. Reinhard Lauth, Joachim Widmann, and Peter Schneider, *Philosophische Bibliothek*, vol. 284 (Hamburg: Felix Meiner Verlag, 1975).

12. *J. G. Fichte/Gesamtausgabe der Bayerischen Akademie der Wissenschaften*, II, ed. Reinhard Lauth and Hans Gliwitzky (Stuttgartt-Bad Cannstadt: Frommann-Holzboog, 1985).

13. I. H. Fichte *Beitrage zur Charakteristik der neueren Philosophie* (Sulzbach, 1841), p. 531 (my translation).

14. Joachim Widmann, *Johann Gottlieb Fichte* (Berlin: DeGruyter, 1982), p. 65 (my translation).

15. Guenther Zoeller, "German realism: the self-limitation of idealist thinking in Fichte, Schelling, and Schopenhauer," in *The Cambridge Companion to German Idealism*, ed. Karl Ameriks (Cambridge University Press: Cambridge, 2000).

16. Breazeale, *Fichte: Early Philosophical Writings* (Ithaca: Cornell University Press, 1988), p. xv.

17. Walter Benjamin, "The Task of the Translator," in *Illuminations*, ed. Hannah Arendt (New York: Schocken Books, 1968), p. 76.

18. Sometimes he also simply writes *"VernunftEffekt."*

Lecture I

1. *SW* and the *Copia* observe different conventions for labeling each lecture. *SW* starts the first paragraph of each lecture with the Roman Numeral designation *"I Vortrag," "II Vortrag,"* etc., while the *Copia* writes out the number of the lecture on a display line and sometimes includes the date of the lecture. The *Copia* also begins with the abbreviation "E.V." for *"ehrwürdige Versammlung"* or "honorable guests." I will follow the *Copia* format, inserting the date of the lecture when it is missing.

2. Paragraph break from *Copia*. *SW* has no break here. When both texts have them, they will be unmarked. When breaks occur in one text only, I will note it. My text will follow the paragraph divisions that best support the sense.

3. Fichte's phrase here *"die Grundzüge unseres gegenwärtige Zeitalters"* mirrors the title of a series of popular lectures that he delivered in 1804/05 *Die Grundzüge des gegenwärtige Zeitalters*. The connection suggests both a point of contact between Fichte's *prima philosophia* and his popular writings, as well as his intention to see the presentation of his philosophy as historically situated. The *1804 WL* is an event of philosophical communication which must be seen within its specific context.

4. Fichte consistently uses masculine forms in contexts where modern sensibility calls for gender neutral pronouns. That Fichte's audience included both men and women provides one reason to think that he may have intended such forms to be gender neutral. However, Fichte's own sexism (e.g., see Dale E. Snow *Schelling and the End of Idealism* [Albany: SUNY Press, 1996] pp. 102ff) and the fact that the style of his day called for masculine pronouns in referring to a person of unknown gender, both favor letting his practice stand to preserve the historical flavor of his text.

5. I have added this paragraph break, which the text's sense calls for and Fichte omits.

6. Fichte's famous term for his distinctively new transcendental philosophical science is *Wissenschaftslehre*. See the Preface for a discussion of its translation.

7. *dass er selbst, die Person . . .*—Copia emphasizes *er selbst*.

8. This emphasis occurs in *SW* only.

9. This paragraph break occurs in *Copia* only.

10. This paragraph break occurs in *SW* only.

11. The "?" occurs in *SW* only.

12. The emphasis on the second occurrence of *"Wahrheit"* in this paragraph is in *SW* only.

13. *Pendant* is added in *SW*. The *Copia* has a blank space.

14. The *Copia* adds a paragraph break here.

15. The phrase "for him" is omitted in *Copia*.

16. This paragraph break occurs in SW only.

17. That is, a thinking or consciousness, which has this being as its intentional object.

Lecture II

1. The paragraph break is in the *Copia* only.

2. This paragraph break occurs in the *Copia* only.

3. Sentence break inserted by the translator. The preceding and succeeding sentences are one long sentence in the original. The structure of Fichte's point here is clearer when the sentence is broken up.

4. This paragraph break occurs in the *Copia* only.

5. The suggestion here is that philosophy requires an inner creative act which goes beyond mere verbal memory. Recalling that the lecturer said A or B is not itself sufficient for understanding.

6. I follow *SW's* wording here, which differs slightly from the *Copia*.

7. This paragraph break occurs in *Copia*. *SW* has a long dash.

8. This paragraph break occurs in *Copia*.

9. This paragraph break occurs in *Copia*.

10. Following *SW*. The *Copia* here reads *"dieses meine Herrn ist eine neuer Punkt."*

11. *"Erscheinung"* in this context refers to the manifestness of what is present to mind rather than any deceptive or merely apparent quality of that something.

12. This emphasis occurs in *SW*.

13. This emphasis occurs in *SW*.

14. This last clause occurs in parentheses in the *Copia*.

15. I have followed the version of this diagram in the *Copia*. Presumably, "A" stands for "the absolute," "B" stands for "being," and "T" stands for "thinking."

16. Fichte's discussion here echoes Spinoza's *Ethics* (Bk. II, P7): "The order and connection of ideas is the same as the order and connection of things."

17. This emphasis occurs in *Copia*. *SW* emphasizes the verb *"enthalten."*

18. *"wieder stille stehen"*—SW has *"irgendwo"* instead of *"wieder."*

19. Fichte's reference here is to his first series of lectures on the *WL* from 1804. Several members of his present audience had also attended the earlier series.

Lecture III

1. This paragraph break occurs in *Copia* only.

2. *"Ich fordre Sie auf, nach der Reihe vorzustellen."*

3. The last sentence is in *Copia* only.

4. "T" stands for "thinking" and "B" stands for "being.

5. The *Copia* includes the following diagram, which is absent in *SW*:

$$T.B.$$
$$K—T.B.$$
$$T.B.\ \text{etc.}$$

6. *SW* has another paragraph break after this sentence. I follow the *Copia*.

7. A synthesis is *post factum* when it works on terms which are factically given.

Lecture IV

1. Different versions of this diagram occur in both *Copia* and *SW*. It is a relative of the simpler diagram in Lecture II (above, p. 13). Fichte may have drawn something like it during his presentation of Lecture II's discussion of Kant, but it was not included in the text. My version is a slight simplification of *SW*.

2. This statement never actually occurs in the written texts of the previous lectures. Possibly, Fichte made it as a side remark not included in his written text.

3. *"genetisch"*—see the Introduction for a discussion of this term.

4. I follow *SW's* emphasis pattern here. In the *Copia*, "genetic," the last word of the preceding sentence, is emphasized, and "mere" is not.

5. Both versions here have the abbreviation *"WL,"* which in this case I take as standing for *"Wissenschaftslehrer,"* practitioner of the *Wissenschaftslehre*.

6. This emphasis is mine.

7. I add paragraph breaks before each of the following numbered points to make the text's structure more evident.

8. *SW* has *"Wissen"* here.

9. Following Lauth, Widmann, and Schneider's preference for *SW's "begriffene"* to *Copia's "unbegriffene."*

10. *". . . eher zu behaupten als wir eingesehen."*

11. Added by Lauth, Widmann, and Schneider in the 1975 Meiner edition (PB 284) as a supplement called for by the sense of the passage.

12. *SW* emphasizes "light" only.

13. This coined term marks the separation between the immediate occurrence of concepts within consciousness and their representation within reason as the necessary counterpart to, and standard for, knowing.

14. *". . . nur von der WL zu intelligienrende Bewusstsein."*

Lecture V

1. This general day of prayer was probably April 25, 1804.

2. This paragraph break occurs in *Copia* only.

3. In *AA*, the page break on the verso side *(SW)* comes $1\frac{1}{2}$ lines earlier.

4. This paragraph break occurs in *Copia* only.

5. This paragraph break occurs in *SW* only.

6. This emphasis occurs in *Copia* only.

7. I follow the wording of *Copia* here.

8. This sentence is found in *Copia* and not in *SW*.

9. This emphasis occurs in *Copia*.

10. The preceding sentence is my rather free reconstruction of a telegraphic and obscure passage.

11. The material in square brackets occurs in the *Copia*, and not in *SW*. Lauth, Widmann, and Schneider suggest that it may be a sketch that Fichte deleted.

Lecture VI

1. The emphasis on "from" is found in *Copia* only.

2. See, Friedrich Nicolai, *"Leben und Meinungen Sempronius Gundlibert's eines deutschen Philosophen"* (*The Life and Opinions of Sempronius Gundlibert, a German Philosopher*), Berlin and Stettin, 1798, p. 122 note: "somewhere in a critical book are to be found *'trichotomies,'* which by a significant ambiguity can also mean *'splitting a hair.'* " GA, II, 8, pp. 84–85)

3. A = A is Fichte's formula for identity in the *Grundlage*. So, the most natural interpretation of the diagram pictured here is as an amplification of that familiar equation. The a's are lower case now, because Fichte is speaking of the general principle of oneness rather than the fundamental identity of the absolute, which is in play in the *Grundlage*. They are in different type faces, because the first "a" is oneness *qua* oneness, and the second "α" is the same oneness differentiating itself into "x, y, and z."

4. This emphasis occurs in *SW* only.

5. The phrase "nor yet by us" occurs in *Copia* only.

6. The phrase, "and we had to declare this inseparability of the distinguishing grounds to be undiscoverable," added in the *Copia*.

7. This paragraph break occurs in *SW* only.

8. This paragraph added in the *Copia*.

9. The bracketed passage occurs only in the *Copia*. The text appears corrupted in places.

Lecture VII

1. Although Lauth, Widmann, and Schneider prefer *Copia* here, I have rendered this numbered sentence according the wording in *SW*. In general, the entire beginning of this lecture is quite telegraphic, and I have translated it freely.

2. The first scheduled discussion section happened after Lecture VII; however, Fichte may have held a conversation with some of the audience on the Day of Repentance and Prayer between Lectures V and VI, enabling him to make this observation.

3. The entirety of 3. added in the *Copia*.

4. This paragraph break occurs in *Copia* only.

5. This paragraph break occurs in *Copia* only.

6. *"vorliegende Schema"*—the emphasis occurs in *Copia* only.

7. That is, the observing of the light.

8. This emphasis occurs in *Copia* only.

9. This emphasis occurs in *Copia* only.

10. This emphasis occurs in *Copia* only.

11. This emphasis occurs in *Copia* only.

12. I follow *SW's* wording here.

13. This would be Lecture III.

14. This emphasis occurs in *SW* only.

15. *Copia* qualifies "completely and unconditionally" by *organisch*. I take that as intended to reinforce the intrinsic character of the way the image posits something imaged, but I have not included it in the text, following *SW* instead.

16. *SW* has "construction" here instead of "abstraction." *GA* notes this as a possible error in *SW*. I think this surmise is correct.

17. *Copia* reverses the emphases on the two preceding terms.

18. The following passage is very sketchy. The editors of *GA* speculate that it is omitted in *SW* for this reason.

19. The following diagram occurs in *Copia*. The text does not indicate what Fichte might intend by the various letters occurring in it. However, "I" and "R" almost certainly mean "ideality" and "reality." At the top, "A" and "E" might be the absolute *(das Absolute)*, or the act *(die Akte)*, and its living appearance *(die Erscheinung)* in their mutual necessity. However, the diagram has many mysteries. What are the B, A, and a, which occur at the bottom? Clearly they are mutually related terms. A under ideality and a under reality are related yet different. But what are they exactly? The general structure strongly suggests, but is not easily reducible to, Fichte's model of five-fold-ness.

Lecture VIII

1. This paragraph break occurs in *Copia* only.

2. This paragraph break occurs in *Copia* only.

3. This presentation of the most fundamental concepts as an inseparable "three-in-one," which leads directly to a discussion of God, is of course suggestive of Trinitarian theology.

4. The verb here *("ginge auf")* is a form of *"aufgehen"* which can mean both to "rise, swell, or dawn," and also to "evaporate or dissolve." I choose the former, but the latter is also possible and not without justification.

5. This emphasis occurs in *SW* only.

6. This emphasis occurs in *SW* only.

7. Alluding here to the Atheism controversy in the Fall of 1798, which led to his dismissal from Jena.

8. The punctuation in both versions is complicated and inconsistent here. I have tried to make sense of it.

9. *anschaulich*—The emphasis occurs in *SW* only.

10. That is, the light's "external and objective expression and existence."

11. The last two words are emphasized in *Copia*.

12. This sentence occurs in *Copia* only.

13. This sentence likewise is in the *Copia* only.

14. This word emphasized in *Copia*.

15. This emphasis occurs in *SW* only.

16. *SW* has a long dash here. *Copia* places it before the next paragraph.

17. I follow *Copia's "gewonnen"* here instead of *SW's "genommen."*

18. Fichte's abbreviations here seem to be: B = being, T = thinking, C = concept and L = light. His formula would then say that the range of differences in appearing reality can only be being/thinking plus the concept plus the light.

Lecture IX

1. The audience mostly consisted of returning listeners, who had already been schooled by that year's first series of lectures in the *WL*. Besides these, there were a group of young listeners who were participating in the discussion meetings. (*GA* II, 8 126 n. 1)

2. In *SW* the term is singular, and in *Copia* it is plural. The editors of *GA* suggest that the *SW* text may be an error, and I follow them here. (*GA* II, 8 126 n. a)

3. This paragraph break occurs in *SW* only.

4. This emphasis occurs in *SW* only.

5. This emphasis occurs in *SW* only.

6. The last two sentences are a single sentence present only in the *Copia*.

7. Instead of *Copia's verhehlen*, *SW* has *verfehlen*. I agree with the judgment of the *GA* editors that this is an error, and that the former makes better sense.

8. This emphasis occurs in *SW* only.

9. This emphasis occurs in *SW* only.

10. Fichte regularly changed his terminology from one presentation of his system to another, in part to discourage attachment to the literal words. He followed this practice in the three 1804 lecture courses on the science of knowing.

Lecture X

1. That is, in the Eighth Lecture.

2. That is, as the object for insight, as it occurs.

3. In this sentence, *Copia* emphasizes the occurrence of "dual" and the two occurrences of "in part," but it does not emphasize "concept" and "being." I follow *SW*.

4. This paragraph break occurs in *Copia* only.

5. The bracketed passage occurs in *Copia* only.

6. That is, in *inwardly* living light.

7. SW expresses this idea symbolically by inserting "= 0." Copia places "= 0" at the end of the previous sentence.

8. *Copia* has a paragraph break here.

9. This emphasis occurs in *Copia* only.

10. Following the wording in *Copia*.

11. *SW* omits the preceding phrase.

12. *Copia* has a paragraph break here.

13. These numbered divisions added by the translator to clarify the structure of this long, run-on passage.

14. *Copia* emphasizes the phrase "only with empirical manifestness."

15. The preceding sentence is from the *Copia*.

16. From the *Copia* only. There is no designation for the second remark in *SW*.

17. *SW* has *"Bild"* here and *Copia* has the abbreviation *"B."* In Fichte's text, however, *"B"* usually stands for *"Begriff"* or concept. "Concept" best fits the context, since it has already been described as the "principle of disjunction." (Please note that *in this translation* "B" always denotes "Being.")

18. Copia has "0." This phrase is replaced in SW by "since otherwise we remain trapped in a synthesis *post factum*."

19. Following the punctuation and paragraphing of *Copia*.

20. 0 = zero, and C = concept.

21. Here, and in every case, B = "Being."

22. Lauth, Widmann, and Schneider add "es" as called for by the sense of the passage; however, the antecedent is not entirely clear. From the sense, it might most naturally be *"das Licht"* understood as "the truly highest term that we are and live" rather than as = 0.

23. See the Seventh Lecture. To indicate that "through" is functioning as a noun and as "a term of art," I will place each of its occurrences in quotation marks.

24. That is, if the internal light (= 0) were this life of the concept as a "through"?

25. I have placed the argument on display lines to make it clearer.

26. Following the *Copia*, as suggested by the editors of *GA*.

27. Here again it is hard to tell what the antecedent of *"es"* should be here. The "through" *(das Durch)* and "life" *(das Leben)* are the most natural candidates. However, one could make a case that the subject under discussion here is the division into being and thinking. Nevertheless, I read this passage as referring to the "through."

28. The bracketed passage is found in the *Copia* only.

29. Following the wording in *Copia*.

30. This emphasis occurs in *SW* only.

31. Following the wording in *SW*.

Lecture XI

1. The text in brackets is found in *SW*. *Copia* replaces this with the following: "Today we begin our explanation directly with the most difficult points and attempt to master these in their inner spirit."

2. "C" here stands for "concept."

3. *SW* has a semicolon here, and *Copia* has a full stop. Neither makes complete grammatical sense.

4. *"Es kommt wirklich zu einem Durch."*

5. This emphasis occurs in *SW* only.

6. *Copia* adds here: "This was the first point. 'a x b' clarified further."

7. *Sehen ein—Copia* substitutes: "We saw into this at once, as I hope."

8. As in note #6, the "a x b" below the line represents the "through" in relation to the original life posited with it. The "a" above the line represents the "through" which posits both in one stroke; and the entire diagram represents "the resulting insight."

9. The *Copia* emphasizes "meaning."

10. This parenthetical addition is omitted in *SW*.

11. This paragraph break occurs in *Copia* only.

12. The *Copia* emphasizes "insight."

13. Here the *Copia* adds the following: "*'Ascending'* I say; to be sure, the historically recognized ideal ordering on a vertical axis is what [we] have understood genetically here. Or the proper standpoint for this ordering considered more deeply."

14. *"Dies, sage ich, wäre idealistisch argumentiert."*

15. *"die Maxime der äusseren Existential-Form"*—this phrase suggests a connection with Kant's analysis of time (and space) as "forms of inner (and outer) sense" respectively.

16. This emphasis occurs in *Copia* only.

17. This emphasis occurs in *Copia* only.

18. *Problemäticitat*—following *Copia*.

19. This sentence, and the paragraph break, are in *Copia* only.

20. *Copia* has a paragraph break here.

21. These are synonyms for inner and outer existence, respectively.

22. The *Copia* has *"aufdecken"* here instead of the probably mistaken *"aufdrücken"* in *SW*.

23. This paragraph break occurs in *Copia* only.

24. This emphasis occurs in *Copia* only.

25. e.g., in the preceding discussion of idealism.

26. An expanded version of a diagram which is in *Copia* only. It suggests that "Living," which is a kind of whole, divides into concept and being. The image, which stands between them, is the site of truth's appearance.

27. In the *Copia*, we find *"schliesse"* instead of *"schärfe"* as found in *SW*.

28. A reference to the phrenology of Franz Joseph Gall (1758–1828).

Lecture XII

1. Sunday, May 6, 1804.

2. This emphasis occurs in *Copia* only.

3. That is, the inward life of the concept in question (trans.).

4. *Copia* emphasizes the verb "be" as well.

5. This paragraph break occurs in *Copia* only.

6. *Die Grundlage der gesamten Wissenschaftslehre* 1794 (/95).

7. This emphasis occurs in *SW* only.

8. I follow *Copia's* parsing of this paragraph rather than that in *SW*.

9. The editors of *GA* suggest that Fichte is referring here to Kant's transcendental apperception, which remains linked to the thing-in-itself.

10. This phrase is added in *SW*.

11. This emphasis occurs in *SW* only.

12. This emphasis occurs in *SW* only.

13. This emphasis occurs in *SW* only.

14. This paragraph break occurs in *Copia* only.

15. "0" stands for being, now understood as the unconceived and inconceivable other = 0. "C" stands for "concept."

16. This word order follows the *Copia.*

17. Copia divides this sentence in two and makes a paragraph break between them.

18. *Copia's "fassen"* instead of *SW's "lassen."*

19. Copia has "what negates its {*sein*} thinking."

20. *Copia* emphasizes *"evident"* rather than *"faktisch."*

21. The emphasis on this, as well as the following, occurrence of *Ansich* is in *SW* only.

22. *Copia* emphasizes this word.

23. This emphasis occurs in *SW* only.

24. *Copia* emphasizes both "intuition" and "construction."

25. This emphasis occurs in *SW* only.

26. This emphasis occurs in *SW* only.

27. This emphasis occurs in *SW* only.

28. I follow Lauth, Widmann, and Schneider's reconstruction of this sentence, which is garbled in both *SW* and *Copia.* The last two emphases occur in the *Copia* only.

29. This emphasis occurs in *SW* only.

30. This emphasis occurs in *SW* only.

31. This emphasis occurs in *SW* only.

32. This paragraph break occurs in *Copia* only.

Lecture XIII

1. The emphasis on these two terms is in *SW* only.

2. The Eleventh Lecture was on Friday, May 4, 1804; however, there is ambiguity about the date of the Twelfth Lecture. *SW* assigns it to Tuesday, May 8, and the

Copia assigns it to May 7. If one accepts *SW's* dating, this sentence should say simply "yesterday."

3. I translate the marked passage—found only in the Copia—from Lauth, Widmann, and Schneider's reconstruction of it. They omit another part of it, which is corrupted with major gaps.

4. I have omitted *Copia's* emphases on several words in this sentence.

5. This emphasis occurs in *Copia* only.

6. *SW* places the emphasis on this occurrence of "one."

7. Instead of *"Wissen oder Denken,"* *Copia* has simply *"Sehen."*

8. At the end of this paragraph, *Copia* adds: "Light shines forth in this same *life* (the self-construction) and united with it. It appears as an immediate synthesis, which is the absolute for the first realism, *deduced from the in-itself.*"

9. *Copia* places emphasis on both preceding words.

10. *Copia* emphasizes this word.

11. *Copia* adds: "Take us to your principle."

12. Followng *SW*. *Copia* has *"herabgesehen"* instead.

13. *Copia* omits "purely" and emphasizes the last two words.

14. Paragraph break in *Copia* only. This is where the SW ends the parenthetical passage begun earlier in this paragraph. In Copia it continues until p. 105 below. I follow *Copia*.

15. At the beginning of this sentence, *Copia* has an "(" here with no corresponding ")." I follow *SW*, which does not.

16. Parenthesis added in *Copia*. The main verb here is the past participle "geschenkt" whose colloquial meaning is "save your breath," or "forget about it." That is the sense *Copia* is calling on here, and I only render it a bit more formally.

17. I have omitted *Copia's* emphases on several words in this sentence.

18. Again, I have omitted *Copia's* emphases on several words in this sentence.

19. *Copia* emphasizes this term as well.

20. *"du dir dessen bewusst bist."*

21. In *Copia*, the preceding sentence is moved to the end of the paragraph, following an em-dash, and no paragraph break occurs before the "historical commentary."

22. In *Copia*, neither name is emphasized.

23. See, J. G. Fichte, *"Antwortschreiben an Herrn Professor Reinhold,"* Tübingen, 1801, pp. 30–35.

24. I have reconstructed the preceeding, very convoluted, sentence rather freely.

25. Parentheses around this paragraph are found in *Copia* only.

26. The last two words are emphasized in *Copia*.

27. This emphasis occurs in *SW* only.

28. "πρῶτον ψεῦδος"

29. *"Tathandlung"*

30. This emphasis occurs in *Copia* only.

31. That is, the same as the refuted idealism.

32. *"intelligieren"*—Emphasis in *SW* only.

33. The emphases in this sentence are from the *Copia* only.

34. *"Ansichgültigkeit"*—This term contains a veiled, punning reference to the validity of the in-itself, which plays such an important role in this juncture of the lectures. This word play is lost in English.

35. In the *Copia* the Thirteenth Lecture ends here, while in *SW*, it continues, with the second paragraph (concerning Schelling) from the beginning of the Fourteenth Lecture. I follow *Copia* here. In *GA*, this passage in the Thirteenth Lecture continues to p. 212. The (*Copia* version of the) beginning of the Fourteenth Lecture begins on 215, and is joined by the *SW* text on the following page.

Lecture XIV

1. This paragraph is missing in *SW*.

2. *SW* has *"Vermittelung"* instead of *"Vernichtung."* I follow the *Copia*.

3. *Zeitschrift für spekulative Physik*, II, 2, par. 6, p. 5. "The sentence A = A is generally taken to mean neither that A in general, nor A as subject, nor A as object *exists*. Rather the only being which is posited in this sentence is that of *identity itself* which therefore is posited completely separately from A as subject or A as predicate. The *proof* for this first claim is conducted in par. 1 of the *Wissenschaftslehre* . . ."

4. This bracketed passage appears at the end of Lecture XIII in *SW*.

5. This phrase is missing in *SW*.

6. The *Copia* has *"ansich Gültigkeit"* here, although *SW* has *"Sichgültigkeit."*

7. This sentence in *Copia* only.

8. *"einsehen"*—emphasis in *SW* only.

9. This passage follows the wording in *Copia*.

10. *Copia* adds "a priori" here.

11. Emphases in this sentence in *SW* only.

12. This is emphasized in *SW*.

13. That is, in (or by means of) the discontinuous projection.—trans.

14. *Copia* emphasizes the two preceding words.

15. *"das Denken"*—that is, the thinking which has this "in-itself" as its object.

16. Following the punctuation of the *Copia*, I parse the last phrase as belonging to the preceding passage rather than to the following. This helps clarify the meaning here.

17. Following the *Copia*, which has *"vorausgesetztes"* (presupposed) for *"Ausgesagtes"* (explicit).

18. I approximate the punctuation of the *Copia*, which uses emphasis to make a parallelism between *"versinnlichte"* and *"intelligierte"* as qualifiers for *"Bedeutung."*

19. Copia adds "... a *not not in-itself* and so ..."

20. This emphasis occurs in *SW* only.

21. *SW* has, "Viewed according its strength ..."

22. This emphasis occurs in *SW* only.

23. This word is emphasized in *Copia*.

24. I have added the bracketed material in keeping with the passage's sense.

25. I follow the *Copia* here, which has *"Seyn"* instead of *SW's* *"Setzen."* However, I keep *SW's* punctuation of the passage.

26. This emphasis occurs in *Copia* only.

27. *"Bestehen."* This emphasis occurs in *Copia* only.

28. SW adds, "and resting of an in-itself."

29. The concluding paragraph is in *Copia* only.

Lecture XV

1. The GA editors assert that "Fichte is speaking about the week of May 6–13. The discussion had taken place on Sunday, May 6, and Lectures Twelve through Fourteen until Thursday, May 10."

2. This discussion was scheduled for the following Sunday, May 13.

3. *Copia* emphasized all three of the preceding words.

4. *Copia* emphasized both of the preceding words.

5. The phrase from "doctrine" to "illusion" is emphasized in *Copia*.

6. This emphasis occurs in *Copia* only.

7. Fichte here writes "... verbaliter, *esse* ..."

8. *"in actu"*—I take his point to be that, in contrast to language's understanding of being as a noun, being is an enactment or event (that is, a verb), which is possible only as living occurrence.

9. The preceding phrase is emphasized in *Copia*.

10. That is, "being" as a verb, or an enactment.—trans.

11. This emphasis occurs in *Copia* only.

12. Following the *Copia*. *SW* omits the first three words and the em dash.

13. SW omits the qualifying phrase "separated by . . . ought to be conscious."

14. SW has *"Wir-in-sich."* *Copia* has *"Wir ansich"* here as well.

15. This emphasis occurs in *Copia* only.

16. This emphasis occurs in *SW* only.

17. *Copia* has *"verbales Leben"* instead of *SW's "actuelles Leben."* The latter makes better sense in the context, and I have chosen to follow it.

18. Copia adds: "where being is, there is I, and the I is being."

19. This emphasis occurs in *Copia* only.

20. This paragraph break occurs in *Copia* only.

21. This word is emphasized in *Copia*.

22. This emphasis occurs in *Copia* only. Parallel structure seems to demand it.

23. Copia adds here: "I say not factically another objectifying consciousness . . ."

24. Instead of *SW's "Bewusstseins, das Wir selber,"* *Copia* has *"Bewusstseins des Wir selber."*

25. *SW* emphasizes the adjective only.

26. This emphasis occurs in *Copia* only.

27. In the Twelfth Lecture.

28. *". . . alles Sehens, in Beziehung auf sich . . ."*

29. i.e., "consciousness."—trans.

30. *". . . diese intelligierend abzuhaltende Nichtgenesis . . ."*

31. This emphasis occurs in *SW* only.

32. This emphasis occurs in *Copia* only.

33. This phrase is emphasized in *Copia*.

34. *SW* has *"bewusst"* here instead of *"bestimmt."* The editors of *GA* mark it as possibly erroneous and I follow them, although the other reading is surely possible.

35. *SW* has *"gerirendes"* here, while the *Copia* has an elision. The context calls for something like the proposed addition.

Lecture XVI

1. Following *SW* which reads *"jetzt"* rather than *Copia's "zuletzt."*

2. *SW* has instead: *". . . a self-enclosed singularity of life and being . . ."*

3. A discussion period was held May 13, after Lecture XV.

4. *SW* does not emphasize the last two words.

5. *Copia* here has *"freie Bemerkung."*

6. *Copia* adds here the following parenthetical remark: "(In brief—the old stands firm and complete;—know that you now begin a separate investigation;—separate as long as, etc. . . .)

7. *Copia* has *"voraus"* instead of *SW's "von uns."*

8. For clarity, I have moved this parenthetical remark from its position near the beginning of the previous sentence, making it an independent, following remark.

9. Fichte uses a colon here and continues his typically long sentence. This perhaps makes sense for a text that is meant for oral presentation, but is ungainly and confusing for written prose.

10. The punctuation here is a semi-colon, and this monster sentence continues.

11. In this passage, "seem," "appears," and "appearance" are part of an extended word play with the German root *Schein*. As seen in the last lecture, Fichte takes the occurrence of separated objects within consciousness as an inevitable appearance that must be discounted to arrive at truth. He is reinforcing, and working with, that point here.

12. Fichte's text marks the subordinate points in this paragraph as 1. and 2. I use a. and b. to indicate their status more clearly as subordinate to the main headings 1. and 2.

13. This word is emphasized in *Copia*.

14. This word is emphasized in *Copia*.

15. *SW* has a period here, but *Copia* a colon.

16. This paragraph break occurs in *Copia* only.

17. Fichte confusingly uses both *"erste"* and *"erstern"* in this clause with the occurrences naming different ones of the two self-constructions under discussion. In the translation, I have tried to arrive at a reading that sorts them out.

18. This sentence is punctuated quite differently in the two versions. I have taken points from both.

19. SW omits *"dadurch."*

20. This emphasis occurs in *Copia* only.

21. This term is emphasized in *Copia*.

22. *Copia* has, "on the condition that the ground be and be assumed."

23. Following the *Copia's* construction of this sentence.

24. *SW* has *"Wie"* here and *Copia* has *"wir."* The *GA* editors query whether the *SW* entry is erroneous. I agree and follow the *Copia*.

25. This is a sentence fragment in both *SW* and *Copia*.

26. This emphasis occurs in *Copia* only.

27. *Copia* adds here "but [have] *never clarified* it."

28. Fichte presents the following explanation as a parenthesis in *SW* and a footnote in the *Copia*: "For now, I will employ the word "existence" exclusively for external being. By contrast "being," which is always to be understood only as a word *{verbaliter}*, is reserved for the inner being posited in the absolute basic proposition, which must be remembered here." In saying that "being" can always only be understood as a word, Fichte is reminding us that the being in question: *"is entirely a self-enclosed singularity* {Singulum} *of life and of being that can never get outside itself."* Thus, this "being" *itself* must be incomprehensible, unintuitable, and so unnamable. Talk about it is always paradoxical.

29. This emphasis occurs in *Copia* only.

30. *SW* omits the parentheses around the preceding paragraph.

31. Fichte begins his important discussion of imperative conditionality (e.g., the "should") in the *WL*.

32. *"Wenn es eingesehen werden soll, so muss. . . ."* The preceding emphases are in *Copia* only.

33. *"absolute non liquet."* SW constructs the sentence's first phrase as a question and the rest of the sentence the answer. I follow Copia's construction, which fits better with the passage's sense.

34. *"problematisch"*—the emphasis occurs in *SW* only.

35. Reading *"Umfange"* with *SW* instead of Copia's *"Anfange."*

36. Following the *Copia's "wenn"* instead of *SW's "von."*

37. This emphasis occurs in *Copia* only.

38. This emphasis occurs in *Copia* only.

39. This emphasis occurs in *Copia* only.

40. This emphasis occurs in *Copia* only.

41. This emphasis occurs in *Copia* only.

42. The preceding two words are emphasized in *Copia*.

43. This emphasis occurs in *Copia* only.

44. *SW* has "constructed" instead of reconstructed." Emphasis in *Copia* only.

45. SW emphasizes "ideality" and "reality" only.

Lecture XVII

1. *SW* has *"innere"* instead of *"nimmer."*

2. *SW* has *"reine"* instead of *"eine."*

3. The word is found in *SW* only. The reference is to the elements (of whatever kinds) that compose "multiplicity," that is, the world of appearances.

4. The emphases in this sentence are from *Copia* only.

5. *Copia* has "*out of them* and from them." Fichte here echoes Kant's famous dictum near the beginning of his Introduction to the *Critique of Pure Reason* (Second Ed.): "But even though all our cognition starts *with* experience, that does not mean that all of it arises *from* experience" (Pluhar 1996, p. 44).

6. *SW* does not enclose this remark in parentheses, and has a paragraph break at this point.

7. Copia adds the following remark: "Because it seemed so to me, I intend that by means of the preceding strenuous ascent, we have been weaned from the inconstant *deliberation* that prevailed here, etc."

8. This emphasis occurs in *Copia* only.

9. Only *Copia* has this sentence in quotation marks.

10. This emphasis occurs in *Copia* only.

11. This implied subject does not actually occur until much later in this complex sentence.

12. This clause's emphases are in *Copia* only.

13. This phrase is in parentheses in *Copia* only.

14. This term is emphasized in *Copia*.

15. This term is emphasized in *Copia*.

16. In Fichte's text, the last three sentences are one long, grammatical complex sentence. I have tried to disentangle its sense.

17. Although the *Copia* gives no indication where this parenthesis closes, this is the most plausible place.

18. Fichte here points out that one key element of the previous arguments has been the hypothetical element marked by the verb *"sollen."* Straightforwardly (and frequently) rendered as "should," it is also sometimes also rendered by "if" clauses.

19. This paragraph break occurs in *SW*.

20. That is, "the insight."

21. This question was probably raised in the discussion periods.

22. This emphasis occurs in *Copia* only.

23. This emphasis occurs in *Copia* only.

24. This emphasis occurs in *Copia* only.

25. The last three words are emphasized in the *Copia*.

26. Fichte's word here is *"Annahme,"* which primarily means "acceptance," rather than the more usual *"Voraussetzung."* The emphases here are from the *Copia*.

27. This emphasis occurs in *Copia* only.

28. Emphases in this sentence are from the *Copia*.

29. Preferring, as do the editors, *Copia's* "*unveränderlichen*" to *SW's* "*unvermeidlichen.*"

30. This emphasis occurs in *Copia* only.

31. *Copia* has "*in*" rather than the "*bei*" from *SW*.

32. This emphasis occurs in *Copia* only.

33. This emphasis occurs in *Copia* only.

34. "*sehr*" added in *Copia*.

35. "*dunkel*" added in *Copia*.

36. *Copia* emphasizes the entire phrase "*as such.*"

37. This prepositional phrase is emphasized in *Copia*.

38. *Copia* has a paragraph break here that seems unjustified, given the continuity of the topic. However, I have followed *Copia* in reading a sentence break at this point rather than *SW's* simple colon.

39. This emphasis occurs in *Copia* only.

40. This emphasis occurs in *Copia* only.

41. *Copia* emphasizes this phrase.

42. Copia adds the phrase: "—and this should is comprehended {*eingesehen*} anew in its nature."

43. The referent here is obscure. It might be "the insight," or it might be "the previous investigation."

44. *Copia* ends with the Latin phrase: "*Haec hactenus,*" which is roughly equivalent to "That's enough for now."

Lecture XVIII

1. For the spaces in the sentence schema, *SW* has *u.s.w.* and *Copia* has *pp* (for *perge perge*). I have chosen a form that should be more perspicuous for contemporary readers.

2. The parentheses are added to clarify the sentence's structure.

3. The two preceding words are emphasized in *Copia*.

4. I follow *SW's* location of the concluding quotation mark. The paragraph break occurs in *Copia* only.

5. The preceding phrase is emphasized in *Copia*.

6. The preceding three words are emphasized in *Copia*.

7. *SW* has a comma and em-dash instead of a full stop.

8. *SW* omits "which," the emphasis on "mere seeing," and the words that follow, up to "should."

9. This word is emphasized in *Copia*.

10. This emphasis occurs in *Copia* only.

11. This emphasis occurs in *Copia* only.

12. In Copia, the parentheses contain the single word "objectivity" and a gap.

13. This emphasis occurs in *Copia* only.

14. This emphasis occurs in *Copia* only.

15. *"Genesis"*—emphasis found in *Copia* only.

16. The *Copia*, however, has *"Forderung"* here instead of *"Genesis."*

17. This emphasis occurs in *Copia* only.

18. This emphasis occurs in *Copia* only.

19. Following the GA editors who prefer *Copia's "unabtrennlichen"* to *SW's "unabtreiblichen."*

20. Following the GA editors who prefer *Copia's "unabtrennlichen"* to *SW's "unabtreiblichen."*

21. Emphasis found in *Copia* only.

22. Emphasis found in *SW* only.

23. Emphasis found in *SW* only.

24. Preferring *SW's "oben"* to *Copia's "aber."*

25. The emphases here are found in *Copia* only.

26. Emphasis found in *Copia* only.

27. Emphasis found in *Copia* only.

28. Emphasis found in *Copia* only.

29. *SW* adds "being and self-construction, being and knowing of itself."

30. In *SW* this was *"unmittelbarer."* The editors, following the *Copia*, changed the word to preserve the sense of how Fichte describes idealism throughout the text.

31. The emphases in this sentence are found in *Copia* only.

32. Emphasis found in *Copia* only.

33. Emphasis found in *Copia* only.

34. That is, a distinction between being and its essence.

35. Paragraph break in Copia only.

36. *Copia* here adds *"als von sich u.s.w,"* a phrase missing in *SW*.

37. The *Copia* adds here *"sahen wir ein . . ."*

38. Emphasis found in *Copia* only.

39. *"genetisch"*—here this elastic term suggests that "seeing" develops something new besides the "unaltered content." Consequently, there are two terms, and hence a connection.

40. Emphasis in *Copia* only.

41. *"aus einem Stücke."*

42. Copia has instead *"verbaliter und agiliter."*

Lecture XIX

1. Reading *"nachweist"* instead of *"nachweise"* with the editors of *GA*, against both *NW* and *Copia*.

2. This emphasis occurs in *Copia* only.

3. This emphasis occurs in *Copia* only.

4. The emphasis in this sentence is found in *Copia* only.

5. I follow *SW's* construal of this passage.

6. The last clause is in the *Copia* only.

7. Following Lauth, Widmann, and Schneider, I read *"sondern"* here instead of *"schon"* in both *SW* and *Copia*.

8. *Copia* has a paragraph break here.

9. This paragraph break occurs in *Copia* only.

10. This emphasis occurs in *Copia* only.

11. I follow *SW's* punctuation here.

12. This emphasis occurs in *Copia* only.

13. This emphasis occurs in *Copia* only.

14. Emphasis found in the *Copia* only.

15. Only the *Copia* puts this sentence in parentheses.

16. Reading *"sichern"* with *Copia*, rather than *"höhern"* with *SW*. The *GA* editors question in a footnote whether the *SW* reading is a mistake, since *"sichern"* seems clearly preferable.

17. I have added these sets of parentheses for clarity.

18. I include here the amplification suggested by the editors of *GA*. SW entirely omits the material in quotation marks, and *Copia* has it in part.

19. *Satz vom Prinzip*. The quoted sentence in the next sentence may be intended as a statement of this "law."

20. Following the *GA* editors who prefer *Copia's "Unphilosophen"* to *SW's "Urphilosophen,"* which is senseless.

21. Here Fichte rehearses the same point that he made in discussing Jacobi at the end of the previous lecture, but without any historical reference.

22. See above p. 163. The two passages are not identical in detail, so Fichte is not quoting exactly. Emphasis found in the *Copia* only.

23. This word is emphasized in *Copia*.

24. The last sentence is found in the *Copia* only as the abbreviation *"W.D.E.W"*: *"Was der Erste war."*

25. This emphasis occurs in *Copia* only.

26. The last two sentences are found in *Copia* only.

27. This emphasis occurs in *Copia* only.

28. This emphasis occurs in *Copia* only.

29. This emphasis occurs in *Copia* only.

30. Following *Copia*. Instead, *SW* has here, "since language is pretty much finished."

31. Reading the antecedent of *"sie"* as *"die Einheit."*

32. The last sentence is found in the *Copia* only.

33. Copia adds a diagram here centered on the line:

$$a - b$$
$$0$$

34. The last sentence is found in the *Copia* only.

35. This emphasis occurs in *Copia* only.

36. This emphasis occurs in *Copia* only.

37. This emphasis occurs in *Copia* only.

38. This sentence's emphases are found in the *Copia* only.

39. This emphasis occurs in *Copia* only.

Lecture XX

1. This emphasis occurs in *Copia* only.

2. *". . . empirisch sprechend . . ."*

3. This emphasis occurs in *Copia* only.

4. This emphasis occurs in *Copia* only.

5. The material in square brackets is absent from the *Copia*.

6. This emphasis occurs in *Copia* only.

7. This emphasis occurs in *Copia* only.

8. This emphasis occurs in *Copia* only.

9. With the *GA* editors, I prefer the *Copia's "Überlegung"* to *SW's "Überzeugung."*

10. This emphasis occurs in *Copia* only.

11. This emphasis occurs in *SW* only.

12. This emphasis occurs in *Copia* only.

13. This emphasis occurs in *SW* only.

14. Reading *"voraus"* here with the *Copia*, instead of the doubtful *"von uns"* in *SW*.

15. The emphasis on the second word occurs in *Copia* only.

16. This word is emphasized in *Copia*.

17. *"Thue es, so thuest du es eben"*—for Fichte, knowing is always above all something that we do.

18. Lauth, Widmann, and Schneider insert this phrase to amplify the passage's sense.

19. This emphasis occurs in *Copia* only.

20. Reading *"nun"* with *SW*, instead of the *Copia's "nur."*

21. This paragraph break occurs in *Copia*. The preceding sentence is obscure. I have given it one possible construal that seems to fit the context.

22. This emphasis occurs in *Copia* only. It also adds the phrase "in our realization" here.

23. *SW* deletes the initial "in our insight," and after "follows" reads "in our insight into . . ." I follow *Copia* here.

24. This emphasis occurs in *Copia* only.

25. I follow *SW's* wording.

26. Following the *Copia's "aus und von dem Von"* rather than *SW's* probably erroneous *"aus einem andern Von."*

27. This emphasis occurs in *Copia* only.

28. The diagram is from Copia only. The two terms of the "from" posited in the first diagram (a and b), are each subsequently divided into further terms (a—b, and a . b)

29. The preceding phrase ("of the original "from"") is added in the *Copia*.

30. I follow *Copia's* wording. *SW* has ". . . 'from,' in an absolutely essential insight . . ."

31. The *Copia* adds here, "because, if content is present, light then does not come purely, thereby not without the appearance of genesis and *vice versa*, to this absolute genesis, that reveals itself as absolutely pure genesis, nor could the latter appear without pure light arising."

32. Copia substitutes the following strange proposition: "This is in a field where the *WL* does not yet stand at the apex."

Lecture XXI

1. I follow the *SW* version here, since the *Copia* text appears corrupted.

2. *Copia* has "from everything relative."

3. In *SW* the term is *"Beweisnervus,"* in *Copia* it is *"Beweisnerven."*

4. I have added the parentheses to make the sentence structure clearer.

5. I take the *"das,"* which stands alone here, as referring back to prior occurrences of *"das Wir."*

6. *Copia* adds here "This would be the first point."

7. This emphasis occurs in *SW* only.

8. *"als qualitative"*—emphasized in *Copia*.

9. I follow the amendment proposed by Lauth, Widmann, and Schneider.

10. There is no indication where "1." belongs, except for the phrase mentioned in note 6 above.

11. Following the *Copia*. *SW* emphasizes the second word only.

12. I follow *Copia's* punctuation here.

13. *SW* has *"sucht"* instead of *"sieht."*

14. The *Copia* inserts *"es"* here, and also encloses the later word "objective" in parentheses.

15. *Copia* emphasizes this last term.

16. Following Lauth, Widmann, and Schneider, who read *"nun"* instead of *"nur."*

17. In the last two sentences, I have rearranged the clauses of one very convoluted Fichtean sentence, in hopes of making better sense in English.

18. This paragraph break is in *SW* only.

19. This paragraph break is in *Copia* only.

20. *SW* omits all parentheses around this passage. *Copia* has the opening parenthesis and omits the last. *Copia* alone sets this apart as a separate paragraph.

21. This emphasis occurs in *Copia* only.

22. *SW* has here *"neuen"* instead.

23. The length and complexity of this sentence makes locating the AA page break in the translation a very approximate matter!

24. The emphasis is in *Copia* only, which also has *"NichtsichGenesis"* instead of *SW's "Nicht-Genesis."*

25. This emphasis is in *Copia* only.

26. This term is emphasized in *Copia*.

27. *SW* has a paragraph break here.

28. That is, "all genesis."

29. Reading *"von"* instead of *"in,"* as does *Copia*.

Lecture XXII

1. Reading *"feinste"* here with the *Copia* and the *GA* editors, instead of *SW's* *"freieste."*

2. Fichte calls knowing in this case *"ein Principiiren."* I take his point to be that this knowing is the site at which absolute self-genesis occurs and is given a principle. I have attempted to capture the sense of Fichte's neologism.

3. The chain of reasoning must be present to us because the "knowing" under discussion is in no sense an object that is present, rather it is the knowing occurring in us here and now, in which whatever is present is present.

4. This emphasis occurs in *Copia* only.

5. Reading *"an"* instead of *"und"* here, with *Copia* and the *GA* editors instead of *SW*. Copia also emphasizes "empirically."

6. Fichte's term here is *"Abschnitt."* A few lines later he uses *"Unterabtheilung"* for the second of the parts of part two, and he follows with reference to a third *"Unterabtheilung."* For the sake of consistency, I call all of them "sub-sections."

7. This emphasis occurs in *Copia* only.

8. This term is emphasized in *Copia*.

9. This emphasis occurs in *Copia* only.

10. There is no obvious indication as to exactly where the 1. should be. Perhaps the beginning of the lecture's second paragraph is the most plausible candidate.

11. *Copia* adds here: "Should such a principle exist or not, and since the second term ____, neither of them."

12. I follow *Copia's* *"gemacht"* instead of *SW's* *"gedacht."*

13. This word is emphasized in *SW*.

14. *Copia* adds: "[we] know directly."

15. This emphasis occurs in *Copia* only.

16. This emphasis occurs in *Copia* only.

17. This paragraph break occurs in *Copia* only.

18. I follow the text of *Copia* here, which makes more sense than *SW*.

Lecture XXIII

1. This emphasis is in *SW* only. *Copia* places the phrase in italics. I have added the parentheses to simplify the structure.

2. Following *Copia* instead of *SW*.

3. I follow *SW* in treating this term as a noun.

4. This emphasis is in *SW* only. I place these qualifications in parentheses to make the sentence structure more perspicuous.

5. *Copia* also emphasizes ". . . support of the 'what.'"

6. *Copia* emphasizes "deducing" as well.

7. This remark occurs in the *Copia* only.

8. *Copia* adds another clause to the two in *SW*. It says: ". . . or to derive whatness, quality."

9. This word is emphasized in *Copia*.

10. *SW* does not place the preceding paragraph in parentheses.

11. This emphasis is in the *Copia* only.

12. I add this emphasis to underline the relation between "that" and "what."

13. I follow the punctuation of *Copia* here.

14. This emphasis is in the *Copia* only.

15. The last two words are emphasized in *Copia*.

16. "Certainty" and "necessity of resting" are emphasized in *Copia*.

17. This emphasis is in the *Copia* only.

18. This word is emphasized in the *Copia*.

19. *Copia* emphasizes the terms "living" and "immanent."

20. This is emphasized in *Copia*.

21. This emphasis is in the *Copia* only. SW emphasizes "as" instead.

22. *Copia* adds, "which is the first point."

23. ". . . and in its proper nature, not through a special act."

24. *Copia* emphasizes each of the last three words.

25. *Copia* emphasizes the last word.

26. *Copia* has a paragraph break here and adds "Which is the second point."

27. *SW* has "which is also self-projecting"—*"zugleich sich projicirend ist."*

28. Emphasis in *Copia* only, which also has *"eine"* instead of *"reine."*

29. *SW* has *"ewig"* only.

30. *Copia* adds here: "Inner life, which is to be lived in living immediately."

31. This emphasis occurs in *Copia* only.

32. Copia emphasizes this term.

33. *Copia* emphasizes this term.

34. Emphasis in *Copia* only.

35. *Copia* emphasizes this term.

36. *Copia* emphasizes "projection" and "intuition."

37. *Copia* emphasizes this term.

38. *Copia* emphasizes this term.

39. *SW* instead has *"genetisch."*

40. *Copia* adds here: "and absolutely."

41. This emphasis is in *Copia* only.

42. Reading *"verholen"* as *"verhohlen."*

Lecture XXIV

1. I follow the *Copia* here. *SW* has no paragraph break and marks this sentence as b. It also omits any 1. for the numbered list that constitutes the rest of the lecture. Although doing this leaves the a. in the first paragraph standing by itself, this otherwise seems to make better sense of the lecture's structure as a whole.

2. *Copia* emphasizes this word.

3. *Copia* emphasizes both quoted terms.

4. *Copia* adds, "or myself."

5. *SW* has "of some."

6. "Predicates do not exist unless they are formally objects." *Copia* has a blank space between *"nisi"* and *"objecti."*

7. Copia inserts a phrase found in the margin here, which may be a note by the transcriber: "Through which the insight can become clearer."

8. *Copia* adds this last question, and the next paragraph as well.

9. *SW* has *"nun"* instead of *"nur."*

10. *Copia* emphasizes this word.

11. This emphasis is in *Copia* only.

12. Both *SW* and *Copia* use 1. and 2. to label the subordinate points in this paragraph. That could create confusion vis-à-vis the four main numbered points Fichte is making in this lecture, so I have used a. and b. for these subordinate points.

13. This emphasis occurs in *Copia* only.

14. This term is emphasized in *Copia*.

15. This term is emphasized in *SW*.

16. This word is omitted in *SW*.

17. This emphasis occurs in *Copia* only.

18. *SW* has here *"Idealistische,"* and *Copia* has *"idealische."* The *GA* editors imply that the latter may be correct.

19. *SW* has *"its"* instead.

20. This paragraph break occurs in *Copia* only.

21. This paragraph break occurs in *Copia* only.

22. This paragraph break occurs in *Copia* only.

Lecture XXV

1. The last sentence occurs in *Copia* only.

2. *SW* has *"jetzt"* instead of *"neu."*

3. This emphasis occurs in *Copia* only.

4. This emphasis occurs in *Copia* only. Copia also inserts the words "this original construction" in the nominative case, which appears senseless.

5. This emphasis occurs in *Copia* only.

6. The last word, *"Bild"* is fundamental in Fichte's lexicon. The emphasis occurs in *Copia* only.

7. This emphasis occurs in *Copia* only.

8. I follow Lauth, Widmann, and Schneider's reconstruction of this passage.

9. *SW* has *"als beweisen übernahmen"* instead of *"zu bewiesen übernahmen."*

10. This paragraph break occurs in *Copia* only.

11. *SW* has *"kommen"* instead of *Copia's "kamen."*

12. This paragraph break occurs in *Copia* only.

13. This emphasis occurs in *Copia* only.

14. *Copia* has *"emanent."*

15. This last sentence is added in *Copia*.

16. This emphasis occurs in *Copia* only.

17. *"... wir daher uns nicht etwa dadurch helfen können, das wir jene Qualität ohne Weiteres einmischen."*

18. This emphasis occurs in *Copia* only.

19. These emphases occur in *SW* only.

20. This paragraph break occurs in *SW* only.

21. *". . . es solle zur W.-L. kommen."* A number of the following lines are omitted in *Copia*. The editors surmise that the copyist skipped from this occurrence of *"es solle"* to another one occurring near the beginning of the following paragraph. This seems the best explanation for the gap.

22. *Copia* has instead, *"qualitative oneness and difference."* The editors ask whether SW's *"Mannigfaltigkeit"* may not be erroneous.

23. *"Position"*—an English speaker might be tempted to write "positing" here, guided by the apparent connection to the language of the Jena *Wissenschaftslehre*. This appearance is misleading. While through its synonyms *"Stellung"* and *"Lage"* Position has a connotative resonance with the *Grundlage's "setzen,"* the term's recognized use as "affirmation" serves well enough here.

24. Fichte refers here to the Gospel of John. One should compare his popular writings from this same period, especially *Die Anweisung zum seligen Leben* and *Die Grundzüge des gegenwärtigen Zeitalters*.

25. This emphasis is in SW only.

26. This paragraph break occurs in *Copia* only.

27. Fichte's word is *"erkennen,"* which most fundamentally means "recognize" rather than "know" as the various English Bible translations I consulted usually have it.

28. John 17:3. The full passage reads: "And eternal life is this: to know you, the only true God, and Jesus Christ, whom you have sent." "The New Testament," *The Jerusalem Bible* (Doubleday & Co.: New York, 1966), p. 183.

29. *Wandel* here, as in some biblical settings, is short for *Lebenswandel*, which means "conduct" or "life."

30. This occurred presumably on Sunday, June 3.

Lecture XXVI

1. At issue in these two telegraphic sentences are the two sorts of knowing—ordinary and transcendental—and their interrelatedness.

2. *SW* has here *"Gegenstände"* and *Copia* has *"Sachen."*

3. *SW* has *"nur"* instead of *"immer."*

4. *Copia* has *"auszusprechen"* instead of *"nachzusprechen."*

5. The last sentence is omitted in *SW*.

6. This paragraph break occurs in *Copia* only.

7. This paragraph break occurs in *Copia* only. I construe the last sentence following the *Copia*.

8. This emphasis is in *Copia* only.

9. Copia adds *"qualitative"* here.

10. These emphases are in *Copia* only.

11. i.e., negating seeing. This negative moment corresponds to the intentionality of consciousness, which Fichte distinguished here from the objectivity of the projection through a gap.

12. I follow *SW*.

13. This paragraph break occurs in *Copia* only. This last sentence also occurs in the *Copia* only.

14. This emphasis occurs in *Copia* only.

15. This emphasis occurs in *Copia* only.

16. This paragraph break occurs in *Copia* only.

17. No emphasis here in *SW*.

18. The last word emphasized in *Copia*.

19. "Seeing" and "being."

20. *Copia* has a word play here, *"ein inneres Aeussern"*; *SW* has *"Projiciern"* instead.

21. *Copia* emphasizes the last three words.

22. I follow *Copia*. SW has "qualities" instead.

23. This emphasis in in *Copia* only.

Lecture XXVII

1. This emphasis is in *Copia* only.

2. This emphasis is in *Copia* only

3. *Copia* has *"gesagt"* here, and *SW* has *"entschieden."* I have combined elements of both.

4. The preceding term is emphasized in *Copia* only.

5. There is no paragraph break in *SW*, which also omits the last sentence.

6. The last sentence is omitted in *SW*.

7. This emphasis is in *Copia* only.

8. This emphasis is in *Copia* only.

9. That is, this fact.

10. This emphasis occurs in *Copia* only.

11. *Copia* has here: ". . . from the objectification of its own freed position . . ."

12. This emphasis occurs in *Copia* only.

13. The last sentence is in *Copia* only.

14. This last sentence is in *Copia* only.

15. This emphasis occurs in *Copia* only.

16. *SW* has *"zeigt"* instead of *Copia's "äussert."*

17. *"Erscheinung,"* here as in Lecture Two with the special meaning of the fundamental manifestness that is the condition for all empirical appearing. This emphasis occurs in *Copia* only.

18. This term is emphasized in *Copia*.

Lecture XXVIII

1. *Copia* emphasizes the two preceding participles.

2. *"begründen"* occurs in *Copia* only.

3. The last word emphasized in *Copia* only.

4. The last word emphasized in *Copia* only.

5. This emphasis occurs in *Copia* only.

6. This emphasis occurs in *Copia* only.

7. I follow Lauth, Widmann, and Schneider in preferring the *Copia's* version of this phrase. SW has *"eine sonach durchsichtige Licht (= Vernunft)."*

8. This emphasis occurs in *Copia* only.

9. This paragraph break and the subsequent "Further" occur in *Copia* only.

10. This emphasis occurs in *Copia* only.

11. This emphasis occurs in *Copia* only.

12. This emphasis occurs in *Copia* only.

13. The last sentence and the paragraph break are in *Copia* only.

14. This sentence is omitted in *SW*.

15. This sentence is omitted in *SW*.

16. *Copia* does not emphasize "self-" and instead emphasizes "fully" and "into our imitative image."

17. This emphasis occurs in *Copia* only.

18. The emphases in this sentence are in *Copia* only.

19. This emphasis occurs in *SW* only.

20. *Copia* adds, "This was the first point."

21. This emphasis occurs in *Copia* only.

22. Only *"principle"* is emphasized in *SW*.

23. *"es ist eben absolut nur faktisch."*

24. This emphasis occurs in *Copia* only.

25. This word only is emphasized in *SW*.

26. *Copia* omits the rest of the quotation after *"I."*

27. *SW* omits "I say."

28. This emphasis occurs in *Copia* only.

29. This paragraph break occurs in *Copia* only.

30. This emphasis occurs in *Copia* only.

31. *SW* has the less pointed "self-making."

32. This last phrase is omitted in *SW*.

33. Dividing one long sentence into two. In the original, the preceding sentence is a confusing relative clause. I take the pronoun's antecedent to be "inner oneness."

34. The occurrences here of "endure" and "hold" all translate forms of *"stehen."*

35. This emphasis occurs in *SW* only.

36. This emphasis occurs in *SW* only.

37. This emphasis occurs in *SW* only.

38. *SW* has *"Boden"* instead of *"Bilden."*

39. Reading "former" as the first fundamental principle, the enduring object or transience in general.

40. This emphasis occurs in *SW* only.

41. *Copia* here has, "Which was the first point."

42. Fichte refers here to Psalms 103:27 and 144:15.

43. *SW* has "act of thought" *(Denkakte)* instead of *Copia's* "decree" *(Dekrete)*.

Appendix I

1. Appia, perhaps: Paul Joseph, 1783–1849, French reformed preacher in Frankfurt am Main.

2. Reading *"Ahnung"* for *"Ahndung."*

German-English Glossary

A

Abgebildete	what is imaged
Absicht	intention
allgemein	general
Anknüpfung	beginning
Anlage	natural tendency
Anschauung	perception, intuition
Ansicht	aspect, view
aufgehen	dissolve
Aufgehen	surrender
Aufgestellte	what has been established
Aufmerksamkeit	attention, attentiveness
Auge	perceptiveness, eye, perspective
Aussagen	assertion, statement, what a sentence asserts
Äusserlichkeit	externality
Äusserung	expression

B

bedingen	qualify
begreifen	conceive
Besinnung	consciousness
Besonnenheit	reflection
Bestehen	persistence
Bestimmtheit	certainty, description (in the sense of determination)
Betrachtung	consideration, contemplation
Bild	image
Bilden	imaging, image making process
bloss	mere, simple
Buchstaben	literal presentation

C

Consequenz	implication, result, consequence
Construktion	construction

241

construierend	constructing, constructive
Conversatorium	discussion

D

Darstellung	exhibition
Denken	thinking
Duplicität	ambiguity (I do not adopt Zoller's more literal "duplicity," which in English connotes deceit and double-dealing)
Durch	through
durchdringen	master, penetrate, permeate
Durcheinander	"through one another"—for Fichte, this names the mutuality of two terms that can be organically constructed *only through one another*. As a noun or adverb, *Durcheinander* usually means "disorder" or "confusion." However, Fichte seems to be appealing to its composition from the roots *"durch"* and *"einander"* to suggest an ineradicable reciprocity. Such reciprocity may sometimes create disorder, but that is not the primary sense in which Fichte uses the term in these lectures.
durchkreuzen	intersect

E

Effekt	effect, power
Einheit	oneness
einleuchten	be manifest, appear
einsehen	see into, understand
einzig	sole
eingeleuchtet	evident, manifest
Empirie	empirical experience
empirisch	empirical
Erläuterung	explanation
Einsicht	insight
Erklärung	clarification, explanation
Erscheinen	appearing
Erscheinung	"appearance" is the standard equivalent. However, Fichte uses *Erscheinung* in a special way in Lectures Two and Twenty Seven to name the fundamental openness or the open, which he understands as the self-created internal realization of philosophical insight. In these contexts, I render it "vision" or "epiphany."
erzeugen	create, produce
Erzeuger	creator

Evidenz	manifestness—For Fichte, this important concept names the clarity of an immediate mental grasping, which cannot be mistaken.

F

Fakticität	facticity
faktisch	factical
Faktische	the factical
Forttragen	carrying forward, continuation
füglich	appropriately

G

Genesis	origin, development. The idea of "genesis" as a self-active process, or unfolding, plays a central from in these lectures.
genetisch	genetic, developing, developmental (modified as "actively" where contextually appropriate).
Geschlossenheit	enclosure
gewiss	certain
Gewissheit	certainty
Glied	term
gründlich	fundamentally

H

Herausgehen	going out
Hiatus	gap

I

Ich	I
Ingredienz	component, part, ingredient
intelligieren	think, intellectualize,
Intelligieren	intellectual activity, thinking
intelligierend	thinking
Intuition	Intuition

L

Lebendigkeit	vivacity, livingness
Leerheit	vacuity
Licht	light

M

mittlebar	mediate, mediately
Mittelpunkt	midpoint
Moment	element, moment, factor

N

Nachbild	copy
Nachconstruction	reconstruction
nachconstruieren	reconstruct
nachmachen	copy, imitate
Nebenglied	subordinate term

O

Objectivieren	event of objectifying
Orient	direction

P

Pendant	counterpart
per hiatum	through a gap, discontinuous
Position	affirmation
Postulat	postulation
Princip	principle
Principiat	something principled, an outcome
Principiiren	Fichte introduces this neologism in the second part of his lectures. It names the self-grounding moment in the immanent, self-enclosed life of light. This life lacks any ground other than itself, and yet it requires a principle, which it itself provides by seeing itself as the reconstruction (or image) of absolute inconceivable being. I translate it as "principle-providing."
Principsein	being-a-principle
Problematicität	hypothetical quality, hypotheticalness
problematisch	hypothetical

Q

Qualität	quality
Quantitabilität	quantifiability

R

raisonnieren	(to) reason
realisieren	realize
Realisierung	realization
rein	pure

S

Schliessen	closing
Sehen	seeing, vision
Sein	Being
Seitenglieder	subordinate terms
setzen	posit
sollen	This term can mean "ought" in the sense of obligation, and it can also express the hypothetical character of a clause in which it occurs. To convey this use, I will translate it as either "should" or "if," depending on the context.
Soll	should, ought. Throughout these lectures, the substantive *"Soll,"* as expressing an essential hypothetical character (together with some degree of imperativeness), plays a major role in Fichte's argument.
Sonderung	division
Stellung	arrangement

T

Tathandlung	enactment
Tatsache	fact
Thun	doing
trieben	pursue, conduct

U

Unwandelbare	The unchangeable
ursprünglich	primordially
Urbegriff	primordial concept
Urlicht	primordial light
Urphantasie	primal fantasy
Urquell	original source

V

Veränderlichkeit	variability
Veränderung	variation
Verfahren	procedure, process
Vernehmen	awareness—this verbal noun comes from the verb *vernehmen*, which means to hear, perceive, become aware of, understand, examine, interrogate, etc. As a noun, it usually occurs in phrases referring to what we know indirectly through its being heard or reported on. Fichte introduces it late in these lectures to name a very deep inner knowing that is not mediated through our usually cognitive means.
Vernünfteffekt	reason's effect, the power of reason
Verständlichkeit	intelligibility
Verwirklichung	actualization
vollziehen	carry out, accomplish
Von	from—usually a preposition, this term is systematically used as a noun by Fichte to characterize the dynamic and developmental (or genetic) character of the absolute, as it is manifested.
Vorconstruction	pre-construction
Vorhaben	project, plan
Vorsatz	intention
Vortrag	lecture

W

Wahrheit	truth
Wandel	change; (metaphorically for *Lebenswandel*) conduct way of life
Wandelbare	the changeable
Wandelbarkeit	changeability
Werden	transformation
Willkür	arbitrariness
wirklich	genuine, actual
Wissen	knowing
Wissenschaft	science
Wissenschaftslehre	*Wissenschaftslehre* is Fichte's term for his distinctively new transcendental philosophical science. I translate it as "science of knowing." (For an explanation and defense of this choice, see the Introduction.)

Z

Zerfall	decomposition
Zuhörer	listener (*pl.* audience)

zurückführen	to trace back
Zusatz	supplement
Zusammenhang	relation, coherence
zusammenhängen	cohere
zweckmässige	appropriate

Index

Absolute, 4; as absolute, 147; appearance, 195; being, 25, 43, 69, 70, 89, 132, 137, 160, 185, 190; certainty, 168; consciousness, 103, 105, 106, 109; disjunction, 57, 64; essence, 123; existence, 124; from-itself, 143; genesis, 123, 145, 150, 156; "I," 105; idealism, 90, 135, 157; inconceivability of, 42, 43; insight, 60, 90, 115, 123; intuition, 98, 105, 186; knowing, 149, 164, 181, 182, 184, 190; law, 174, 175, 177, 178; life, 90, 91; light, 43, 52, 60, 82, 99, 102, 146, 149, 160; located in being, 25; love of, 49, 50; manifestness, 42, 149; multiplicity, 55; non-being, 117; oneness, 28, 41, 63, 64, 136; presentation of, 24; primordial, 90; proof regarding essence of, 148; reality, 85; reason, 88, 89, 142, 198; reflection, 102; relation, 115; science as expression of, 51; self-construction of, 98; self-genesis, 161; should, 132; spirit, 4; substance, 71; through, 91; in transcendence, 4, 7; truth, 75, 91

Action/activity: priority over fact of, 13; self-making, 197

Adorno, Theodor, 8

"Aphorisms on the Essence of Philosophy as a Science," 20

Appearance: absolute, 195; absolute idealism and, 135; of absolute knowing, 181; as absolute's internal construction, 128; as appearance, 61, 84; as basis for disjunctions, 20, 160, 162; of being, 128; deducing, 167; doctrine of, 20; of freedom, 70; of inner energy, 89; light and, 61, 66; of light from the light, 147; primordial, 61, 146; principle of, 20, 125, 149, 160, 162; of reality, 85; in science of knowing, 115; the should of, 5, 138, 141

Appia, P.J., 20

"Atheism Controversy," 1

Attention: complete, 47, 48; distraction and, 48; need for, 47, 48; total, 49

Awareness: consciousness and, 9; contradictions arising in, 4; modern rejection of, 10; occurrence of, 9; philosophical insight and, 8; as test of truth, 10

Being: absolute, 25, 43, 69, 70, 89, 132, 137, 160, 185, 190; analytic/synthetic principle of, 123; appearance of, 128; categoricalness and, 131; closed into itself, 167; concept of, 54, 64; construction of, 121, 122, 123, 124, 127, 129, 134; dead, 161; deposing/deposed by doing, 53; duality with thinking, 38; enduring, 161; essential, 123; factical, 122, 130; genesis of, 156; immanent, 128, 186; immanent essence of, 123; inconceivable, 44, 52, 92; independent, 75; in-itself, 114, 116; inner, 109, 114, 117, 126, 129, 131, 132, 136, 143, 147, 161; intrinsic, 52; of knowing, 158, 161, 162, 163; light and, 61, 167; in living, 116; location of absolute in, 25; making into, 19; need for thinking and, 30; needing no other being for existence, 114; negation of self, 54; non-genesis and, 164; objectifica-